SOUTH SHIELDS:

ITS PAST, PRESENT, AND FUTURE!

BEING

A LECTURE,

DELIVERED IN THE CENTRAL HALL, SOUTH SHIELDS,

ON WEDNESDAY, THE 9TH APRIL, 1856,

TO A CROWDED AUDIENCE.

BY

THOMAS SALMON, ESQ.,

TOWN CLERK:

AND PRINTED IN COMPLIANCE WITH THE UNANIMOUS
VOTE OF THE MEETING.

"A chiel's amang you, taking notes,
And, faith, he'll prent it."

SOUTH SHIELDS:
PRINTED AND PUBLISHED BY HENRY HEWISON, MARKET PLACE.

1856.

INTRODUCTION.

AFTER having tried the patience of my hearers for three long hours in the delivery of this lecture, *de omnibus rebus et quibusdam aliis*, there was still much that I had in readiness, which unavoidably remained unsaid. Without that additional matter, the lecture would have remained imperfect as a record of incidents connected with South Shields, and I, therefore, find it necessary to introduce it now, with further additions and some tabular statements of interesting importance, in completion of my humble undertaking. For the honor bestowed by the publication of the lecture, I feel indebted to the kind partiality of my townsmen, rather than to any merits of my own, or of my unpretending production. It was, however, their loudly declared wish, most unmistakably expressed, that I should rush into print; and with a full knowledge of the risks and consequences of authorship, I felt that it would be ungracious not to accede to the request. Whether I acted wisely or unwisely in thus subjecting, by its publication, an ephemeral lecture, of hasty preparation, to the ordeal of criticism, as a printed work, remains to be seen. I shall certainly feel gratified by its favourable reception, but will not complain if its fate should be otherwise.

THOS. SALMON.

Mr. Salmon died in 1871. See post. p. 75 & 76.

N.B.—The annexed being a Plan of the date of 1768—the same year as that in which the Market Place Act was passed—it becomes necessary to call attention to the fact, that the Market Place and Streets adjacent are those which were *dowled* out, but *not then erected*.

SOUTH SHIELDS:

ITS PAST, PRESENT, AND FUTURE.

THE PAST, THE PRESENT, AND THE FUTURE! are words of serious signification, the consideration of which if entered upon in a wide and general sense, would lead me to remarks, and you to reflections, of a very grave and extensive nature. But my intention in adopting them as my motto on this occasion, was foreign to any such ambitious design, the Past, the Present, and the Future of South Shields being the more humble limit to which my subject will be confined. Indeed, I may perhaps, notwithstanding this moderate restriction, be still considered presumptuous in offering thus publicly to intrude my notions upon you. It is, however, my first appearance as a Lecturer upon this or any other stage, and I crave from you that favourable indulgence which is usually extended to incipient actors, under similar circumstances and upon like occasions. At the same time I unhesitatingly give, as one of my reasons for that appearance, my earnest desire to make more extensively known to the public at large, through the medium of this lecture and of the press, the shipping, manufacturing, commercial, and mining importance, and the future prospects of this happily situate borough, in order that it may take that high and conspicuous rank amongst the kindred boroughs of the kingdom, to which it is, in reality, most justly entitled, but which I am sometimes mortified to discover, is not at all times conceded to it by strangers. But whatever others, in their ignorance or conceit, may think of South Shields, and however it may be their custom or their fashion to speak in disparagement of it and its institutions, I love it as the place of my birth and the residence of my forefathers,

"Land of my Sires, what mortal hand,
Can e'er untie the filial band."

I value and respect the sterling worth of its inhabitants, amongst whom I am proud to reckon many, very many, friends; I admire it for much in its character, that is worthy of all honour and praise, and possessed of those feelings I give expression to them in those

A

4

beautiful and poetical strains of the sweet singer of Israel, which are familiar to you all—

"Peace be within thy walls, and plenteousness within thy palaces.
For my brethren and companions' sakes, I will wish thee prosperity.
Yea, because of the house of the Lord our God I will seek to do thee good."

With these preliminary remarks, I now proceed on my way, and *first*—with respect to South Shields and its past—I could, if it were necessary, go back into a very remote antiquity—I could picture to myself, in imagination, the Legions of Imperial Rome encamped at the Lawe in their military station, on the site of the native fortified town of the Britons—the march of those Roman soldiers in all the proud panoply of war, on the Wreken-dyke military way, leading from that station by a route which, even at the present day, can be traced by Antiquaries to their other station then in existence at Lanchester—the Tyne, that ancient river, the river Tyne, pursuing its sullen silent course through banks as yet undisturbed by the works of man, or the busy hum of Industry, and with foreshores so completely unappropriated as would have given satisfaction even to a minority of a River Tyne Improvement Commission, had any such existed in those ancient days—the Slake of Jarrow, not then as now, half filled by deposits of sand and mud, but deep and actually sustaining on its waters, the Royal Navy of the Saxon King Egfrid, whose haven it undoubtedly was—the far-famed Monastery of Jarrow, standing in solemn and monastic seclusion on that elevated spot which is still marked by its ruins—the devastating inroads of the Danes—the twice repeated burning and reduction to ashes of that sacred edifice (endeared to us by the life and death of the learned and venerable Bede), by the piratical and unenlightened barbarians of the Baltic—and its subsequent sacrilegious destruction by the fierce and enraged Normans, under the Conqueror, William, notwithstanding they boasted of the Gospel Dispensation.

But these, the events of by-gone ages, are all matters of history, and I, therefore, pass on to a period of a much later date, as connected with South Shields and its past, in doing which, I must, of necessity, connect it with its present.

South Shields (anciently written Le Sheeles), originated with the fishermen of the Tyne who built here, along the southern shore, sheds, provincially termed "Sheels" or "Shields," to defend themselves from the weather. Subsequently, and for some few centuries, the place became known for its Salt Works, nearly two hundred pans having been at one time employed, paying on the salt boiled therein, no less an annual duty than £80,000; but that branch of industry became extinct, its place having happily been supplied by others of more real importance. So recently, however, as the year 1740, one hundred and sixteen years ago, only four vessels, according to Hutchinson, the historian of this and the neighbouring county of

Northumberland, belonged to South Shields, an extraordinary fact from which may be judged, the amazingly rapid increase which has since taken place in our shipping.

The increase of the town was consequent on that of the shipping, but its sanatary and other condition, up to the year 1829, when an Act was first obtained for "paving, lighting, watching, cleansing, regulating, and improving" it, was anything but satisfactory. The streets, as well carriage-ways as footways, were badly paved, insufficiently cleansed, and totally unlighted. Without police, the safety and protection of the inhabitants and their property, were left to the parish Dogberries by day, whilst at night, during the winter, the Waits, with their melancholy music, were our only security against burglary, molestation, and fire—numerous swine, of the most disgusting description, some of them with their "nine farrow," wallowed unmolested in the unwholesome sump-holes of the public thoroughfares—foul water and filthy offal were cast with impunity upon our streets—the public and private middens were full even to overflowing—and in the absence of scavengers' carts for the daily reception of the ashes, dirt, and refuse of the inhabitants, the state of such of the houses, and they were very numerous, as were destitute of yards, middens, and conveniences, may readily be conceived—streets were laid out of insufficient width, without regularity, and with no provision of any kind for sewerage, footpaths, and pavement—houses were built, in too many instances, according to the interested motives and plans of those who obtained building sites from the Dean and Chapter of Durham, and they were undrained, unventilated, and too frequently without yards or out-offices—no regulating or restraining authority existed on the part of the public, with respect to any of such things —and much of our town, and many of our dwellings, came to possess in consequence, that narrow, crowded, and ill-ventilated condition, which is so unsightly to the eye, so detrimental to health, and so inconvenient for traffic—in addition to all which subjects of mortifying retrospection, artificial hills of huge size, and unsightly appearance, were suffered to be created in many of the best and most desirable situations of the town, by deposits of refuse from the salt-pans and glass-houses, and of ballast from the ships, conspicuous and, I fear, lasting reproaches to those in whom, as owners of the soil, powers of prevention were undoubtedly vested ; a remark which applies with equal force to most of the other evils of which I have complained ; for it is certain that the Dean and Chapter of those days (I speak of a period more remote than the agency of Mr. Stoddart), could, with their proprietary powers, equal in many respects to those of a modern Town Improvement Act, have stipulated in the bargains which they made with those to whom they granted leases of ground to be built upon, for wide streets, houses of an uniform character, suitable out-offices, spacious yards, paved carriage-ways, flagged footpaths, public sewers, and connecting drains. That no such stipulations were made, affords matter now for just complaint, for it has left to be done by the present inhabitants of this borough, much of that which ought to have been done by their predecessors, and hence the unjust entailment upon the former of a local taxation, which, in some degree, may be considered as an accumulation unfairly imposed upon them; but which they must now of necessity submit to, for the health and comfort of our people cry aloud for the effectual sewerage of the borough, and it is the determination of the municipal authorities, acting as the local board of health, with my progressive friend, the Mayor, as their encouraging head, that the boon shall not be unnecessarily delayed.

Taking a retrospect as regards the past, to the year 1768, a distance of 88 years only, it is wonderful to reflect on comparing it with the present, that at that time, the eight acres upon which the Market-place and its adjoining streets now stand, were a green field in the very centre of the town—that Ogle's freehold, Green's freehold, Alderson's freehold butts, and the Glebe, were unbuilt upon—that there were no Corstorphine-town, East Jarrow, East King-street, Queen-street, North-street, Thames-street, or Keppell-street—no Wellington-street, Heron-street, Palatine-street, houses or street, on any ballast-hill—no Green's-place, Green's-terrace, Blumer's-terrace, Lawe-cottages, Waterloo-vale, Coronation-street, Oyston-street, Albert-terrace, or Commercial-road—*that the town of South Shields, in fact, consisted of the narrow street only, next the river*, with no docks; there having been only at the later period of 1782, three docks in existence at South Shields, viz., those at present occupied by Mr. Edwards, the Middle-dock Company, and Thomas Barker and Son—that the Jarrow Chemical works, Westoe Soda works, and Hilda Colliery, the Ballast wharves (with the exception of Cookson's), public and private railways, coal-staiths, glass-manufactories (with an exception again of Cookson's), patent slipways, shipbuilding-yards, cast iron foundries, roperies, breweries, and all our other present manufactories, were not then in existence—that Saint Hilda was the only church—and that with one solitary exception (the old Presbyterian chapel, of which the late respected father of Mr. Ald. Toshach, was so many years minister), the present dissenting chapels, had not then been built—that there were no Water works—no Gas works—and no Steam-ferry—no Mechanics' Institute—no Subscription Library—no Dispensary—no Savings' Bank—no Theatre—no Town-hall—that, in short, much of the properties which are now most valuable, and highly prized in our borough, were then either unappropriated foreshores, useless embankments, or lands unconverted to building, manufacturing, or other useful purposes—and that no one at that time could have formed the slightest conception of the rapid advance which has since been made by South Shields, in shipping, manufacturing, commercial, and general prosperity.

In the year 1768, a period to which I have already specially referred, an Act of Parliament was obtained, at the instance of the Dean and Chapter of Durham and the Incumbent of Saint Hilda, intituled "An Act for vesting in the Dean and Chapter of Durham, a certain piece of ground adjoining to the town of South Shields, and for making an adequate compensation to the Curate of the chapel of Saint Hild's and his successors for the same, and for enabling the said Dean and Chapter to remove the fairs and markets out of the said town of South Shields, and to cause the same to be held on the said piece of ground."

The piece of ground alluded to, consisted of eight acres, in the very heart of our present town.

The alleged adequate compensation made to the Curate of Saint Hild's and his successors, for alienating the same to the Dean and Chapter, was a paltry annuity or yearly sum of £30.

The name of the Curate, who was a party to this one-sided bargain, by which the living of Saint Hilda was so irretrievably injured, and through it the public, stands recorded in the Act, to his everlasting shame, as the Rev. Samuel Dennis.

And the fairs and markets were removed, from the narrow streets, to the spacious Market-place in which they are now held, and which, as being one of the finest squares in the kingdom, is justly the pride and boast of our town.

No sooner had the Act passed the Legislature, than armed with the powers which it carefully conferred, the Dean and Chapter of that day, with a full knowledge of all which the Curate had lost, and they themselves had gained, proceeded to avail themselves, after a most business-like fashion, of their advantageous position; and soon was this splendid and extraordinarily eligible building ground covered with houses and shops, built at the cost, not of the Dean and Chapter, but of those lessees to whom building leases, for forty years each, had been granted by the former; the loss to Saint Hilda, and the gain to the Dean and Chapter, having been enormous by this most astonishing transaction.

That this was so, may well be understood, when it is known that the Market-place, King-street, Dean-street, Chapter-row, Church-row, East-street, West-street, and Thrift-street, (none of which were in existence before 1768), were erected on the area of these eight acres, the Dean and Chapter having, be it also remembered, profited largely, not only by the surface, but by the valuable coal which was under it.

Impressed with a feeling of attachment to the Established Church, and ardently desirous to extend its efficiency and usefulness in South Shields and the neighbourhood, certain memorialists, in the year 1834, brought under the notice of the then Dean and Chapter, that the limited income of the incumbency of Saint Hilda was wholly inadequate to the spiritual wants of the chapelry, and prevented the resident minister giving that efficiency to the establishment which was requisite in so populous and important a place; that this arose chiefly from the unwise alienation in 1768 of property of such immense prospective value, whereby the Dean and Chapter were enriched at the expense of Saint Hilda; and that the memorialists laid the facts before that reverend body, in the firm persuasion, that they were not acquainted with the manifest advantages they derived, and continued to derive, from property, originally and recently, belonging to the chapel of Saint Hilda, and of the great public disadvantage the people in consequence sustained, at the same time referring the matter to their own conscientious decision, confident that as no other construction could fairly and equitably be put on the Act, than that it was intended for public accommodation, without injury to the incumbency of Saint Hilda, the right reverend body would at once perceive, that they might fairly be expected to see that the public suffered no loss and the chapel of Saint Hilda no further detriment.

The prayer of the memorial, that the Dean and Chapter would adopt measures for a grant of such an equitable and just restoration to the living of Saint Hilda, as the case imperiously demanded, and the duties required, was not granted; but the spiritual wants of the chapelry have since been considered by the erection, at the cost of the Dean and Chapter, and endowment by them of Holy Trinity Church; the erection of Saint Stephen's Church at their chief expense, and its endowment at their entire cost; and their intended erection and endowment of a new church near the Jarrow docks; all which, though of no pecuniary benefit to the living of Saint Hilda which suffered the loss, is yet an advantage to the members of the Established Church generally, and was probably meant, in some degree, as a restitution, in part, for the injury done by the proceeding of 1768, and an indirect admission of the just demands of the memorialists.

The Town-hall, in the centre of the Market-place, was erected, it should be stated, by and at the expense of the Dean and Chapter, it and the market, fairs, and tolls, having been lately purchased of them by the Corporation of South Shields, for the moderate sum of £500, under the provisions of " The South Shields Improvement Act, 1853." The Town-hall, market, fairs, and tolls, are consequently now, as they ought to be, in the absolute ownership, and under the entire control and management, of the Corporation as our governing body, who derive, I am happy to say, considerable advantage from the possession of these valuable properties. As a consequence of which I look forward with confidence to the pulling down, at no distant period, of the present Town-hall, and its replacement by a building, architecturally ornamental, and adapted in every respect to the municipal and public requirements of the borough. This can be effected on a self-supporting principle, through the medium of the tolls, and without the cost of one farthing to the ratepayers, and it is an improvement very greatly necessary, most anxiously looked for, and which cannot much longer be withheld.

In the year 1788, an Act of Parliament was obtained, intituled " An Act for supplying with water the town of South Shields, and parts adjacent, and the shipping resorting to the said town ;" by the preamble of which it is set forth, that the town of South Shields and parts adjacent were not sufficiently supplied with fresh water ; and that the conveying a sufficient quantity of fresh water into the town would be a great benefit to the inhabitants and the shipping resort- ing to the harbour of the town. George Rippon, Richard Armstrong, William Taylor, Edward Hall, John Rippon, and William Watson, all of North Shields, brewers, and Charles Cockerill, of South Shields, gentleman, and their respective successors, executors, administrators, and assigns, together with such person or persons as they should from time to time nominate and appoint under their hands and seals, were united into a company and corporate body for supplying with water the inhabitants of South Shields and parts adjacent, and the shipping resorting to the harbour of that town, by the name of " The Company of Proprietors of South Shields Water Works," with powers of a very extensive nature, for obtaining and supplying water in man- ner aforesaid.

Under this Act the supply of water was made for many years, but insufficiently, as was shown by the pant system and the existence of water-carts, the Water Works having been, beyond doubt, absurdly behind these later times, and quite inadequate to meet the wants of the community; so much so that on the 24th of April, 1845, the South Shields Improvement Commissioners resolved, in meeting assembled, " That a plentiful supply of pure and wholesome water was so essentially necessary to the health and comforts of the inha- bitants of South Shields and the security of their buildings from fire, that a committee be appointed for making a searching inquiry into the quantity, quality, and other particulars of the then supply ; and the practicability, expediency, and mode of increasing and improving the same, with a request to report fully thereon to a future meeting of the commissioners." The committee to consist of Geo. Potts, John Toshach, Henry Briggs, James Mather, and W. Alfred Swinburne, with myself as their secretary.

The committee, impressed with the important duties assigned to them, carefully inquired into and investigated the several branches of the subject referred to them, and made an elaborate and very able report thereon to the commissioners ; but as the Act in question no longer exists, and our supply of water now comes from an entirely different source, and under very altered circumstances, it would be an unnecessary waste of time to trouble you with the particulars, but rather to proceed at once to the Act under the provisions of which the present excellent and abundant supply of South Shields is derived; and which received the Royal Assent on the 28th of May, 1852, its title being " An Act for better supplying with water the boroughs of Sunderland and South Shields, and other places in the county of Durham."

By that last-mentioned Act the existing Sunderland Water Works Acts, and the South Shields Act, were repealed, and a new incorporated company formed for the supply with water of Sunderland and South Shields and the intermediate places, under the name of " The Sunderland and South Shields Water Company."

By that Company Sunderland and South Shields have since been connected by means of water-pipes laid down in the turnpike-road, and in addition to the supply from the Humbledon-hill shaft, on the south side of the Wear on the Durham-road, another abundant and inexhaustible one has been obtained of the most wholesome and satisfactory quality from the new shaft at the bottom of Fulwell-hill, the buildings, reservoir, and beautiful machinery connected with which are well deserving of a visit, in order that it may become known how great the obligations of the people are to the Town Council of this borough, for the wise and far-seeing judgment with which they joined with Sunderland in the successful parliamentary attempt, to secure for both boroughs, and the intermediate villages of Westoe, Harton, Cleadon, Whitburn, and Fulwell, and their respective farm-houses, the invaluable blessing of a copious and wholesome supply of pure and uncontaminated water.

Jarrow and its neighbourhood, with their rapidly increasing manufactories and population, are also now being placed by the company in a position to benefit by and partake of the water, the scarcity of which had become inconveniently felt in that locality.

And though last not least, the source of the supply at a high elevation enables us here, in case of fire, to use our hose effectually and without the intervention of a fire-engine.

South Shields is represented in the Board of Directors of the Company by Thomas Forsyth and James Cochran Stevenson, Esqrs.

And now comes the turn of my east end friends the Pilots, for a *Fisher* and not a *Panner* in my younger days, they have always been the familiars of my youth, and I know that a more brave, hardy, humane, and adventurous body of men is not to be found within her Majesty's wide dominions. The Life-boat never proceeds on her frequent errands of mercy without a willing and a gallant crew of these noble men, whose skilful daring cannot be surpassed, and who are undeterred by the fatal and still deplored catastrophe of 1849.

They reside mostly, if not altogether, at the eastern extremity of the town, and are under the peculiar jurisdiction of the Newcastle Trinity-House, Mr. Pearson being their present ruler. Their numbers here are for the sea one hundred and sixty, and at Cullercoats fifteen.

As Pilots in the management of vessels leaving or entering the port, sometimes under trying circumstances of difficulty and danger, they command our admiration for their coolness and skill; while with their cobles under sail, a craft which only they themselves can manage, they are most wonderfully dexterous.

The subject that follows the Pilots cannot be any other than the *South Shields Life-boat,* and to it, as a native of this town, I proceed with pride and exultation, for to whatever individual or individuals that noble and humane invention may be attributed, it is a certain and admitted fact, that to South Shields, and South Shields alone, is the honour and the debt of gratitude due. I never cast my eyes upon its model, in Saint Hilda's Church, without a feeling of thankfulness for the prevention of suffering and affliction which was consequent on the discovery; for I know that by it the lives of thousands have been saved and rescued from a destruction that would otherwise have been inevitable, and that dearly beloved husbands, fathers, brothers, and relatives, have been enabled, through its blessed agency, to return in safety to their welcome homes.

The original Life-boat was built at South Shields by subscription, under the inspection of Henry Heath, Michael Rockwood, Cuthbert Marshall, Thomas Masterman, Joseph William Roxby, and Nicholas Fairles, the latter gentleman being their chairman. The scheme was suggested by the melancholy loss of the crew of the "Adventure," at South Shields, in Sept., 1789. The men dropped from her rigging, one by one, exhausted by cold and fatigue, as she lay stranded on the Herd-sand, near the entrance of the harbour, in the midst of tremendous breakers, in the presence of thousands of spectators, not one of whom could be prevailed on by any rewards to venture out to her assistance in any boat or coble of the common construction. The above committee was formed in consequence at the Lawe-house, the place at which the subscribers to the Exchange News-rooms (who afterwards removed to the Town-hall) then met. The following is the history of the invention, which I am enabled to lay before you in the words of the chairman of the committee himself, as extracted from his own written account, in a letter of his, bearing date the 4th Feb., 1806, and as it corresponds in every particular with that of my late father, who was himself an original trustee of the South Shields Life-boat Fund, and well acquainted with the circumstances of the invention, I place the most implicit reliance on Mr. Fairles' facts :—

"I shall confine myself to what came within my own knowledge. I have no ambition to be considered the inventor of the life-boat; and for any active part which I took upon me with other gentlemen, I am fully compensated by its general utility.

B

Could I render you the information required, without having recourse to the name of the assumed inventor or his competitor, I should do so. But to be as brief as possible, I do declare, that neither Mr. Greathead nor Mr. Wouldhave was the inventor of the life-boat. The truth stands thus—several gentlemen formed themselves into a committee, of which I had the honour of being chairman, for the purpose of obtaining information and models most proper for saving persons from ships wrecked at the entrance of this harbour; in consequence of which an advertisement appeared in the Newcastle paper. Much information was received by letter, and two models were produced; one of them by Mr. Wouldhave, which was not approved of by the committee; and on my suggestion, Mr. Wouldhave was presented with one guinea, as a compensation for his trouble. Mr. Greathead's model was next taken into consideration, and was also considered an improper one for the purpose wanted. Not any compensation was voted to Mr. Greathead for his trouble, as he was the only professional man who exhibited a model, the committee considered they had it in their power to compensate him by employing him to build a boat as they should hereafter determine upon. At this time much conversation took place among the committee on the subject, and Mr. Michael Rockwood, an intelligent member of the committee, described a boat by which he was saved at Memel in a most tremendous sea : she resembled the Norway yawl. But the committee were of opinion that a boat entirely of that description would not answer for the local purposes of this harbour, as she would draw too much water. The committee then endeavoured to combine, with their own knowledge on the subject, the various information they had received, and out of the whole to produce a something which might answer the purpose. In one idea they all agreed, that the boat should be formed at each end alike, as described by Mr. Rockwood; that the bottom should be something in form between the coble and yawl, with a proper breadth for two persons to row abreast, and a proportional length, with great elevation at the ends. Here rested the idea of the committee for some time; until by accident, Mr. Rockwook and myself met, when the conversation turned upon what should be done in forwarding the proposed boat. I proposed that we should enter an adjoining tile-manufactory, and there endeavour to explain to each other our ideas of the boat, by making a model in clay. In this we succeeded to our entire satisfaction, and the boat was ordered to be built by Mr. Greathead under the direction of the committee. At the commencement of building the boat, Mr. Greathead proposed that the keel should be curved, and this part is the whole that Mr. Greathead has any claim to as the inventor.

"Some years after, I was not a little surprised at an application from Mr. Greathead to sign a certificate, purporting that he was the inventor of the boat. My reply was—that I could not consider Mr. Greathead the inventor, nor would I sign any certificate separately from the committee: that I would do anything consistent with truth, in presence of the committee; and it would be necessary for him to exhibit his original model, when it would be seen whether it resembled the life-boat or not. Some time after this the committee were summoned by Mr. Wm. Blackburn to meet at a Mr. How's, when a certificate was produced for their signatures, purporting that Mr. Greathead was the inventor of the boat. This matter was fully canvassed, and the certificate rejected. I then proposed that the committee should go as far as they could in giving Mr. Greathead a certificate, acknowledging him much credit in the execution of the work as a professional man, and admitting the curve of the keel to be his invention. This was done and signed by the committee, considering that they could go no further to be consistent with truth. If any other certificate was ever obtained, it is unknown to me. In a letter from Mr. Burdon, M.P., he asked me why I would not sign Greathead's certificate? My reply was, I could not do it consistant with truth; and enclosed him a copy of the one signed by the committee, and recommended Mr. Greathead to be noticed by Mr. Burdon in some other way."

Mr. Fairles concludes his letter by solemnly declaring it to be the truth, and no one who knew him could doubt that it was so.

The opinion of the individual, to whom the foregoing letter was addressed, being still at variance with that of Mr. Fairles, to whom he had expressed his continued doubts, pointing out at the same time the alleged trivial difference between Wouldhave's model and the boat, Mr. Fairles, on the 9th of Feb., 1806, replied to those doubts as follows:—

"I do admit, that if a similarity exists between the model exhibited by Mr. Wouldhave to the committee and the first life-boat built at South Shields, you have some foundation for an argument in favour of Mr. Wouldhave against mere assertion on my part, consistent with truth, viz., that the model exhibited by Mr. Wouldhave did not appear to me adequate to the purpose, nor did I derive any assistance from it in making up my ideas on the subject. To the best of my remembrance the model was of tin or copper, painted (this is of no consequence), and in form much resembled the coal-keel: the ends were alike—had, what professional men call, little rake—and fully below. These two points required particular attention, as, in my opinion, the whole depended upon it; and here it was that the committee paused for some time, until the model in clay, formed by Mr. Rockwood and myself, represented the entrance and rake which you termed dead-wood.

"Before any model was exhibited, cork was recommended by a Mr. Hays, of Alnmouth, in a letter to the committee; but prior to that, the idea of cork existed with them, and was strongly recommended by me.

"The following points were laid down by the committee as absolutely necessary to be attended to in the formation of the boat:—Buoyancy, and the ability to divide the water with the least possible resistence—each end of the boat to be similar, that in leaving a wreck there might be no occasion to turn the boat about; and thereby the danger of being laid athwart, or in the hollow of the sea, would be avoided—that great elevation at the ends was necessary, to prevent agitated broken water from entering the boat, when contending against a head sea and wind—and, finally, the local situation required an easy draught of water. These points combined were to constitute the intended boat.

"Now, Sir, these points being necessary, every man who ever saw the boisterous sea on the Herd Sand during a storm, and had turned his mind to forming a boat to contend with that sea, must have determined upon the very points described as absolutely necessary. And as one of the committee, I must declare, I was astonished to see such models exhibited.

"It may be necessary for me to say something on Mr. Greathead's model. It was a long flat boat, and I think was to row double, that is, two persons on each thwart; nor were the ends alike. He described it as being similar to a boat in which he had been accustomed to go up the rivers of America, in the night time, under the command of some naval officer. This model had no buoyancy or cork, nor did it resemble the life-boat. But when I speak of a resemblance in boats, I beg to be understood generally; for as all boats, more or less, possess some of the properties of each other, they must, in some degree, be similar in some respects; and the rudest boat, in the interior, will resemble all the boats in the kingdom in some particular part."

The tile manufactory alluded to in Mr. Fairles' letter, as the place (now memorable) in which the clay model of the Life-boat was made, was in East King-street, behind the Brick and Tile Inn, now occupied by Mrs. Pickering, and which was then the only house in the street. Upon the site of the tile manufactory stand now the new Court-house and the houses in Smithy-street, &c., lying between it and East King-street.

I shall not at this distance of time, when all the parties are dead, and no further information can be received, enter further into the still vexata questio of the Life-boat invention. It is, undoubtedly, my own opinion, that to no single individual did the sole honour of the invention belong; and, therefore, that though Mr. Greathead was fortunate enough to receive several flattering compliments from

persons of the highest rank, a diamond ring, in particular, from the
then Emperor of Russia, a parliamentary grant of £1,200, 100 guineas
from the Trinity-house, 60 guineas and their silver medal from the
Society of Arts, and other gifts, (notwithstanding all, which he died
a bankrupt), no other credit is due to him than that of being the
builder, and of having suggested the curvature of the keel, a main
element, by the way, as I was always given to understand, in the
success of the invention, and one to which much of the safety of the
Life-boat is said to be attributed.

The Life-boat was first used on the 30th of June, 1790, when
several seamen were brought off in safety from a wreck in the offing.
The crew of the Life-boat were provided, on the first trial, with cork
jackets, but these were found to be quite unnecessary. Since then,
hundreds of valuable lives have been saved at the mouth of the Tyne
alone, and the Life-boat with various improvements or alterations,
has been adopted in the ports of Great Britain, and in many foreign
ports also.

Greathead was well known to me as a boatbuilder and an inhabitant of Wellington-street, opposite to my father's.   Wouldhave
was a house painter, and for many years clerk of St. Hilda's Church.

"Alas! poor Yorick!—I knew him well, Horatio: a fellow of infinite jest,
and of most excellent fancy."

He died poor, in this town, on the 28th of Sept., 1821, aged 70, and
was distinguished during his lifetime for his eccentricity of manners,
versatility of mind, and a peculiarly inventive genius.

"Great wits to madness nearly are allied,
And thin partitions, do the bounds divide."

Honest as poor, and almost communicative as ingenious; he was
always employed, yet always changing his employment; sometimes
with shouts, as if speaking to a deaf person, arguing on music with
the organist, and philosophising at other times with a keelman.
Yet his mechanical genius was often usefully employed.   He suggested an important improvement in the building of docks, and he
weighed up a ship that had been sunk, and was abandoned, at the
mouth of the harbour.   He amused himself, also, by constructing
various curious instruments, amongst which were an organ, a clock,
and an electrical machine.   He was as original in appearance as
manners.

The figure of his proposed Life-boat is cut upon his tombstone,
in Saint Hilda's Church-yard, and he is described thereon, by some
undoubting admirer, as "inventor of that invaluable blessing to mankind, the Life-boat."

The Life-boat, forms a conspicious part of the South Shields
Borough Arms, as the same were designed by our highly gifted townsman, Robinson Elliott, who, as an artist, has done much correctly to
preserve "a recollection in his habit as he lived," of many a deserving

and well-known citizen—The motto *" Always ready "* having reference to the promptitude with which the boat is launched and eagerly manned on every occasion which arises for help,

" When the stormy tempests blow."

Courage being represented on one side by a South Shields sailor as a supporter, commerce by commerce herself, in propriâ personâ, as a supporter on the other side, and humanity in the middle, by the Lifeboat itself, and her gallant crew of South Shields Pilots.

In the year 1801, Saint Hilda's Glebe of two acres which is now covered with houses and chapels, to the east of the church, was a public garden, to which our citizens resorted for fruit and recreation, and from which there was an uninterrupted view of the Milldam lake, then unpolluted by its present lamented appropriation. The Rev. Richard Wallis was, at that time, the Incumbent of Saint Hilda, and by agreement between him and the late Henry Robson and Nicholas Fairles, an Act of Parliament was obtained for enabling the former to grant to the latter a lease of the Glebe for 999 years at a yearly rent of £115 payable to the Incumbent and his successors, and with powers for the erection of houses thereon by themselves or those to whom they might grant under-leases. The lease for 999 years was granted accordingly to Messrs. Robson and Fairles, and bears date the 24th of June, 1801, by virtue of which and of the under-leases granted afterwards, the present erections on the Glebe were made and streets created, viz., Barrington-street, Cornwallis-street, Wallis-street, and Nelson-street. The Incumbent of Saint Hilda was considered to be much benefited by the transaction, and this gave rise to the following couplet by a talented legal predecessor of mine, the late Mr. Blackburn, the harmless repetition of which here will give offence, I trust, to no one :—

",Long Harry and little Nick,
Were both outwitted by skinny Dick."

But even witty lawyers cannot escape from the inevitable fate of man, as is evidenced by a handsome monument with the following inscription, which may be seen on the walls of Saint Hilda's Church, by those who are curious in such matters :—

WILLIAM BLACKBURN, Esq.,

OF

SOUTH SHIELDS,

Died Feb. 1818, aged 43 Years.

In testimony of splendid talents, and independence of mind,
most zealously exerted in acts of benevolence and eminent
services rendered to the shipping interest of this port ;
his friends, by whom he was highly esteemed,
erected this tribute to his memory.

To which might have been added, in the words of Hamlet, when apostrophising in the presence of the sexton, on what he conjectured to be the skull of a lawyer—

"Where be his quiddits now, his quillets, his cases, his tenures, and his tricks? Why does he suffer this rude knave now to knock him about the sconce with a dirty shovel, and will not tell him of his action of battery?"

This appropriation of the Glebe of Saint Hilda to building purposes, when the want of it for an additional churchyard has since been so seriously felt, has from time to time been complained of; but it is better that, by the carrying out of the arrangement between the Incumbent and his two lessees, we have one unsightly intramural graveyard the less, and have instead, well-formed streets, respectable dwelling-houses, a handsome Savings'-bank, and chapels dedicated to the worship of Almighty God.

This town has also the honour of originating an invention, by which the means of safety, in cases of shipwreck, by tempest or fire, *is put into the hands of mariners themselves.* My talented and philanthropic friend, Mr. James Mather, was the undisputed inventor of this, he having, in 1826, caused a boat to be constructed at South Shields, successfully uniting the qualities of a life and a ship's boat.

This boat underwent a severe and successful trial in the midst of a heavy six feet sea on the bar, during a strong wind from the north-east, and was found, undoubtedly, to answer the purpose contemplated by the ingenious inventor.

In order, likewise, to avoid the awkward and ill-devised mode of lowering a boat over the vessel's side, which, in a rough sea, exposes it to the danger of being stove, and has, indeed, in many well-remembered cases of melancholy interest, caused a terrible loss of valuable lives under the heart-rending circumstances of ships foundering or being burnt at sea, Mr. Mather invented a launching-frame of the most simple construction, taking up no extra room, with which he himself, unaided, in one minute, and in the presence of a number of spectators, launched a ship-life-boat, containing four men, from the deck of a vessel called the "Mary," belonging to his father. This vessel was wrecked the same year on the coast of Norway in a heavy gale, when the ship-life-boat, safely projected from the launching-frame, saved the entire crew, after every effort of the Norwegians *from the shore* had failed in their well-managed and storm-accustomed sea-boats, thus practically proving the utility of the invention.

I am informed that ship-life-boats of this description have since formed part of the appendages, and are now on board of many large steamers and foreign-going passenger vessels; but surprize is felt that they have not become universally adopted, their value as ship-life-boats being undisputed, and their cost only £10 more than that of an ordinary long-boat; and I, therefore, take this opportunity of recalling them to the notice of my hearers, in connection with the ever ready exertions of the inventor in the cause of humanity.

In Denmark, the Admiralty, with great care and attention, made themselves masters of the most trivial details of the plan; and his Danish Majesty's Minister for Foreign Affairs instructed his Ambassador to transmit to Mr. Mather a letter of thanks for having communicated it to them.

Thus does it appear that by either of those inventions shipwrecked mariners, when stranded, can be rescued; and that by one of them, they also can be saved, under circumstances when, only to the crew themselves and their own ship-life-boat, all hope of safety is confined. Verily, of both inventions, South Shields has reason to feel justly proud.

The filling up with ballast, in the years 1816-18, in spite of all remonstrances to the contrary, of the Mill-dam, which, in my recollection, existed as an inland lake, having access to the river Tyne, and upon which I have skated in my boyhood, has always been to me, and to my brother citizens, a matter of the most bitter regret, for the invaluable opportunity, which once existed, of coverting it into a wet-dock was thereby unhappily lost. The Corporation, of Newcastle, were the lessees of the Dam under the Dean and Chapter of Durham, but it was the inexcusable act of the former, and not of the latter, which deprived South Shields, in the first instance, of a central dock, in a situation so admirably adapted for it; though the subsequent erection upon it of houses and manufactories under leases from the Dean and Chapter, certainly rendered still more unlikely the creation of a dock upon its site. What is also matter for much dissatisfaction is the low, swampy, unhealthy site, upon which the erections were suffered to be made, the Waterloo-vale district being notoriously, that (with the exception of Corstrophine-town) with which South Shields has most reason to be dissatisfied in a sanatary point of view.

Some inhabitants still cling with a "lingering hope, a fond desire," to the possible existence of a dock in this once well-adapted locality; but with the mass of buildings by which the site is now covered, (including the gas-works and glass-house,) the churchyard on the north, the colliery on the south, and the railway mound on the east, the area for a dock is now so circumscribed as to make it certain that with Jarrow-docks alone we must at present be content, whatever may arise out of the future requirements of our trade.

During its existence as a sheet of water, passengers and carts crossed over the Mill-dam by means of two bridges, one at its eastern and the other at its western end, and there was also a cart-road across it, passable at low water.

With respect to the mode in which, within my recollection, communication was kept up between South Shields and Newcastle, there have been many vicissitudes and progressive improvements. By

land, the unquayed state, previous to 1826, of the whole of the road
round Jarrow-slake, frequently covered as it was by the tide, and
sometimes in winter by masses of drift ice, rendered a steady
passage for travellers in that direction by means of public vehicles,
out of the question. The passenger traffic between the two places
was, therefore, of necessity, carried on by land in stage coaches and
gigs from North Shields, or by water, from South Shields and North
Shields, in wherries, comfortables, and steam-boats, such having been
the order in which the means of passenger transit, on the river Tyne,
was progressively improved. The wherries were, as they still are,
open and used not only in the carriage of passengers, but of goods also.
The comfortables, an imitation as it would seem of the Noah's Ark of
the toy-shop, was a decided improvement upon the wherries; and
the establishment of steam-boats, in the year 1814, was hailed with
delight, as unquestionably superior to both. The steam-boats, in
their turn, have yielded, in great measure, to the railroads—and in
asking the question, which naturally suggests itself—" What next ?"
—it is wonderful to reflect upon the increase in the number of passengers, who now avail themselves of the safety and despatch of the
railroad, as compared with the insignificant numbers, by whom the
previous modes of conveyance by land and water, were used.

> " Our lot is given us in a land,
> Where busy arts are never at a stand;
> Where science points her telescopic eye,
> Familiar with the wonders of the sky;
> Where bold inquiry, diving out of sight,
> Brings many a precious pearl of truth to light;
> Where nought eludes the persevering quest,
> That fashion, taste, or luxury suggest."

The " Tyne Steam Packet," afterwards named " The Perseverance,"
was the first built upon the river Tyne for the conveyance of passengers between Newcastle and Shields, and it commenced its course on
the 19th of May, 1814. Being Ascension Day, it joined the procession of barges and boats, and was a great novelty. I was one of the
multitude of wondering spectators, who witnessed its performances
from Newcastle Bridge, and it is impossible to look back without
amazement upon the vast improvements which have since taken place
in all things connected with steam navigation. By it, the duration
of voyages between the most remote regions of the earth, has been
advantageously and agreeably shortened, in spite of adverse winds
and opposing tides, while the merchant and the consumer have largely
benefited by the regularity and rapidity with which merchandize has
been conveyed to its destined market. Our colonies and distant
possessions have become converted into one great and compact em-
pire, by this wonderful discovery; and in war, the modus operandi
has been thereby changed, this country strengthened, and her power
better developed. In this particular locality, to which only I confine

myself, its adaptation to purposes of towage, through the agency of steam-tugs, has caused the foy-boats to be looked upon as things of the *Past ;* and instead of those congregated fleets of vessels within our crowded harbour, for periods of long duration, owing to long continuance of contrary winds, the only stoppages now arise from the bar and the sea. The consequence is, that the continually increasing demands of the London coal market, are met with a supply more steady, and prices less fluctuating, than in former years, an advantage certainly to the London consumer, but perhaps not equally so to my coal-carrying friends, who used to benefit largely, as merchants, by the fluctuations in prices, arising from those detentions to which I have alluded; and who are, I fear, doomed as coal-carriers, to still further revolution, not only through the dangerous and encroaching rivalry of the quick and burthensome screw steam colliers of modern invention, but by the substitution of railways for ships, as a means for the conveyance of coal to London and many other British markets, which formerly were supplied by collier vessels only. This is gradually being effected, as was wisely foretold by Mr. Mather, in that patriotic and cautionary work of his on " Ships and Railways," which, ever alive to our maritime interests, he published in the year 1846 ; the truth of his prophecies and the reasonableness of his doubts, having since been proved by the admitted and alarming fact, that of all the coals now brought to London from the various parts of the kingdom, amounting, according to the returns of 1855, for the preceding year, to 4,378,732 tons, there *were actually conveyed by railway the serious proportion of* 979,171 *tons,* or nearly 29 per cent. In 1846, when " Ships and Railways " was published, there were little more than 3 per cent. of the whole London supplies conveyed by railway, an almost imperceptible item in the great account.

Here, also, it was my pleasant lot to aid Mr. Mather in his important object, his work on " Ships and Railways," having, from its commencement and during its progress, been confided to me only by its talented author.

South Shields is so deservedly eminent for its chemical and glass manufactures as to render them deserving of special notice. Both are of ancient date as to their establishment, but the chemical manufacture was not fully developed till about the year 1827.

The first record of a chemical work in South Shields, is of one at the *Alum House-ham,* about the year 1720, when the Mr. John Cookson of that day, a name which has remained ever since in prominent manufacturing connection with South Shields, had some small vessels fitted with tanks for the reception of alum liquor from the Whitby alum works. These craft were kept constantly employed in carrying the liquid solution of that which is the basis of the article called alum (viz. alumina), to a small factory, situated at what is now the foot of Dean-street, where the liquor was afterwards treated in

c

the proper manner for the production of alum, and hence the shore or landing place came to be designated, as it still is, the *Alum House-ham*; Glue, fig-blue, sulphate of soda, and chrystals of soda, were made by the Cookson family during the middle of last century. All these substances were then largely imported from Holland and other parts of the continent, and it was in the nationalising of these products that the Cooksons founded their expectation of profit. Glue and fig-blue were made from the substances now used—sulphate of soda was made by means of copperas and chrystals of soda from barilla, both of which modes are now disused.

In the year 1822, a manufactory, on a small scale, was established at Temple Town for the manufacture of carbonate of soda, otherwise called alkali. The process was then little known, and the results were unsatisfactory until the year 1827, when an improved process was firmly established, and a marketable article produced. The works were enlarged, year by year, until the year 1844, when Messrs. Cookson and Cuthbert discontinued the works, and let the premises to the Jarrow Chemical Company, who now conduct them on a scale, and in a manner far surpassing their predecessors, both as regards scientific appliances and quantity of produce.

During the occupation of Messrs. Cookson and Cuthbert, various chemical substances were produced at the works at Temple Town, viz., sulphate of copper (blue vitriol), iodine, bleaching powder, and alum. The latter was produced without the use of the natural deposit, which the former John Cookson of my lecture, was at the pains of bringing at such expense from Whitby, and is a striking instance of the substitution of artificial for natural processes. At the time when that John Cookson made alum at the Alum House-ham, the manufacture of this article formed a considerable item in the revenues of the Pope of Rome on the coast of Italy, and after the fashion of those by-gone days, a bull was issued anathematising the competitors of his Holiness.

The history of the manufacture of carbonate of soda, or alkali, forms a most interesting episode in our industrial annals, and in every step and stage of its progress, it has been made at South Shields. It was first made from barilla, a sort of kelp, brought from Alicante and Teneriffe—then it was made, at the suggestion of the Earl of Dundonald, by the decomposition of common salt, by pearl ashes or carbonate of potash,—and lastly it was made by the present process, which was first known in Europe at the time of the French Revolution. The English cruisers prevented foreign importations to the ports of France, and, in consequence, its inhabitants found their supply of sugar, alkali, and saltpetre, suddenly cut off. The Committee of Public Safety, supposing that these articles could be produced by artifical means, issued a chemical commission for the examination of the subject, and the result of their labours was a detail of processes for the manufacture of sugar from beet-root, saltpetre from the refuse of stables, and alkali from common salt, all which processes are now in full operation in France, and the last has been introduced with incomparable success into this country.

For many years the carriers on of these chemical works were almost continually subjected to legal proceedings, both of a public and private nature, by way of indictment for nuisance, or actions for private damage, but owing to a more perfect and careful condensation of the injurious gases arising from the processes, such proceedings are now unheard of, and the company carry on their works undisturbed by legal annoyance.

The first *Glass Work*, in Great Britain, for the manufacture of window glass, was established at the Ouseburn, near Newcastle-upon-Tyne, in the year 1630, and letters are extant in which John Cookson dates from his glass works at South Shields, in the year 1690. The ancient books of the South Shields plate and crown glass works for 1728 are in existance, and the wages book of that year contains the names of the ancestors of many families who still earn their bread at the same manufactory.

A detail of the improvement in the art would fill a volume. Originally the sizes of the glass, particularly the plate, were very small, and the latter was laboriously polished by manual labour. During the whole of last century the process was little understood, and the mixing book, or account of the mixtures of plate glass made at South Shields, dated 1650, is such as to make the merest tyro in the art laugh with amazement. Substances long since discarded, and many of them highly inimical to the process, were then liberally used, and it is a subject of wonder how glass could be made from such materials.

In the middle of last century the use of Scotch kelp became more general in the manufacture of crown glass, and the consequence was, that lands in Scotland unproductive of almost anything else, became of great value. During the summer the sea-weed was collected from the rocks, and burnt in ovens on the shore. The result was large cakes of kelp, which, without further preparation, were shipped off to the English glass works. So valuable was the weed, that, during the winter, the poor inhabitants have been known to roll stones within the tide-way, on which weed grew during the succeeding summer, and thereby their crop was increased—an instance of agricultural enterprise worthy of commendation.

Kelp in its turn has been superseded by alkali, and the kelp farms are now valueless, their populations having, in many instances, emigrated to America. Although the mutations of science and commerce often inflict great individual suffering, it appears to be a condition of our commercial progress.

The duty on glass of all kinds was long an incubus on its manufacture, and the revenue derivable from this branch of industry, prior to the abolition of the duty, amounted to £600,000 per annum. The works carried on by Messrs. Cookson and Cuthbert, and by Messrs. Shortridge & Co. frequently paid the large sum of £150,000 or nearly £3,000 per week, and in the case of crown glass, the duty, in some cases, amounted to nearly 300 per cent. on its value.

On the abolition of the duty, the produce of window and plate glass and bottles, was nearly quadrupled, but with the exception of plate glass and bottles, the manufacture of glass in this town and this river, has materially declined. Formerly there were, on the river Tyne, twelve furnaces in operation for the manufacture of crown glass, now there is only one, that of Messrs. R. W. Swinburne & Co., the head of which firm worthily occupies, through his own merits and abilities, the high position as a plate and crown glass manufacturer and merchant, which was previously held by his well-known predecessor, the late Isaac Cookson, in South Shields and Newcastle-upon Tyne. This decay is attributable to many causes—a preference for a superior quality or larger size of glass—the general introduction of plate—and the use of sheet glass, which is now made in England in large quantities, at prices which are kept exceedingly low by foreign importation, and the establishment of large window glass works in the manufacturing districts of Lancashire, where there is a great demand for glass, and where coal is now raised in abundance. It is understood that the glass trade is at present depressed beyond all former precedent, it having been greatly injured by the dearness of building materials, the effects of the war, and the competition of the foreign manufacturer.

The only other crown glass work ever established in South Shields, was the extensive one near the Mill-dam, first carried on as crown and bottle works by Simon Temple, then by Shortridge, Russell, and Barras, afterwards by Richard Turner Shortridge, since by Richard Shortridge, followed by the South Tyne Glass Company, and now as bottle works by Hudson & Co. These particular works are pleasingly connected in our minds, with our neighbour, Richard Shortridge, who, as a resident townsman amongst us from his youth upwards, almost even to the present time, and a successful manufacturer and merchant, has obtained, by his many public services, mercantile character, and private worth, our respect and regard, so much so as to justify me in the conviction, that I shall be joined by every one who has honoured me with his attendance this evening, in an earnest with, that in the beautiful and well-selected retirement which he has earned and recently secured, he may enjoy with those whom he loves and by whom he is so well-beloved, health of body, peace of mind, and continued prosperity, certain that, when fallen into the sear and yellow leaf, he may well look to have and surely will receive

> " All that should accompany old age,
> As honor, love, obedience, troops of friends."

The ancient and extensive bottle works of Messrs. Cookson and Cuth-

bert, in East Holborn, only remain to be mentioned in completion of
my list of South Shields glass works, the flint glass works so long
carried on by Shortridge, Sawyer, & Co., in West Holborn, and lately
by Cooke & Co., being unfortunately not a current going concern.

Of which brittle portion of my subject I now take leave with a
feeling of pride, that South Shields still continues to possess the
advantages of a high position in the glass trade of the United Kingdom; and of hope that it will speedily recover from its present
depression, and, like a giant refreshed with sleep, be carried on with
renewed vigour in all its pristine magnitude and prosperity.

To be reckoned amongst the things which are past, is the patriotic and warlike spirit by which the inhabitants of this town were
actuated, in common with those of the whole kingdom, when threatened with invasion by the first Napoleon Buonaparte, and

"When we alone amongst the nations, were found to withstand his violent
and unjust ambition."

That spirit displayed itself in our locality, by the formation of two
effective and well-disciplined volunteer corps—the South Shields
Loyal Volunteers—and the South Shields Loyal Independent Armed
Association—the former under the command of Lieut.-Colonel Sir
Cuthbert Heron, baronet, and the latter of Lieut.-Colonel Joseph
Bulmer—a corps of Sea Fencible, composed chiefly of pilots, and
commanded by Capt. Praed, having also been organised. By drilling
and frequent exercise, these corps had all arrived at a high state of
discipline, and, it cannot be doubted, that had opportunity presented
itself for a meeting with the enemy, South Shields would not have
had cause to blush for her sons. Well do I recollect the eagerness and
delight with which, as a boy, I listened to the rattling drums and the
merry fifes as they summoned to parade the members of the respective
corps—still do I recollect the gallant bearing of the soldier-like Sir
Cuthbert Heron, as he proudly rode at the head of his regiment, "the
observed of all observers"—"In my mind's eye" yet, I have before
me, the well-known Dalgetties of their day, Majors John Thompson
and Christopher Bainbridge—nor have I forgotten the evolutions of
the wiry and active fugleman, as in front of his regiment, he signalled
his comrades, and at the same time astonished the admiring spectators. Alas! alas! it is melancholy to reflect, that of all that imposing force, few only of the privates survive, and that of the officers,
two only remain to remind us, by their still welcome presence, of the
stirring events of that stormy period, Capt. John Paxton and my
valued friend, Lieut. George Potts.

"His master's gone, and no one now,
Dwells in the halls of Ivor,
Men, dogs, and horses, all are dead,
He is the sole survivor."

A disappearance which is by no means a poetical fiction, for many of the leading shipowners of that day hunted regularly with the late Sir Hedworth Williamson, of Whitburn, and his pack of harriers; and often was the neighbourhood enlivened with the sound of the merry horn, the music of the dogs, and the cries of the hunters as they swept along, in eager pursuit of some timid and unoffending hare.

An extensive reform in the representation of the people in the Commons House of Parliament, having been one of the conditions upon which the late Earl Grey accepted office in 1830, and it being then generally understood that the noble Earl's pledge would be redeemed by the introduction to parliament of a measure sufficiently comprehensive to meet the wishes of the people; the attention of the inhabitants of South Shields (who laboured, under a more serious destitution of the elective franchise, than the inhabitants of any other town in Great Britain, of equal trade and magnitude), was promptly called (I am proud to say by me) to the subject of its claims to a direct share in the representation; and the inhabitants were not wanting in their constitutional exertions for the furtherance of the good cause. Several public meetings, of a numerous and very influential character were held, at which able and spirited resolutions, of a nature to meet the various difficult and perhaps dangerous exigencies which arose during the tantalising progress of the Reform Bill, were passed, and petitions to both Houses of Parliament, with addresses also to King William himself, unanimously agreed to. It is superfluous now to state, that those exertions were eventually crowned with success, the claims of South Shields to that place in the Reform Act, to which its population, trade, and increasing importance, so justly entitled it, having been clearly established and conceded.

The Reform Act passed in 1832, and a contest of a most spirited and determined nature took place for the honour of becoming the first representative of our maiden borough in parliament, during which the wit, intelligence, and controversial talent of the town, were shown to great advantage in the numerous squibs and electioneering articles which appeared on behalf the various candidates. The contest ended in the return of Robert Ingham, Esq., of Westoe, our present member, on the 12th day of December, 1832, the numbers being as follow—

VOTES.

For Robert Ingham, Westoe............ 205 (returned)
" George Palmer, London 108
" William Gowan, London............ 104
" Russell Bowlby, Cleadon Meadows.... 2

There having since (with the exception of 1837) been other contested elections for this borough, with the following results, viz. :—

VOTES.

1835.—Robert Ingham................ 273 (returned)
Russell Bowlby................ 128

1837.—Robert Ingham.................... (returned)
(no contest.)

VOTES.

1841.—John Twizell Wawn, West Boldon   240 (returned)
Robert Ingham................   207
George Fyler, London   34

1847.—John Twizell Wawn ....   333 (returned)
William Whateley, London   176

1852.—Robert Ingham................   430 (returned)
Hon. Hen. Thos. Liddell, Eslington 249

During the whole of these contests, the conduct of the electors of
South Shields was such as to show how well they were deserving of
the franchise which they had gained—no open public-houses—no
treating—no bribery or corruption—disgraced our borough, or the
the candidates for the representation. The electors exercised their
franchise with deliberate independence; while, with a purity of
conduct which was beyond suspicion, they performed the electoral
duties, which had been entrusted to them by the legislature, with
disinterested faithfulness and truth. None had better means than
I had of arriving at a knowledge of all this, and I pronounce it as
my opinion thus openly before you, and without fear of contradiction,
that in none of the parliamentary boroughs of the United Kingdom
is there to be found a constituency more pure and independent, or
more anxious for the proper discharge of their electoral franchise than
that of South Shields.

Again, while other boroughs have been driven to the disagreeable
necessity of seeking at a distance for a stranger as their representative, South Shields, since her enfranchisement, has been satisfactorily
represented by her own sons only. This is to her a source of motherly
pride and honest exultation, for in Robert Ingham and John Twizell
Wawn, she found two zealous and faithful servants acquainted with
her wants, devoted to her interests, and capable of protecting and advancing them. In his retirement the one is looked upon with respect
and rewarded with thanks for the services which he has rendered,
while the other is receiving, as a reward in his present parliamentary
position, the confidence and encouragement of his brother electors,
the constituency of this borough, and the love of all for his kindness
of heart, courtesy of manners, and neighbourly good qualities.

> " A man of letters, and of manners too,
> Of manners sweet as virtue always wears,
> When gay good-nature dresses her in smiles—
> He graced a college, in which order yet,
> Was sacred; and was honoured and beloved
> By more than one, themselves conspicuous there."

In 1832, the number of parliamentary voters on the list for the
borough was 540. Now, in 1856, it is 1,073, showing an increase,
in twenty-four years, of 533 voters.

Up to a not very late period, the entire intercourse between the inhabitants of South and North Shields was entirely carried on by means of sculler-boats, manned each by a superannuated seaman, rowing two oars, one in each hand, and not unfrequent were the accidents and loss of life, in thus crossing the river when the tides were strong, more especially when passenger and tug steam-boats became numerous. This led first to the thought of a tunnel under the river, from one town to the other; and then to that of a chain suspension bridge, by which Capt. Brown, of the royal navy, proposed to connect the two towns at a very high elevation, sufficient above the water to admit ships to sail thereunder without striking their masts, starting near the Library, at North Shields, and near the north end of Westoe-lane, at South Shields. The estimated cost of it was £150,000, but owing to a want of sufficient support, arising chiefly from a dread of the stability of the structure when exposed to gales of wind, at so high and exposed an elevation, and with such an enormous span across, the project was wisely abandoned; a powerful letter of warning which appeared in the "Tyne Mercury" newspaper of that day, having, in a great degree, been the cause of that determination.

Still the necessity of obtaining a safe, commodious, and expeditious conveyance across the river for passengers, carriages, and cattle, was generally admitted and it was finally resolved to make use of steam for effecting so desirable an object. Accordingly, on the 1st of June, 1829, an Act of Parliament was obtained, entituled "An Act for establishing a Ferry across the river Tyne, between North Shields and South Shields, and for opening and making proper roads, avenues, and passages to communicate therewith." By the preamble it is set forth that there was at that time no convenient means of conveyance or communication across the river Tyne between those two towns; and that from the greatly increased and increasing population of them, there was much necessity for convenient means of intercourse between the inhabitants thereof; and that it would greatly contribute to the advantage, accommodation, and safety of such inhabitants, and be of great public utility, to have a convenient Ferry established for carriages, horses, cattle, goods, wares, merchandise, and other portable articles, and foot passengers, over the river, between North and South Shields aforesaid, and to have a good road, avenue, way or passage, from such Ferry at North Shields to, and into the main street of, the low town of North Shields, called Duke-street, and from such Ferry at South Shields to and into the street called Dean-street, communicating with the Market-place, in South Shields;

Certain shareholders, with all necessary powers for the making, establishing, and maintaining of the Ferry for the purposes aforesaid, were united into a company by the name and style of "The North and South Shields Ferry Company;

A maximum scale of toll to be taken were fixed;

And the setting up and using of any other Ferry across the river Tyne within the limits of the parish of Tynemouth, in Northumberland, and of the townships of South Shields and Westoe, in Durham, was prohibited, with an exception in favour of boats, barges, floats, rafts, or other vessels of the burthen of four tons or upwards; and with a further exception in favour of boats, barges, or vessels aiding or assisting any boat, barge, ship, or vessel, in navigating the river, and for the purpose of going to or from any such boat, barge, ship, or vessel, whether they be laying near the river, or going in or upon the same.

Never was preamble more truly stated, as will be admitted by all persons, who, like myself, have experienced the dangers and delays of crossing the river at Shields, when it could only be accomplished in the boats of the scullermen;

And great was the boon conferred upon the public at large, and the towns of South and North Shields in particular, when passengers were relieved from those dangers and delays by the enterprize and capital of the spirited individuals who originally formed themselves into The North and South Shields Ferry Company, to whom we are indebted for the safety and accommodation afforded by the Ferry-boats which first steamed between the two towns.

On the 30th of June, 1848, another Act of Parliament was obtained, entituled "An Act for establishing *direct* steam communication, between the towns of North and South Shields, and between other places in the counties of Durham and Northumberland," in which after reciting that the towns of North and South Shields and the parishes, townships, and places adjacent thereto upon the river Tyne, had, of late years, much increased in population, and that frequent and easy communication with each other had become essential; and reciting the Ferry Act of the 1st of June, 1829, and the incorporation thereby of "The North and South Shields Ferry Company," and that certain provisions were contained in the said last-mentioned Act, restricting the establishment of any other Ferry within certain limits, and imposing a penalty upon any person carrying passengers for hire across the said Ferry within such limits in vessels of a burthen of four tons and upwards; and that it had become expedient and requisite for the accommodation of the public, that further accommodation should be provided for conveying passengers across the river Tyne both within and beyond the limits of the last-mentioned Act; that powers should be given for constructing certain stations, wharves, landing places, approaches, and other works, for the accommodation of passengers and goods; that provisions should be made for arrangements with the North and South Shields Ferry Company established by the last-mentioned Act; and that the several persons thereinafter named, together with others, were desirous of being united into a company for the establishment of *new* steam communications, and for the execution of the works connected therewith.

D

They were so incorporated by the name of "The Tyne Direct Ferry Company," with a capital of £9,300, divided into 1,860 shares of £5 each, with powers to enter on lands and construct works according to the plans and book of reference lodged with the respective Clerks of the Peace for Durham, Northumberland, and Newcastle-upon-Tyne; and to establish and maintain steam or other boats for the conveyance of foot passengers over and across the river Tyne, between the several places described on the said plans, and also to convey carriages, horses, cattle, goods, wares, merchandise, and other portable articles by means of such steam and other boats across the said river Tyne, between the stations at Willington-quay and Jarrow, and, also, if they thought fit, between the stations at Whitehill-point and Penny Pie-stairs, and to construct and maintain good and substantial stations, wharves, landing places, approaches, and other works, within the limits described on the said plans, in the several parishes thereinafter mentioned, or some of them, that is to say, Tynemouth and Wallsend, or either of them, in the county of Northumberland, Jarrow and the parochial chapelry of Saint Hilda, in the parish of Jarrow and county of Durham, and Saint Nicholas, in the town and county of the town of Newcastle-upon-Tyne.

· Power was given to levy tolls according to a fixed maximum rate;

And after reciting that the North and South Shields Ferry Company were desirous of establishing the said additional Ferries authorised by that Act, and that inasmuch as the exclusive right of Ferry was at present vested in such company, and it had been deemed more advantageous to the public that the whole of the Ferries should be constructed and worked by *one company*, it was expedient that the North and South Shields Ferry Company should be empowered to purchase the undertaking by that Act authorised; *It was therefore Enacted*, That it should be lawful for the North and South Shields Ferry Company (in manner therein mentioned) to purchase and accept the undertaking, and "The Tyne Direct Ferry Company" were authorised and directed, when thereunto directed by the "North and South Shields Ferry Company," to convey the undertaking and all the powers and authorities conferred upon them by virtue of that Act (but subject to the existing mortgages, contracts, agreements, and liabilities affecting the same);

That every such transfer should be deed;

That on the completion of such transfer, the North and South Shields Ferry Company might have and hold the undertaking, and use, exercise, and enjoy the rights, powers, and privileges conferred by that Act on the Tyne Direct Ferry Company, as well as the rights, &c., conferred by the recited Act upon "The North and South Shields Ferry Company," and be subject to the same provisions and restrictions with respect to the Ferries thereby authorised to be established, as were imposed on the Tyne Direct Ferry Company.

That when such purchase should take place the North and South

Shields Ferry Company should purchase the boats, vessels, gangways, and other the working stock and plant of the Tyne Direct Ferry Company.

That, after the completion of the purchase of such undertaking, the easternmost Ferry, by that Act authorised to be made, might run to the station of the North and South Shields Ferry Company at the Comical-corner, South Shields;

And that if the North and South Shields Ferry Company should neglect or omit to purchase the undertaking for twelve months after the passing of the Act, then, and in that case, it should be lawful for "The Tyne Direct Ferry Company" to proceed themselves in the execution of the undertaking, without being subject to any of the restrictions, or liable to any of the penalties contained in the said recited Act of the North and South Shields Ferry Company.

The North and South Shields Ferry Company *did* purchase of, and have conveyed to them, by "The Tyne Direct Ferry Company," the undertaking, and have since worked the whole of the Ferries to the great safety, comfort, and convenience of the public. They being now engaged in the establishment of a Steam Ferry between White-hill-point and Penny Pie-stairs, which will be a great and an additional public accommodation, and of particular advantage to this borough, by the facilities and inducements which it will afford for visits to South Shields, by the working population of Whitehill-point and Hayhole, to the benefit, it is hoped, of our shops and markets.

These dry details I would gladly spare you, but it would be foreign to my object if I were to slim them over, and I, therefore, pray you to excuse me, and to submit to them patiently as an inevitable infliction.

I have before alluded to the old Improvement Act of 1829. The powers for executing it were vested in commissioners, self-elected, the only requirement in regard to whom, being a property qualification of £2,000, or a yearly £30 occupancy or possession, and the taking of an oath to that effect. The Act contained the usual powers of that day for lighting, watching, cleansing, regulating, improving, and rating, and under it the town was governed and very much improved. The powers of the Commissioners were formally transferred to the Corporation by deed, dated the 31st of Dec., 1850. The transfer was made under the 75 sec. of the Municipal Corporation Act, 5 and 6 Wm. IV. c. 76, and the powers and provisions of the Act of 1829, were executed by the Council of the borough until its repeal on the 8th of July, 1853, by the new Improvement Act, which, on that day, received the Royal Assent.

The reasons for the repeal of the old, and the obtaining of the new Improvement Act, were weighty and sufficient; but it is not necessary to recapitulate them here, it being sufficient to say, that the valuable and extensive provisions of the latter and its incorporated public Acts, viz., the Public Health Act, Town's Improvement Clauses Act, Town's Police Clauses Act, Markets and Fairs Clauses Act, Cemeteries Clauses Act, Gas Works Clauses Act, and Lands Clauses Consolidation Act, are being carried out by the Town Council, and the several committees, with a judgment, diligence, and determination, which are deserving of the confidence and thanks of the burgesses. The thorough and entire underground sewerage of the borough is receiving their attention, and preparations are in actual progress in the making, by Mr. Thompson, the borough surveyor, of surveys, plans, and sections, of a very scientific and able character, for that important work, according to the assurance given by his worship, the Mayor, on his first entering into office. The village of Westoe has already been drained as a special district, and the Ogle estate, with its many streets, is likewise in rapid course of sewerage as a special district also. The rest of the town will follow in due time, and there will then be no necessity for the use of surface drains, at present so offensive both to the sight and the smell.

The new Improvement Act does not quite include the whole of the township of Westoe, but it will do so at the expiration of three years after the completion of the Jarrow Dock, now happily in course of construction, and then there will be embraced within its boundaries the whole of the townships of South Shields and Westoe.

Amongst our public undertakings, most deserving of notice, is that of *The South Shields Gas Company* which was formed by deed of covenants, bearing date the 17th day of March, 1824, with a capital of £4,000 divided into 160 shares of £25 each. The works are situated in St. Hilda's Lane, and gas was first supplied therefrom to the shops and houses on the 1st of Oct., 1824, and to the public street lamps on the 1st Nov., 1829, the number then of thirty-eight only, having since increased to three hundred and eighty-six. Benjamin Tyzack, of North Shields, was the engineer employed in their construction, and Mr. Sanderson was the first, and is still, the engineering manager, John Walker having been the first secretary, succeeded on his death by Jas. Anderson, who was succeeded on his resignation by John Dixon Lister, the present secretary.

The wants of the public, and the prosperity of the undertaking, rendered necessary an extension of the works, and this is now being effected by means of the acquisition by purchase of Mr. Wm. Allon's soapery and extensive premises, in immediate proximity to the original works. By this acquisition the company will be enabled to lay down immediately a gasholder capable of containing 200,000 cubic feet of gas, in addition to the 80,000 cubit feet, of the previous gasholders.

There are about 2,000 consumers of gas at present, 900 of whom burn by meter, and the remaining 1,100 by scale.

The present price of gas is 4s. per 1,000 cubic feet.

The company are about to lay down a large main from the gas

works to Edwards's dock, there to join the new main laid down from thence to Jarrow-slake last year, with a view to the supply of that locality and the Jarrow docks, now in course of formation, with gas.

By a fresh deed, dated the 26th of Dec., 1855, and registered 23rd January, 1856, under the 7 and 8 Vic. c. 110, the company was reorganized with a capital of £20,000, divided into 2,000 shares of £10 each, with power of increase by the issue of new shares or otherwise, to the amount of the further sum of £15,000.

It will not be considered out of place for me here to state, that the existence and inflammability of coal gas have been known for upwards of two hundred years, but no one thought of applying it to a useful object until the year 1798, when a gas work was put up at the manufactory of Bolton and Watt, at Soho, and this was the first application of gas in a large way; but excepting in manufactories and amongst scientific men, it excited little attention until the year 1802, when the front of the great Soho manufactory was brilliantly illuminated with gas, on the occasion of the public rejoicing at the peace. The superiority of the new light over the dingy oil lamps used at that day, when thus brought into public view, produced an astonishing effect. All Birmingham poured forth to view the spectacle, and strangers carried to every part of the country an account of what they had seen. It was spread about everywhere by the newspapers, easy modes of making gas were described, and coal was distilled in tobacco-pipes at the fire-side, all over the kingdom. Soon after this, several manufactories, whose works required light and heat, adopted the use of gas. But although the use of it was thus spreading in the manufacturing towns, it made, owing chiefly to the want of purification, little progress in London; Pall Mall, which was first lighted up in 1807, having continued for some years to be the only street in London in which gas was used. I believe, however, that it may be asserted that every street and alley in London is now lighted with gas, the consumption of the metropolis being many millions of cubic feet every twenty-four hours.

The great success which attended gas light in London, has extended itself throughout Great Britain. Every town (including, I am happy to say, our own,) has long been blessed with gas. The smaller towns followed, and there is now scarcely a place in the kingdom without it.

To those of my fellow-townsmen who had to perambulate our dark and narrow streets, at night, in the olden times, when lanterns *were*, but cabs were *not*, in common use, and servant-maids were in all quarters to be met, bearing their gaily painted green and red lanterns in solemn state before their equally solemn mistresses, on their way to or from some favourite gossip, the safety and comfort derived from the lighting of the streets with gas may readily be imagined. To the South Shields Gas Company we are indebted for a change so satisfac-

tory, and it is pleasing to perceive that, by the extension of their
works, such as we have already mentioned, they are alive to the requirements of a rapidly increasing population, and are prepared to
meet them with promptitude and liberality.

By our new Improvement Act, the Corporation are empowered to
purchase, by agreement, the gas works, gasometers, machinery, and
apparatus, belonging to the Gas Company, and such company are
thereby authorised to sell and transfer the same to the Corporation,
but as the Corporation are limited by the Act to the raising of
£10,000 only for this purpose, it is not likely now, that with such
a recently extended capital as we have before brought under your
notice, any such change of property will or can be effected.

On the 3rd of Sept., 1850, a memorable day in the annals of
this borough, her Majesty, Queen Victoria, was graciously pleased to
grant to it a Royal Charter of Incorporation, under which, and the
Municipal Acts, the mayor, aldermen, and burgesses, have since discharged the functions of a Municipal Corporation, with credit to
themselves, and the advantage of the borough. Two former attempts
had failed, owing to the opposition of the chief ratepayers, but the time
for incorporation was admitted to have arrived, when the third application was made, and the Charter was applied for and obtained, with
the universal consent, and hearty good wishes of the inhabitants, who
had become dissatisfied with the irresponsible constitution of the
Commission, and the unequal rating, provided by the old Improvement Act of 1829.   The principal grounds upon which the promoters
rested their petition for incorporation, were as follow :—

1. The want of responsible local government, with sufficient power to promote improvements and prevent nuisances.
2. The want of a medium of concentration for public opinion in the borough, and of a recognized head, for communication with government, and other public bodies.
3. The want of a proper machine for the adoption and carrying out of sanitary measures. And
4. The want of a Municipal body, out of which to elect such commissioners on the part of South Shields, as were rendered necessary by the changes in the Conservancy of the River Tyne.

By means of the Charter, these wants were all supplied, and the
Corporate body now consists of a mayor, aldermen, and councillors,
there being three Wards, viz., South Shields Ward, with three aldermen, and nine councillors; Westoe Ward, with two aldermen, and
six councillors; and Jarrow Ward, with three aldermen, and nine councillors; making a total of thirty-two.   One-third of the councillors go
out of office every year, and one-half of the alderman every third year,
all the retiring aldermen and councillors being re-eligible.   There are
also a town clerk, appointed by the Council, and borough assessors,
revising assessors, and auditors, elected annually by the burgesses,
together with a Mayor's auditor, appointed annually by his worship
the Mayor—and a staff of officers, consisting of treasurer, borough

surveyor, rate collector, inspector of nuisances and of common lodging-houses, and high constable.

In the watch committee, by the Municipal Act, the appointment and management of the police-officers are vested, and the force consists at present of a superintendent, an inspector, a night sergeant, and thirteen police constables; the police-station, lock-up, and superintendent's dwelling-house, being in the court-house, Waterloo-vale, where both the county and borough magistrates hold their sittings, and in which the county court for the South Shields district is held.

In the Council, as a responsible body, the local government of the borough is safely placed. But the powers of its members, for good or for evil, are of the most extensive description, and it, therefore, well behoves the burgesses of the different wards, to whom the privilege of election is confided as a sacred trust, to take care that no man is sent, as their representative to our local parliament, who is not in every respect qualified, by intelligence, character, habits of business, stake in the borough, and respectable position, for the discharge of his important duties. The levying of taxes, and the spending of them, the public lighting, the police, the sewerage, the scavenging, the streets themselves, are all placed absolutely under their management and control; while as the Local Board of Health, the comforts and health of the inhabitants may be said in a great measure to be dependant on them. The proceedings of Parliament, by means of which our interests as a shipping and trading community might in many ways be injured or affected, receive from them a watchful care. And in their hands is placed the important appointment of three Improvement Commissioners who are sent as the representatives of this borough to the River Tyne Improvement Commission, there to take care that no detriment is done to that noble river, in the preservation and improvement of which, as a public highway, the inhabitants of this borough are so deeply interested. So great indeed are those, the powers and responsibilities which I have named, that it has always been to me a matter of surprise and dissatisfaction, that many who are interested in the trade, prosperity, and good government of this borough, and upon whom the public had a right to look for assistance, should have studiously kept aloof, and abandoned to others the performance of duties which they themselves should have joined in discharging. Property has its duties as well as its rights, and I purposely declare, without any intention unnecessarily to offend, that in too many instances, those duties have been unfairly avoided by those who are the possessors of property within the borough, and who profit largely by its local position, and their connexion with it. But that is happily, no longer of moment; for it has been found, that without the aid of those to whom I have alluded, the affairs of this borough can be managed by others to whom the burgesses have confided the trust, and by whom it has been so ably, so prudently, and so industriously discharged, as to have placed the Town Council of South Shields in a position undoubtedly second to none of the neighbouring boroughs, as possessors of all those good qualities for which the governing body of a corporate town should be most highly prized.

The number of burgesses on the roll in the first year of incorporation, was 879; and it is now, in 1856, 1570: the following being the rotation in which the mayors have held office, viz.:—

1st year.—Alderman John Clay.
2nd year.— Do.
3rd year.—Alderman George Potts.
4th year.—Alderman John Robinson.
5th year.—Alderman John Toshach.
6th year.—Alderman Thomas Stainton,

our present able, public-spirited, and energetic chief magistrate who stands forth conspicuously in proof of what can be accomplished and won in a manufacturing and commercial community, by industry, integrity, and determined perseverance.

And now that I have got thus far on my journey, you will perhaps allow me to relieve its tediousness by the following clever jeu d'esprit from the pen and manufactory of our friend Councillor Armstrong, the production of which arose from the circumstance of Alderman Potts following Alderman Clay (both of whom will enjoy the joke) in the office of Mayor, and which is headed—

THE BOROUGH'S BOAST.

My factories I've hatch'd and nursed,
    Till fam'd for operative skill;
I take the *raw material* first,
    Then shew the *finished article*.

My Council, too, a fact displays,
    That beats the neighbouring boroughs hollow:
To wit, in choosing Mayors, it says,
    First give me *Clay* and *Potts* shall follow.

Clay from the *bank*, all hands declare,
    Is good *material* for the *mould*;
Press'd, he came out a *model* Mayor,
    And *Potts* came after, as foretold.

A separate commission of the peace for the borough, bearing date the eleventh day of July, 1851, and consisting at present of the following magistrates, may also be reckoned as one of the benefits derived from its incorporation; viz., the Mayor, for the time being, John Twizell Wawn, Richard Shortridge, John Robinson, James Stevenson, James Young, Thomas Forsyth, and George Potts. They hold their sittings in the Police Court on the Monday, Wednesday, Thursday, and Saturday of each week, the Local County Magistrates administering justice in Petty Sessions on every Tuesday and Friday. James Lamb Barker is the efficient Clerk to both Benches of Magistrates.

The proceedings of the local committee, which was appointed at a public meeting in South Shields, held in consequence of the dreadful loss of life by the explosion of Saint Hilda Coal Mine, on the 28th of June, 1839, must not be overlooked, when we consider the honor which we, as a community, derived from them. The committee consisted of Robert Ingham, chairman, Thomas Masterman Winterbottom, Richard Shortridge, James Wardle Roxby, John Clay, Errington Bell, Robert Walter Swinburne, William King Eddowes, Anthony Harrison, James Mather, and myself, the two latter having been the honorary secretaries. The laborious investigations of the committee were almost unexampled, and their report, as prepared by Mr. Mather, (whose services, in a cause for which he was peculiarly adapted, were most energetic, scientific, and valuable) was of no ordinary character. It was translated into foreign languages, became a text book for the scientific enquirer, and is thus made honorable mention of in the report of the Parliamentary Committee of 1852, appointed to enquire into the causes of the frequency of explosions in coal mines, with a view to prevent the appalling loss of life arising from them :—

" The report from the South Shields committee, appointed to investigate the causes of accidents in coal mines, was brought under our notice; to which report the attention of the House of Lords' Committee was also directed in 1849. On examination, this report proved to be a repertory of information so extensive, important, and apparently so accurate, that it seemed to supersede, in a measure, the necessity of examining very numerous witnesses. This committee continued its labours for three years; visited in person various mines; communicated with many of the most scientific and practical men of the day, at home and abroad; and terminated its labours by that report."

The labours of Mr. Mather, in this interesting cause of humanity, being justly alluded to in that Parliamentary Report as " Worthy of the highest praise." So much value, indeed, did that Parliamentary Committee attach to the report of the South Shields committee, that they added it, in extenso, in an appendix to their own report.

Never shall I forget, as connected with the subsequent labours of that committee, the harrowing spectacle that presented itself at the mouth of Saint Hilda Pit, when on that day, so sad and melancholy in the annals of our borough, one scorched and blackened corpse after another was brought to bank, amidst the wailings and lamentations of surrounding relatives ; and never, while memory holds her seat, will the heart rending glance, and despairing recognition, which told in language not to be misunderstood, that all hope had fled, be banished from my recollection.

" A voice was heard in Ramah, lamentation and bitter weeping; Rachael weeping for her children, refused to be comforted because they were not."

But not only was Rachael weeping for her children, " refusing to be comforted," but wives for their husbands, children for their fathers, sisters for their brothers—all of whom " were not "—" In the midst of life they had been in death"—and nothing remained but to allevi-

E

ate by worldly means, the wants of those who had so suddenly been deprived of their natural supporters. This was nobly and bountifully done, and though the bereaved ones could not altogether " refrain their voice from weeping, nor their eyes from tears," they were grateful to a generous public, and to the kind distributors of its bounty, for that alleviation, without which their mental agony would have been aggravated greatly, by unavoidable recourse to the parish workhouse or the relieving officers' limited and scanty pittance ; and also for that deep and universal sympathy of society which was expressed for the mourners, and which was, perhaps, more consoling to them than any other offering.

Since then, legislation (in aid of which Mr. Mather, with untiring energy and neverfailing ability, had previously published, in 1853, his work on " The Coal Mines, their Dangers, and Means of safety,") has been at work with a view to the prevention of the like deplorable catastrophes, and it cannot but be gratifying to South Shields, that a committee originated in her bosom, and guided by her good sense, should have laid down principles and explained views, that have been not only enforced by the legislature, but willingly adopted by practical men as guides for their mining operations.

On the recommendation of that report, Inspectors of Mines have been appointed who are subjected to a searching examination before their appointment, and who have already adduced many valuable facts relative to the various phenomena that present themselves in Mines.

Scientific Instruments have also been introduced into the Mines so important in their investigations, and giving a new and more penetrating sense of coming danger, and the means of averting its terrible consequences.

Schools of Mines are developing themselves at Durham, and Newcastle-upon-Tyne, and the Government Institution of Economic Geology in London, has grown into a great Mining School, since the publication of the South Shields report.

Children under eleven years of age have been withdrawn from mines; where, entrusted with some of the most delicate and ingenious machinery,—the very lungs of the mine workings,—their inexperience and boyish carelessness led to the most lamentable catastrophes. Better systems of ventilation, so urgently demanded by the South Shields committee, have been adopted in most of the mining districts of Britain; and last session, the legislature passed an act, compelling the adoption of a system of improved ventilation in all mines, in many of which no means of ventilation had previously existed.

A great, but practical, safe, and vast revolution, is progressing in mines, that will eventually render this dangerous scene of operations as safe and healthy as any other field of labor. This source of the chief strength and success of the country will no longer be wasted.

The dangers, that perpetually occurring, laid a whole district in mourning, will cease to a great extent; and society be spared the dreadful pangs which are consequent upon such catastrophes:—and thus will this dark and dangerous art, rise into a great and safe practical science, shedding lustre as well as strength, instead of bringing mourning and opprobrium upon our land.

These, and many others, are the fortunate results of the labours of the South Shields committee, which grow in importance as time more and more developes their truth; and it is an honest pride and a pleasure to me, to have, with my whole heart, co-operated from its commencement in this great work of humanity and usefulness.

On the 15th of July, 1850, after a most memorable parliamentary struggle, of long continuance, on the part of South and North Shields against the Corporation of Newcastle, an Act of Parliament was obtained "for the improvement and regulation of the river Tyne and the navigation thereof, and for other purposes," whereby the Conservancy of the river Tyne was taken out of the hands of the Corporation of Newcastle, and transferred to those of Commissioners, viz., four Life Commissioners, and the successors of two of them, six persons to be appointed annually by the Newcastle Council, two by the Gateshead Council, three by the Tynemouth Council, and three by the Improvement Commissioners of South Shields, or by its Council, if incorporated.

Before the passing of that Act, the whole of the coal dues were received by the Newcastle Corporation; but by the act, three-eighths of those dues are to go to the "Tyne Improvement Fund Account," and the remaining five-eighths to the credit of the Newcastle Borough Fund," and to be applicable generally for the purposes to which that Borough Fund is by law applicable, and exempted from all liability in respect of the conservancy, or the maintenance and repair, of the port and river, and the quays, banks, and shores thereof, save the public quay of Newcastle-upon-Tyne. An attempt is being made to alter this arrangement, by the Government Bill for the regulation of local dues on shipping, as founded on the report of the Harbour Dues Commissioners, with what success remains to be seen: but it is more than probable, that notwithstanding the determined opposition of Liverpool, Newcastle-upon-Tyne, Hull, and other interested places, all local charges on shipping, or on goods conveyed in ships, applied to other than shipping purposes will be abolished, or transferred to the harbour authorities for application to their legitimate objects; and that boroughs which have hitherto enjoyed such extensive privileges in aid of their borough rates, will, very properly, be placed in the same position as other boroughs which are subjected to a local taxation.

The other financial arrangements of the act can be ascertained by reference to it; but there is one clause to which I particularly call your attention, in connexion with our *Future*, and that is the 57th, whereby it is enacted, That when the Mayor, Aldermen, and Burgesses of South Shields shall have opened, within their borough, a quay of not less than one hundred yards in length, for the use of the public, subject to the payment of quay dues thereat to the parties erecting such quay, the goods, wares, and merchandize landed thereat shall thenceforth be exempted from the payment of one-half of the dues, which are described in the Act as the Import Dues.

The enormous cost at which these changes were effected amounted to many thousands of pounds, which were charged upon, and have been paid out of, "The Tyne Improvement Fund," but they were the unavoidable penalty for the advantages which were gained, and it is now hoped that, in future, "the funds of the Conservancy will be husbanded and devoted to the permanent improvement of the river;"

"And," further to use the words of the Royal Commission, in the report made by them to Her Majesty, in 1855, on the state of the river Tyne, "that the differences and disputes which have prevailed in the Tyne Improvement Commission, and so much interfered with its usefulness, may cease to exist; and that all its members may be induced to bury in oblivion those local jealousies and animosities, which can only prejudice the community to which they belong."

South Shields is, for the current municipal year, well represented in the river Commission by his Worship, the Mayor, Alderman Robinson, and Mr. Jas. Mather; Mr. Jas. Cochran Stevenson, of the Jarrow chemical works, being a life commissioner, appointed by the Act, who discharges his duties with an ability and sincerity of purpose, which are admitted even by those who are opposed to his views.

On the 17th June, 1852, an Act of Parliament was passed, having reference to the four important subjects of moorings, river police, piers, and Hayhole dock, being intituled, "An Act for repealing an Act of the 9th year of the reign of her present Majesty, relating to *moorings* for vessels in the river Tyne, and the *river police*, and for transferring the powers of the said Act to the Tyne Improvement Commissioners; for enabling the said Commissioners to construct and maintain *piers* at the mouth of the said river, in the counties of Durham and Northumberland; and to construct and maintain *docks* and other works on the *north* side of the said river in the last-mentioned county; and for other purposes.

Under this and the preceding Act, *moorings* have been judiciously laid down in front of the whole line of river frontage at South Shields, by which, instead of the rickety posts upon which, and their own anchors, ships had formerly to rely, they are now placed, not only in safety, but in readiness to be unmoored for sea with facility and dispatch, undetained by the raffled anchors of former days.

An effective *river police* has been established, the want of which had long been felt on the river;

And the Commissioners are empowered to demand and receive for every vessel which enters within the limits of the port of Newcastle-upon-Tyne, the sum of one farthing for every ton burden which such vessel shall measure or contain.

Such tonnage rate of one farthing is to be applied as follows: viz., 1-3rd to the maintenance of the *river police,* and to the other purposes of the Act connected therewith; and the remaining 2-3rds in payment, first, of interest on the existing debt of £17,000, and the principal when required; second, in paying interest upon any money which might be borrowed for *mooring* purposes, and the principal when required; third, in laying down and placing *moorings,* under the authority of the Act, and in maintaining the *moorings* laid down under the former Act; and fourth, in an accumulation and investment, for the purpose thereinafter mentioned;

The Tyne Improvement Commissioners, out of the ship and boat due, part of the Tyne Improvement Fund, being required to pay 1-3rd of the expense of maintaining the river police, or otherwise in relation to such police.

Provision is made for reduction, partly or in toto, of the farthing tonnage rate, in manner therein mentioned.

And the Commissioners are empowered to construct docks at Hayhole, and piers on both sides of the entrance of the Tyne.

The Piers to be commenced within two years from the 17th June, 1852, and the Piers and Hayhole docks to be completed within seven years from that date.

The estimated expense of the Piers is stated at £180,000, and power is given to borrow £200,000 on mortgage.

The *Pier* Rates are for every vessel which shall enter the port of Newcastle from any part of the United Kingdom, or the Isle of Man, the sum of *one penny* for every ton burden which such vessel shall measure or contain; and for every vessel that shall enter within such limits, from any other port or place, the sum of *twopence* for every ton burden which such vessel shall measure or contain; with a proviso that every sailing vessel in respect of which such payment shall have been made seven times, and every vessel propelled by steam in respect of which such payments shall have been made fifteen times in any one year, shall be exempted from any further payment for the remainder of such year;

And vessels propelled by steam and used only as tugs for vessels, are not to be liable to the Pier rate.

When the Piers are finished, and all monies borrowed for the purposes of them, and interest paid off, the Pier rates to cease to be levied.

The appropriation of the Pier rates is as follows:—First, in paying the interest of monies borrowed on the rates; second, in the formation and repair of them; and lastly, in appropriating and setting apart £2 10s per cent. upon the whole of the sums borrowed on the credit of those rates, as a sinking fund in paying off the principal.

And by the 74th clause, which is specially worthy of notice, jurisdiction is given on the river Tyne, between Spar Hawke-in-the-Sea and the east side of Newcastle bridge, to justices acting in and for the counties of Northumberland and Durham, and the boroughs of Tynemouth, *South Shields*, and Gateshead, *as well as those for Newcastle-upon-Tyne.*

To those who are aware of the danger, delay, and inconvenience of sending to Newcastle for magistrates, in former times, during the not unfrequent strikes of the sailors, the great public advantage of this extension of magisterial authority, will be at once apparent.

The provisions of the Act having reference to Hayhole-dock, not coming within the scope and object of this lecture, I refrain from adding them to the dry details, of which, I fear, you are already weary. I must, however, state, with joy, that the Piers from the formation of which so much improvement to the bar and harbour, and so great a consequent increase to our trade are expected, will, simultaneously with the construction of the northern Pier, be substantially, effectually, and safely proceeded with; and that the southern one will *now*, thanks to the vigilant watchfulness which was exercised at South Shields, at a very critical juncture, and the proceedings which were taken there by the Council and the Shipowners' Society, aided in their efforts by the Tyne Improvement Commissioners, be such as will be satisfactory to the inhabitants, and of a nature to be looked forward to with hope and gratification, as a component part of our promising and encouraging *Future*.

In connection, not only with the *Past* and the *Present*, but also with the *Future* of South Shields, it would be an act of wilful injustice not to notice, with all honour and gratitude, one who has, by his liberality and charitable deeds of no ordinary character, deservedly secured for himself a place in the hearts and affections of the inhabitants of this his native borough.

> " All our praises why should Lords engross?
> Rise honest muse! and sing the Man of Ross;
> Thrice happy man! enabled to pursue,
> What all so wish, but want the power to do!"

Happy, indeed, is it for himself—happy is it for South Shields—that Thomas Masterman Winterbottom, the individual to whom I allude, has possessed the " power," as well as the " wish," to gratify the promptings of his benevolent heart, by the exercise of the kindliest feelings of humanity. While some men carry out their charitable designs through the medium of executors, when they themselves are laid in the cold and silent tomb, incapable of witnessing the blessings which their bounty has left behind, Dr. Winterbottom,

> "The friend of man, the friend of truth,
> The friend of age, and guide of youth;
> Few hearts like his with virtue warm'd,
> Few heads with knowledge so inform'd."

Has pursued an opposite and a wiser course. He has *himself* been the dispenser, with no niggard hand, of his own bounteous gifts; he has *himself* caused the widow's heart to rejoice, and her children to be glad; and he has *himself* been the recipient of her grateful thanks. Many are the lasting and substantial memorials which he has in this manner raised to his own memory, by the funds which he has invested for charitable and useful purposes; and it is to me a pleasing satisfaction that I am enabled to enumerate them on this public occasion, with an earnest prayer that the venerable Nonogenarian may, even at his present advanced age, still continue to contemplate, with ease and complacency, the good which he has done, and the happiness which he has created.

1st. *"The Master Mariners' (enrolled) Asylum and Annuity Society,"*

> "That Alm's House, neat but void of State,
> Where age and want, sit smiling at the gate."

Created by him in the year 1846, at a cost of £2,300, having for its object the providing a fund for paying annuities to aged, infirm, and poor master mariners, their widows, and orphans, and building asylums for their occupation. To which he has added a further investment since of £403 17s. 4d., three per cent. consols, for keeping in order the pleasure grounds in front and the paint work of the cottages.

2nd. *"The Winterbottom South Shields Fund for the Relief of deserving Widows of Seamen,"* with a magnificent investment of £5,000, and two shares besides in the Newcastle and Carlisle Railway, for paying to fifteen such widows as aforesaid, natives of, and residing within, this borough, an annuity of £10 each. The surplus of the interest, as it amounts to £20, to be divided, from time to time, amongst five such widows likewise.

3rd. *"The Unmarried Female Servants' Rewards Fund,"* created by him in 1849, with an investment of £200. the dividends of which are to be paid and applied on New Year's-day in each year, in bestowing two separate rewards of £4 and £2 each on two unmarried female servants in the borough of South Shields, or township of Harton, who come within the meaning of the conditions prescribed by the deed of trust of the 7th of December, 1849.

And an additional investment since of £150 by a subsequent deed, for the purpose of being applied in a similar manner.

4th. An investment of £150, producing an interest of £7 10s

to be divided as rewards amongst the four best ploughmen at the East Chester Ward annual ploughing match.

And an investment of £150, producing a similar interest of £7 10s. to be divided in like manner, as rewards amongst the four best plough boys, under eighteen years of age, at that same annual ploughing match.

5th.   An investment of £200, with the annual interest of which, coals are purchased and divided at Christmas amongst the poor of the village of Westoe.

6th.   The arrangement he has made by deed, under date of the 28th August, 1837, and enrolled in the High Court of Chancery, for founding within this borough a school, to be called *"The Marine School of South Shields,"* which is to be conducted according to certain statutes or rules laid down by the deed, some of the most important of which are as follow:—

"That every person chosen to be a master of this school, shall be a Master of Arts of one of the universities of Oxford or Cambridge.

"That any person who can write a good and legible hand, and is acquainted with the first four rules of arithmetic, and shall have served one whole year at sea, or have attained the age of seventeen years, or spent at least one year in the pilot boats, shall be admissible into the said school as a scholar; it being the opinion of the said Thomas Masterman Winterbottom, founded on much experience, that the knowledge of navigation acquired by boys previous to their fifteenth or sixteenth year is seldom retained or improved.

"That the instruction afforded in the said school shall be wholly gratuitous, and without any charge whatever to the scholars; save and except, the scholars shall be bound to provide themselves with such elementary books, and such mathematical instruments, as the master of the said school shall require.

"That the instruction in the said school shall consist of every part of mathematical or other learning, which can interest or be useful to a mariner, and *fit him for the higher duties of his profession*, according to the system pursued for the time being in the best marine schools in the Kingdom: and to further this purpose, a lecture, not less than an hour in duration, shall be given four evenings in each week during the winter months in each year, beginning in October, and terminating with the end of March; in which lectures, such branches of natural philosophy shall be treated of, and illustrated by experiments, and a suitable apparatus, as shall be thought interesting to the sailor. The laws of mechanics shall be particularly attended to, magnetism, hydrostatics, pneumatics, the principles of optics, electricity, meteorology, or the science which treats of the atmosphere and its phenomena, shall be clearly and particularly explained; and the elements of maritime law, such as the power of raising money on the ship, and the master's duty as to the freight and insurance, shall also be explained.   And as it is of the utmost importance that the sailor should be made a proficient in that most sublime of all sciences, astronomy, a science which can alone enable him to form some idea of the magnitude of the works of his Creator, it is the particular desire of the founder, that the whole of Saturday shall be devoted to the study of astronomy and geography, aided by the use of the celestial and terrestrial globes.

"It shall be permitted to any person, with the approbation of the Committee, to attend any or all of the lectures, on paying such a gratuity to the lecturer as shall be fixed by the Committee; as it is the wish of the said T. M. Winterbottom, that the benefits of the said Marine School, should be like the light of heaven, equally distributed to all.

"That if any young person in South Shields shall wish to have private instruction in the use of the globes, it shall be permitted to the master, or to the second master if there should be two, to form a class for that purpose, he receiving from the pupils a sufficient gratuity for his trouble, provided it be done with the full concurrence of the Committee, and during such hours as shall not interfere with the usual routine of the school. Moreover should any young sailors, during the private course of such lectures, not amounting to more than six or eight persons at a time, wish to attend, he or they shall be admitted gratuitously. If, however, the private class shall be formed entirely of young females, then, and in that case, no young man shall be allowed to attend, without the especial permission of the whole Committee."

The scholars to be examined periodically, viva voce, or by written questions and answers, and a certificate given.

"That it shall be lawful for the Governors to make or sanction such rules or regulations as they shall think proper for ensuring the moral conduct and correct deportment of the scholars.

"That the several statutes and rules herein-before contained, shall be deemed fundamental and unalterable. *Provided always*, and in case after seven years' strict observance of the foregoing statutes and rules respecting the admission of scholars into the said school, the terms of such statutes or rules shall be deemed by the Governors to militate against the general utility of the said school, as a school for the instruction of seamen in the higher branches of nautical knowledge, it shall be lawful for the Governors, with the consent in writing of the Visitor for the time being, from time to time to make such other regulations as to the admission of scholars into the said school, as shall seem to them best adapted to promote the utility of the institution, ever bearing in mind that the object of the said school is to render the sailor accomplished in those branches of knowledge which are especially required *in the higher stations of his calling*, rather than to afford merely elementary instruction, which may be equally well obtained in the ordinary schools of the town, and with which schools there ought to be no interference.

"*Provided also*, that in case the endowment of the said school shall not alone be sufficient to carry it on in the liberal and efficient manner intended by the Founder, according to the provisions of these presents, it shall be lawful in that case, and in that case only, for the Governors of the said school, to require the scholars in the same, to pay a moderate sum for their education, but not exceeding what shall for the time being be charged in other schools of navigation in South Shields: *provided*, nevertheless, that no scholar shall be charged with any such payment during his apprenticeship.

"The Trustees to proceed under the trust when they are of opinion that sufficient funds have been obtained for the erection of a suitable building or buildings, and for the maintenance of the said school."

Robert Ingham, Richard Shortridge, Joseph Hargrave, Robert Anderson, and Terrot Glover, are the original trustees named in the deed, with provisions for fresh appointments in case of death, non residence, or resignation.

The Bishop of Durham for the time being, is to be the visitor of the school.

The Dean of Durham and the several Incumbents for the time being of the parishes or parochial chapelries of St. Hilda, Jarrow, Boldon, Whitburn, and Monkwearmouth, together with the trustees for the time being, and six merchants or shipowners to be chosen as therein mentioned, are to be the Governors of the school.

And the six merchants or shipowners so to be chosen, are to be the Committee thereof.

A piece of freehold ground on the east side of Mile-end-road, lying between Alderson-street and Ingham-street, and containing in length from north to south on the west end eighty three feet, and on the east end eighty two feet, and in breadth or depth from east to west on the north side seventy eight feet, and on the south side sixty nine feet, is conveyed to the Trustees by the deed, for the purposes of the school, and also two shares of the Founder, and other his shares in the

F

Imperial Fire Office Company, London; five shares and other his shares or interest in the Union Fire and Life Insurance Company, London; and one moiety of a share and other his share or interest in the Royal Exchange Insurance Company London; and all profits, &c., due, or to grow due, for, or in respect of the same.

Upon trust for the Founder during his life, after his death for his sisters, Ann Masterman Stewart, (since deceased,) Elizabeth Masterman Winterbottom, (still living,) and Mary Masterman Winterbottom, (since also deceased,) during their respective lives, in equal shares, as tenants in common, with benefit of survivorship; and after the death of the survivor, *in trust* for the said school.

Having thus purposely set forth at length, for public information, the main provisions of the South Shields Marine School Deed of settlement, the wise and practical intentions of whose founder are so clearly explained by its statutes and rules; and having thus enumerated the many useful and benevolent acts "past, present, and to come" of the good old Doctor, I shall pass on to the subject which next demands my attention, first remarking, that although we have it on the high authority of Shakespeare's Hamlet, that "there's hope a great man's memory, may outlive his life half a year"—but then only be it recollected, on the express condition that "he build churches"—I have a better knowledge of my fellow-townsmen than to suppose that any such brief duration will attend the memory of our venerable friend. He, I feel assured, will prove an exception to this cynical rule of the philosophising prince, and that his memory will, in connection with his acts, outlive his life, not for "half a year," but for so long as South Shields shall continue its existence as an English borough, embracing, I hope, a period of many, very many, prosperous years of advancing improvement.

About three thousand seamen belong to South Shields who still are inferior to none in the world for skill, hardiness, and intrepidity. The intricate, dangerous, and stormy navigation of the east coast of England, much of the trade of which is now carried on during the winter season, still requires all the attention and dexterity which a seaman can possess; and therefore the coal trade has always been considered, and still is, an excellent school for seamanship, and one from which the ablest seamen of Her Majesty's fleet could be obtained, it being certain that it was this class that constituted during former wars the pride of our naval service;

> The mariners of England,
>   That guard our native seas;
> Whose flag has braved a thousand years
>   The battle and the breeze.

With which defenders, as has again been well sung by Campbell,

> Britannia needs no bulwarks,
>   No towers along the steep:
> Her march is o'er the mountain waves,
>   Her home is on the deep.

But retaining a vivid recollection of the scenes of impressment which I have witnessed in my youth in the streets of this very town; the screams of the women, the shouts and imprecations of the men, and the curses of the press-gang, who were tracking like bloodhounds the flying steps of some unhappy sailor, just returning perhaps in joy and expectation to his wife and children after an absence of years; I cannot wonder at the abhorrence of the impress service which always prevailed amongst the north country seamen, and I rejoice that a necessity no longer exists for the exercise of such tyranny. Amongst the gallant fellows by whom Her Majesty's present magnificent fleet is so effectually manned, not an impressed man is to be found, and it is earnestly to be hoped that on no future occasion will recourse be had to the brutal violence of impressment.

Better fed, more liberally paid, with kinder treatment, and with the horrid lash scarcely ever used, and even then under guarded restrictions, the naval service of the country has the happiness now to obtain by its popularity, the voluntary service of the British sailor, and ever may it continue to be as it now is, a *free* service for a *free* man.

I have not spoken rashly or in ignorance of these matters, for a relative of mine had the misfortune to undergo impressment, and a long service on board the Alarm frigate, "when George the Third was king;" from which I think he was right in availing himself, as he certainly did, of the first favorable opportunity of escape from the compulsory service of the crown, notwithstanding the prospect of promotion and the inducements which were held out to him. This was a very common case for impressed men, for they did not scruple to leave a service without ceremony, into which they had been forcibly dragged at the sacrifice of all their domestic happiness and comforts.

Commencing at 1768, there have been many strikes of the South Shields and other seamen of the Tyne, and disputes with their employers, sometimes so alarming, as to render necessary the protection and active interference, not only of the civil, but of the naval and military powers. Increased intelligence and a more correct knowledge of the rights of property and of labour, will however, it is hoped, prevent a repetition of such violent and illegal proceedings, than which nothing would be more at variance with the growing intelligence of the age, participated in, as it has been by the employed as well as the employer.

The South Shields Loyal Standard Association or Benefit Society was established at South Shields, on the 5th of Oct., 1824, and its rules after certain previous corrections, were again revised and amended in conformity to law, in the year 1853; the members having (to use their own language) "by experience seen and felt the sad and disappointing evils attending upon bad customs and calculations in former Seamen's funds, where those who have contributed for the space

of twenty or thirty years and then become claimants, find that the
funds for support have been solely exhausted in relieving early
claimants, hundreds of cases now appearing in this town of great
distress from that cause." Its objects are to make provision for the
members and families, in case of shipwreck, death, sickness, superan-
nuation, or other infirmities; and it is duly certified and enrolled
according to law. The members must be mariners or sea-going
carpenters, and none are to be admitted who are above forty years of
age. The terms and benefits are to be found in the printed rules.
Its present trustees are Robert Wallis, John Robinson, and Errington
Bell; the Committee consisting of eleven members, who are chosen
quarterly by the members who may be then in port. Mr. John
Jobling is the excellent secretary, and there are auditors and arbitra-
tors.

The *receipts* for the past year ended 1st Dec, 1855, arising from
contributions, rents, subscriptions, donations, &c., amounted, according to the published statement, to £1109 12s. 8d.; and the
disbursements, for death benefits, sick members, widows, shipwrecked
mariners, secretary's salary, and sundries, to £853 6s. 1d.; leaving
a Gain, I am happy to say, of £256 6s. 7d.

£37,311 7s. 4d. has been paid to members for benefits since
1824, and the capital and stock of the association amounts to £1471
15s. 6d.

One hundred and eighty seven members entered during the past
year, the total number on the books of the association being seven
hundred and thirty, which includes thirty two superannuated and
sixty-five land members.

To make provision in this manner for the dangers and uncertainties of a sea-faring life, is a wise and prudent forethought, and it is
therefore gratifying to find that so many seamen have secured for
themselves and families, the benefits of an institution "to which they
may have recourse in the hour of necessity, and where their wants
will in some measure be relieved, whether in time of sickness,
misfortune, or the decline of life." I quote from the feeling "address"
of the members themselves, and cordially agreeing with it, that, for
the reasons therein set forth, it is "well doing" for sailors "to enlist
under the banners" of such an association as this, I exhort them to
do so without hesitation or delay, for no one knows what a day may
bring forth.

In 1854, South Shields had the honour to be selected by Professor George Biddell Airy, the Astronomer Royal, as the locality for
pendulum experiments, the ultimate purpose of which was to give the
means of weighing, by the use of a pound weight, not only the earth,
but also the sun, Jupiter, and all the principal bodies of the solar
system. These experiments were made during three weeks, in Harton
pit, belonging to Messrs. Blackett, Anderson, Wood, and Philipson,

whose conduct, in the granting of all necessary facilities to the learned professor and his assistants, was of the most liberal character. The pit is of the depth of one thousand two hundred and sixty feet, and is connected, in its workings below, with those of Saint Hilda colliery, the subterraneous workings of both extending to upwards of eighty miles, and some of them being more than three miles in a direct line.

The experiments were completely successful, and a very interesting lecture, in explanation of them, and of the object sought to be obtained through their means, was delivered by Professor Airy, in this hall, on the 24th of October, 1854, to a numerous audience, the lecture having afterwards been printed in extenso, at the request of a deputation who waited upon the Professor, for the purpose of conveying to him the desire which prevailed for the publication.

In the language of the introduction to the printed lecture,

"The experiments with this instrument (the Pendulum), at Harton pit, by the Astronomer Royal, were of a different nature from those made by Kater, Sabine, Foster, and others. The former were intended to discover the exact number of vibrations of the invariable pendulum upon the surface, and at the lowest ascertainable depth below it. The latter to ascertain the actual length of the seconds pendulum, or the number of vibrations at different places of the Earth's surface. One to discover the absolute density of the Earth; the other its form, and the relative position of its parts.

"Since the time of the discovery, by Galileo, that the vibrations of the pendulum are nearly equal in time whatever the extent of the arc,—its application to clocks, in 1649, by his son, Vincent Galileo, at Venice, and its successful development by Christian Huyghens, this little instrument, based on a great law of the Universe, has been growing in importance and value, till now, in its employment by the Astronomer Royal in the South Shields experiments, it has achieved new and unexpected results."

It cannot be otherwise than gratifying to South Shields, that for the solution of so important a question in the sublime science of astronomy, as that now sought to be solved, it should have possessed in its district such facilities; nor is it otherwise than honourable to the town and a matter of distinction, that its inhabitants and neighbours, appreciating the great object, should have merited, by their conduct and proceedings, the confidence and unusual compliment paid to them by the Astronomer Royal.

Mr. Thompson, the borough surveyor, has, with the permission of the Corporation of South Shields, prepared, gratuitously, a plan of levels of the district around Harton pit, which is highly valued by Professor Airy for the processes of his calculations. From this plan —from specimens of the strata through which the shaft of Harton pit is sunk—and from the state of his pendulum experiments, the learned Professor has a certain hope of working out the great astronomical results of which we have so satisfactory an assurance in his printed letter appended to the lecture; and thus science will add one more triumph to its already glorious achievements.

In this matter, too, thus has South Shields well performed its duty.

The boundaries of the parliamentary and municipal borough and market town of South Shields are co-extensive, the whole of the townships of South Shields and Westoe being comprised therein. It is situate in, and forms the north eastern extremity of, the county palatine of Durham, adjoining the river Tyne on the north, the German ocean on the east, and other parts of the county of Durham on the south and west, its extent being a mile and eight-tenths along the southern bank of the river Tyne from near its mouth upwards, in a westerly direction, as far as Jarrow-bridge, the *town* of South Shields, properly so called to distinguish it from the borough, consisting of the whole of the township of South Shields, and a portion of the township of Westoe, the residue of the latter township being an agricultural district, with the exception of East Jarrow, the village of Westoe, and some other outlying suburbs.   Lying immediately opposite to the sister borough of Tynemouth, the two boroughs of South Shields and Tynemouth form together the deep water basin and harbour of Shields, where all the large vessels lie and take up their berths, and in which many hundreds of ships are frequently congregated together.

Such are its advantages, that South Shields has been selected as the site for gigantic operations in the shipment of coals, its population being large, its docks and manufactories extensive, prosperous, (with the exception, perhaps, of the temporary depression of the glass trade,) and increasing, and its amount of shipping nationally important.

The following brief detail will clearly prove the importance of the borough, and its claims for that high position amongst the boroughs of the kingdom, for which I, and you, and every inhabitant should ever most strenuously contend.

The population of the borough amounted, according to the census of 1841, to 22,908; and according to that of 1851, (a period of ten years,) to 28,293, showing a *decrease* of 142 in the township of South Shields (the area of which has long been fully occupied by dwelling-houses, shops, docks, shipbuilding-yards, and manufactories, thereby rendering *its* population nearly stationary), and an *increase* of 5,527 in the township of Westoe, the latter being the only area on which future buildings within the borough can be erected; and it is, therefore, in that direction that the urban population is so rapidly extending outwards.   These numbers are exclusive of the maritime absentees at the respective times of the census, but by the addition of whom the total population of the borough would be considerably increased.   The permanent population of the place, however, by no means constitutes the whole of the persons immediately connected with and dependent upon it, for there is a very great and constant concourse of mariners and others engaged in maritime pursuits, who, although not residing in, nor belonging to, the borough; yet tend very materially to increase the traffic of the place.

The quantity of *coals and coke* shipped in 1854, at South Shields, at her fourteen staiths, from forty-four coal mines, amounted to *one million two hundred and eighty thousand and eighteen tons.*

The quantity of *ballast* discharged there amounted 94,263 tons, the *total* quantity discharged in the *Tyne* (including 49,629 tons in the Jarrow and South Shields Tyne Police District), having been 242,198 tons.

The length of her quays and moorings are about 9,500 feet, or a mile and eight-tenths.

Her registered tonnage of shipping being.... 126,096 tons.
Valued at........................£1,008,768

South Shields also possesses, as I have already brought under your special notice, a large portion of the plate, crown, and German sheet glass and bottle manufactories of the kingdom.

The three chemical and soda manufactories, within this borough, (a fourth not being carried on at present,) are also, as I have before mentioned, on a very extensive scale, and there are fifteen iron works of various descriptions; four rope manufactories; four oil, paint, and varnish manufactories; a large earthenware pottery; four ballast wharves of great extent, with their corresponding machinery for the delivery of ballast from ships; six timber yards; a public railway, with its appurtenances; fourteen staiths or drops, for the delivery of coals, having river termini at South Shields, and four private railways; together with a valuable sea-sale and land-sale colliery, within the borough, and another at Harton, immediately adjoining, whose coals are of excellent quality, well known as Hilda Wallsend and Harton Wallsend, in the London market, and adapted, and extensively used, for household and manufacturing purposes.

In addition to all which, South Shields possesses graving docks and slipways, suitable to her extent of shipping, and capable of accommodating, at one time, for repairs, twenty-five ships; and she also possesses fifteen building yards, capable of the construction of twenty-seven ships.

At the South Shields moorings during the year 1855, there were moored 65,359 ships; the total number moored in the Tyne at the whole moorings, having been 178,812.

On the 7th January, 1856, every berth in the harbour being then filled, South Shields had moored at her moorings, 485 ships; the total number then moored at the moorings in the Tyne, being 984; showing the moorings at South Shields to have accommodated *on that day* very nearly *one-half of the ships then in the Tyne.*

The *value* of the shipping property *so moored on that day*, was as follows:—

	Ships.	Average Tonnage.	Total.	£	Value.
In the whole of the Tyne ..	984	200	196,800.. at 8..		1,574,400
At South Shields	485	200	97,000.. at 8..		776,000

Than which nothing can be more satisfactory, as demonstrating our magnificent river frontage and its mooring facilities.

The first Mutual Ship Insurance Company was established by shipowners in 1788, upon a plan which was found so useful and advantageous as to have since caused their general adoption in the borough, not only for ships, but for freight and cargo also. There are now several of such insurances here, the affairs of which are ably conducted by intelligent secretaries and committees of management. I give a list of them as follows, viz. :—

NAME OF CLUB.	NATURE OF INSURANCE.	NAME OF SECRETARY.	AMOUNT OF CAP.	
			In Money.	In Kls.
Anchor	On Ship, according to Classification	George Stout	50,000	
Atlas Al	On Ship	Geo. D. Robeson	40,000	
British Insurance	On Ship	George Stout	50,000	
British and Friendly	On Freight and Outfit	Wm. Bainbridge, jun.		1,100
British and Friendly Protecting Society	Casualties not covered by ordinary Insurances	George Stout	400,000	
Coal Trade	On Ship	John Davison	125,000	
Eligible	On Freight and Outfit	John Davison		2,600
Friendly	On Ship	Wm. Bainbridge, jun.	50,000	
Imperial	On Cargo, Freight, and Outfit	George Potts		2,000
Maritime and Mercantile	On Ship	John Walker Lamb	68,000	
Maritime and Mercantile	On Cargo, Freight, and Outfit	John Walker Lamb		1,100
Marine Safeguard Protecting Society	Casualties not covered by ordinary Insurances	George Potts	125,000	
Nautical	On Ship	George Potts	72,000	
Port of Tyne Al	On Ship	Geo. Stout and Wm. Bainbridge, jun.	40,000	
Shields Marine	On Ship	Geo. Alex. Tate	40,000	
Standard	On Ship	John Walker Lamb	68,000	
South Shields Protecting Society	Casualties not covered by ordinary Insurances	John Walker Lamb	1,200,000	
Star Al	On Ship	George Lyall	75,000	
South Shields Al	On Freight and Outfit	George Lyall		700
Sun	On Ship	Christ. A. Wawn	75,000	
Sun	On Cargo, Freight, and Outfit	Christ. A. Wawn		1,000
South Shields Demurrage	For Recovery of Demurrage	Geo. Stout and Wm. Bainbridge, jun.		{ 150 Ships
Total Loss	On Ship	Wm. John Stout	10,000	
Unanimous	On Ship	George Potts	54,000	

In addition to what has been already enumerated, South Shields can reckon within her boundaries many other establishments, viz: those of brewers, spirit merchants, provision dealers, boat builders, blockmakers, sailmakers, painters, coopers, braziers, tin-plate workers, cum multis aliis: the numerous, handsome, and well-filled shops of the town, being now of a nature to bear comparison with those of any neighbouring town, and capable of supplying all the wants of our community without recourse to Newcastle, North Shields, Sunderland, or any other rival; a very different state of things from that which prevailed when the mayor and burgesses of Newcastle would not permit the inhabitants of South Shields to sell either bread, beer, or fish to strangers; when no ship could be laden or unladen there, and no "shoars" or quays built there.

The annual gross estimated rental and ratable value of property within the borough, as taken from the existing poor rates, are as follow:—

Townships.	Gross estimated value.	Ratable Value.
South Shields	£30,869 0 0	£23,024 10 0
Westoe	£45,923 10 0	£34,386 0 0
Totals	£76,792 10 0	£57,410 10 0

And the area of the borough is as follows:

	A.	R.	P.
South Shields Township	89	2	20
Westoe Township	1691	0	0
Total..	1780	2	20

The whole borough is within the South Shields poor law union, of which Wm. Anderson, Esq., J.P., is chairman; and its affairs are ably, prudently, and humanely managed by a board of guardians, with even handed justice as well to the unfortunate objects of relief as to the ratepayers, by whom they have to be supported.   By the ratepayers of South Shields nine guardians are elected annually as their representatives at the board, and a similar number by the ratepayers of Westoe; the remaining seven guardians being elected by the following parishes and townships of the union, viz.: by Hedworth, Monkton, and Jarrow, four; Harton, one; Whitburn, one; and Boldon, one.

On the formation of the union in 1836, the old and very insufficient township poor houses of South Shields, Westoe, and Harton, were sold; and their places supplied by the present extensive, commodious, and well-arranged workhouse for the whole union: the debt of £2400 which was contracted to make the erection, having been gradually reduced by annual instalments of £120 each, to its present amount of £480 only.

G

The South Shields Literary, Mechanical, and Scientific Institution
was established November 23rd, 1825. Several of those who took an
active share in its formation continue still zealous officers of the society.
It is not always easy to originate a society. It is vastly more difficult to give it any degree of permanence, especially when that is
dependent upon voluntary support. To them, however, belongs the
credit not only of originating this institution, but also by their perseverance and judicious management, of securing for it the stability
it possesses. It is a material feature in the history of this institution,
that unlike the majority of kindred institutions established about the
same period, it has ever retained its pristine vigour, exhibited no
marks of decay, has retained a large number of supporters, and has
gone on year after year adding to its valuable literary stores.

The gentlemen to whom the distinction of having been officers of
the society from its beginning and continuing such is due, are Robert
Ingham, Esq., the venerable Dr. Winterbottom, and Messrs. Matthew
Hutchinson, Christopher M'Donald, Evan Hunter, and John Nevison.
These gentlemen with George Townsend Fox, Esq., and the late secre-
tary, George Pringle, took a leading part in forming the society.

The society met for a few years after its formation in a school
room under the Primitive Methodist Chapel, Cornwallis Street, and
there kept its library. It received a material impetus at its first formation, by gifts of many valuable works. Among the donors to whose
liberality the society were much indebted, were the late Bishop
Barrington, Mr. Ingham, the late Mr. G. T. Fox, Dr. Winterbottom,
my late brother John Salmon, and Mr. Robert Walter Swinburne.
At this time there was a little prejudice against the society in the
minds of some who were jealous of the progress of knowledge. It
was regarded and spoken by such as a society with infidel tendencies.
The able management of the committee speedily dissipated the silly
calumny, and secured for it the goodwill of all classes of their fellow
townsmen,—a goodwill which continues to manifest itself up to the
present period.

Mr. G. T. Fox was the first president and continued so until
1831, when Mr. Ingham was elected. He has remained president
since then. The vice-presidents were Dr. Winterbottom, Mr. Ingham,
Dr. Thorburn, Mr. William Bell, and Mr. Archibald McRae. Mr.
R. W. Swinburne was elected in 1835, and is a vice president still.
Dr. Winterbottom is the only one of the original vice-presidents who
has continued to the present time.

Joseph Hargrave was appointed first treasurer, and was succeeded by Thomas Scott in 1842. The latter was followed by F.
Stephenson, and again became treasurer in 1850.

The first secretaries were the Rev. S. Pears and George Pringle.
The latter acted as sole secretary from 1826 till 1835, when John
Nevison was elected. In 1838 John Pearson Elliott took the place of

George Pringle; and in 1855, Christopher Tate that of John Nevison, who had resigned.

Some of the members of the committee have continued in office from the society's formation. Two of them, Messrs. Christopher M'Donald and Evan Hunter, are now vice-presidents.

It was soon felt that more accommodation was required than could be had in the school room where the society was formed, and after much discussion it was resolved to build the hall which the society now occupies. It was built by Mr. William Alderson, and formally taken possession of by Evan Hunter, George Pringle, and myself, as trustees, on behalf of the society, on the 20th of February, 1835.

The building was leasehold. Since then it has been enfranchised, and is now the property of the society, without incumbrance.

Classes have been established for the study of the following subjects :—grammar, arithmetic, mathematics, geometry, chemistry, the French and Latin languages, geography, drawing, and music. Some of these were carried on by mutual instruction, and some under the superintendence of teachers.

Lectures on a variety of subjects, literary and scientific, have been given almost yearly, and by gentlemen eminently distinguished in literature and science. Among the many to whom the society is deeply indebted, I may be permitted to mention the late lamented Professor Johnston, Professor Chevallier, Dr. Townsend, Mr. Ingham, Dr. Winterbottom, Dr. Embleton, Dr. George Fife, Mr. G. Y. Heath, Capt. Collinson, Capt. B. Ibbotson, Rev. Robert Gillan, Dr. Glover, and others.

The society has occasionally had exhibitions of industrial art, and it has its yearly festivals. The number of members has ranged from one hundred and twenty to about two hundred and seventy. This, it must be confessed, is but a small number, when we take the population of the place into account : and it is matter, I know, of deep regret to the committee and friends of the institution, that comparatively so few join. Still the number, such as it is, has been steadily sustained.

The society is now in possession of a library consisting of three thousand five hundred valuable works. Very many of them are standard works, both in science and literature. A variety of the first class periodicals is an attractive feature in the library. The periodicals taken are the Edinburgh Quarterly, the Quarterly, Blackwood, Fraser, Tait, Bentley, the Eclectic, Athenæum, Art Journal, Mechanics' Magazine, Builder, the Dublin, Punch, &c.

The most of these works are purchases, although the society has from time to time to acknowledge with pleasure the liberality of friends in making presents of works. This result could only have been accomplished by the most rigid economy in keeping down the current expenses, so as to leave a good purchase fund.

The position the society now holds in public estimation, can only have been achieved by their pertinacious adherence to what the committee has deemed its proper duty,—the selection of the best works in literature and science, as free as possible from what is purely controversial in divinity or politics. This is the feeling expressed in one of their reports :—

That "it is by acting thus, by enabling their members to keep pace most effectually with the progress of society, by placing books in their hands which are the highest efforts of genius, or which display the most recent and widely-extended conquests of science, or which laying hold of these grand results, shew by what skilful appliances these are made so to subserve the purposes of life, as to give redoubled energy to industry and enterprise; that they have preserved the high character of this institution as purely literary, scientific, and mechanical."

The subscription is 8s. per annum—a sum which can scarcely offer a hindrance to any one. It is much to the credit of the body of managers, that, with such a moderate subscription, they have been able to form so valuable a library.

It is now intended to enlarge the building, which is felt to be inadequate to supply the present wants of the society ; and the determination is a wise one.

I have the honour to be one of the original and present trustees, in whom the building is vested ; and I have further, the pride and satisfaction of being an honorary member of the Institution—a distinction conferred upon me in the most gratifying manner by the members, as being the highest which it was in their power to bestow. I avail myself of this opportunity thus publicly to thank them for it, and at the same time to express a hope that, in raising the funds for the necessary enlargement of their building, the members may be encouraged by the voluntary assistance from without, of those who are favourable to mental improvement and progress, and to an institution especially intended for the benefit of the working classes.

The South Shields Working Men's Institute was established on the 11th of March, 1850. Its affairs are managed by a president, vice-president, treasurer, two secretaries, and twenty members as a committee, who are annually elected by ballot ; Mr. Councillor Solomon Sutherland having been the president of the society from its commencement. The duties of the office are still ably and zealously discharged by him. The objects for which the society was formed were, as explained by the president in his eloquent and sensible address to the members at their meeting on the 13th of April, 1855, of a twofold character,—partly recreative, and partly educational ; the one being to furnish comfortable and commodious apartments suitably supplied with books, newspapers, periodicals, and other means of mental enjoyment and relaxation,—the other, the establishment of classes for instruction in the various departments of literature and science, in which, by the assistance of competent teachers, the seeker after self-improvement might, at the smallest possible charge, find such direction and help, as would greatly facilitate his onward progress. Both these objects have been efficiently carried out by a very moderate subscription of one penny per week, and the number of members on the books of the society at the last anniversary was 600, being a satisfactory increase of 150 since the preceding one. The library of books is well-selected and continually increasing, and eleven weekly, and one daily newspaper, besides periodicals, are now regularly on the table of its news-room, while the issues from its as yet limited stock of useful and general literature, have reached in the last year, the astonishing number of nearly 5,500 volumes.

It was at one time thought that this comparatively modern society would prove injurious to the much older institute of the Mechanics', but such an apprehension no longer exists; for, notwithstanding the rapid success which has attended the former, .the latter has steadily maintained its position—the political information furnished by the Working Men's Institute supplying a want which had not been provided for by the rules of the Mechanics'.

Measures have been organised for obtaining a building, suitable for all the growing requirements of the Working Men's Institute, and I would gladly see its members aided by the friends of popular education, in their laudable endeavours to secure for themselves, the necessary accommodation in the shape of class-rooms, a reading-room, and a lecture-room. The inauguration of the opening of such a building in South Shields, would be an event of which the borough might, in connection with its working classes, feel justly proud; and, I trust, the day is not far distant, when amongst the things of the *Present*, and not of the future, will be reckoned "The Hall of the South Shields Working Men's Institute," in which will be carried out the great and praiseworthy object of making still more ample provision for the increasing educational wants of the working classes of this great and important town.

"Happy is the man that findeth wisdom, and the man that getteth understanding.

"For the merchandise of it is better than the merchandise of silver, and the gain thereof than fine gold.

"She is more precious then rubies: and all the things thou can'st desire are not to be compared unto her."

There is one subject in connection with our literary institutions to which I would call your attention with much anxiety, and that is, the *South Shields Subscription Library*, which was established so far back as the year 1803, and contains a large and very valuable collection of books. Owing to the want of support, it is sick even unto death—so much so that if our *Future* be not more encouraging, we shall have nothing to boast of in that direction. With an existing debt, and a current expenditure, considerably more than its income, it cannot without assistance go on, and it will most certainly be closed forthwith, unless it is invigorated by many additional subscribers. It would truly be a disgrace to the town in the present day, if a literary establishment, of so old and extensive a character, should be suffered to expire, owing to the indifference to literature, or the apathy of that upper 'class of the inhabitants by which it has hitherto been supported; and I trust that this well-meant remonstrance will have its effect, and that, resuscitated by public encouragement, it may continue to afford that information and instruction by which so many have been improved and benefited since its original establishment.

By the 26th rule, it it enacted—

"That in case the society shall be reduced so as not to be supported by the annual income, then the books shall devolve upon the Incumbents of Saint Hilda's Chapel, of Westoe Parochial School, and the Trustees of the South Shields Charity School, and remain with them, *in trust*, for the benefit and use of any future re-establishment of the library."

The contingency thus provided for has now arrived, and it remains to be seen whether the library is to be re-established upon its ancient footing, or its literary treasures are to be altogether withdrawn from perusal or use, and placed under lock and key, as useless as if they had never been published. The decision rests with the inhabitants and to them I leave it; not doubting but that the literary character of the town will be thereby rescued from the passing cloud, which, in this instance only, overshadows it, and that, by the restoration of the library, through public support, to its former position, the intentions of the founders may again be carried out by the diffusion of that knowledge which its volumes contain.

The South Shields and Westoe Dispensary, established in 1821, for the purpose of supplying the poor inhabitants of South Shields and Westoe with medical and surgical aid, ranks, deservedly, amongst the most beneficial institutions of the borough, having since the commencement to the 6th of February, 1856, a period of thirty-five years, dispensed its benefits to 37,183 patients, in manner and with the results following, for the last year, viz. :—

Admitted by ticket 567
Casualties 700
—1,267
Cured......................... 1,116
Relieved........................ 69
Dead ...`...................... 22
Remaining on books 60
—1,267

It is supported by annual subscriptions, donations, congregational collections, dividends on stock, and interest, which, for the year ended February last, amounted, with the balance of the previous year, to £192 14s. 2d., the disbursements for the same period having been £201 2s. 10d., a balance against the charity being thus left of £8 8s. 8d. The Dean and Chapter of Durham are the patrons, and

William Anderson, Esq., of Bent-house, as treasurer, is deserving of honourable mention, for his praiseworthy services, and the interest he takes in the well-being of the institution. By a committee of nine subscribers the affairs are managed, and the following are the medical gentlemen, who, to their honour be it recorded, attend the dispensary without fee or reward, viz. :—Dr. Brown, of Sunderland, Mr. Toshach, as consulting surgeon, and Messrs. Robert Wallis, Joseph Frain, and Henry Birkett, as surgeons, Mr. Charlton being the house surgeon, with a salary of £80 a year.

To no benevolent object could superfluous wealth be better applied in South Shields, than in extending by donations and legacies, the usefulness of this most excellent charity, and 1, therefore, earnestly call the attention of the opulent to the subject, in the hope that its claims may not be overlooked. Poverty, itself, is a misfortune of no common magnitude, but when accompanied, as it too frequently is, by sickness and bodily affliction, the sufferings of the poor are increased to an extent of which their affluent brethren have little conception. It is true, that for many of such cases of indigent sickness, the Union Workhouse may be had recourse to as a fitting receptacle, or the services of the district medical officer obtained; but such assistance is confined to paupers in receipt of indoor or outdoor relief, and there are many families in possession of means for their *ordinary* support, who cannot find any for *extraordinary* demands, occasioned by loss of health with which they may be unexpectedly overtaken. It is on behalf of this latter class that I venture to make this appeal, and having done so, I leave it for the consideration of those who, having the means, ought not to lack the inclination to lend a favourable ear to the wants of their suffering neighbours, by willingly affording to " The South Shields and Westoe Dispensary " that liberal support to which its merits and usefulness so deservedly entitle it.

> " Oh, ye! who sunk in beds of down,
> Feel not a want but what yourselves create ;"

Think that—

> " Affliction's sons are brothers in distress,
> A brother to relieve, how exquisite the bliss."

The founding of an hospital or infirmary, with adequate funds of a permanent nature, for the reception, *within its walls*, of patients requiring medical or surgical aid, would be a God-like act, by which an existing want in the borough, not provided for by the Dispensary, would be removed, and I bring it under notice, in connection with our *Future*, in the hope that, by the appropriation of a fund sufficient for the purpose, some good Samaritan may thus, with a portion of his riches, acquire an immortality for his name more lasting and satisfactory than that which is frequently attempted by man with short-sighted wisdom and in the pride and vanity of his heart. By thus following the example, which in so many already enumerated instances, has been set by the venerable philanthropist of Westoe, another charitable institution, of no common description, would rise up within the borough in grateful remembrance of the benevolence of its founder, and by it a blessing would be bestowed upon those whom it would seek to relieve and benefit—the sick and needy, and he who has no helper.

The South Shields Indigent Sick Society, next claiming my attention, was established in 1818, and is under the management of Mrs. Roxby and sixteen other ladies, who truly may be designated Sisters of Mercy,—its object being the alleviation of the sufferings of the poor when attacked by sickness and disease. Its income is derived from voluntary subscriptions and donations, congregational collections, and interest of capital, and it amounted last year to £99 17s. 3½d., the expenditure having been £97 17s. 9½d., and the number of sick persons relieved 204. I am sorry to perceive, from the published accounts, that there is a balance of £49 8s. 11½d. due to the treasurer, a financial deficiency which ought not to exist in connection with a charity so eminently useful. The committee and managers, in consequence of this have, by their last report, drawn the attention of the inhabitants to the operations of the society, and the state of the funds, which, from the increased number of applicants for relief, consequent on the increase of the population of the town, they declare to be insufficient adequately to meet the pressing cases which are often brought under the notice of the visitors. They, at the same time, express a hope that, in making the state of the funds more generally known, additional subscriptions and donations may be obtained so as to enable them more effectually to carry out the object of the society. In making this public, I most cordially assist, and I, at the same time, bear my willing testimony to the claims which this society also has, as a valuable auxiliary to the Dispensary, upon the rich, for pecuniary aid. If it were only in compliment to the softer sex, this assistance should be gallantly afforded, and I shall feel disappointed if, in answer to this appeal, it be not made manifest by the improved condition of the society's funds, that in South Shields, at least, the age of chivalry has not departed.

The South Shields Savings' Bank was established on the 27th of October, 1817, and is one of the most useful institutions in the borough, its object being the safe custody and increase of the savings of industrious persons, the funds of friendly societies, and of charitable institutions, in the town of South Shields and its neighbourhood. Its funds and concerns are under the control and management of a committee of managers, consisting of ten trustees, a treasurer, secretary, actuary, three auditors, and twelve or more directors; and as vacancies occur in the committee, they are filled up forthwith by the remaining members. A general audited statement of the funds of

Yesterday (May 22nd. 1933,) was the hundreth anniversary of the laying of the foundation stone of Holy Trinity Church, South Shields. The stone was laid by the Rev. James Carr of St. Hild's, and in the absence owing to illness of Bishop Van Mildert, Dr. Sumner, of Chester, afterwards Archbishop of Canterbury, performed the consecration on the 18th of Sept. 1834.

A HUNDRED YEARS AGO.

(FROM THE NEWCASTLE COURANT, OCTOBER 30, 1817.)

SAVINGS BANK FOR SOUTH SHIELDS.

This day a Savings Bank begins its beneficial operations at South Shields under the patronage of the magistrates of the district. Measures are in progress for establishing one of these admirable institutions in this town.

the bank for each year is published annually, and it will be seen from the one ending the 20th of November last, that the number of depositors then amounted to 1,747, making with eight charitable institutions, a total of 1,755, the amount deposited by them being £47,312 6s. 2d. The business is well conducted in a handsome building built by, and belonging to, the institution, in Barrington-street, and attendance is given at the bank every Saturday night from 7 to 8 o'clock, and on every Monday from 12 o'clock, at noon, to 1, for the purpose of receiving deposits, and paying money due to depositors. The rate of annual interest allowed to depositors is £3 per cent. No sum exceeding 12s. 6d. can be withdrawn without one month's previous notice; but, in cases of great emergency, the directors present may dispense with the notice. Mr. Nevison is the secretary; and, as a director, I can myself bear willing testimony to the value of his services, and those of the actuary, as being of a nature to give confidence to depositors. I only wish that the advantages of the institution were still more generally sought by the working classes, as a place of deposit, for earnings which are otherwise too frequently wasted; and I would earnestly entreat the masters of manufacturing and other establishments to bring prominently and continually under the notice of their workmen the South Shields Savings' Bank, as a place in which can be safely and conveniently deposited their surplus earnings,—and the duty which devolves upon them, the industrious classes, to secure a provision in the time of their youth and strength, for the days of their age and decline; and while yet unencumbered, to invest the surplus of their earnings to meet the wants of those who may become connected with, or dependent on, them in after life.

The Theatre, in Wellington-street, was erected in 1792, by Edward Giles, who was contractor for the whole, from a plan by Thomas Thwaites, painter, Whitby. It is not well attended, except on special occasions, owing chiefly to the present inconvenience of its situation. I am inclined to think that its removal to King-street, the Market-place, or some other central site, would prove a remunerative speculation, and this, perhaps, may be looked forward to as a portion of our *Future*.

Considering it of importance to put on record information which may be relied on as to the present educational condition of the borough, in connection with its churches and chapels, I have submitted, with great care, written queries to, and obtained, with a readiness which deserves my thanks, written answers from, every clergyman and minister within the limits of my inquiry, the particulars of which I have thought it most convenient to concentrate in a Tabular Statement, which will also be found to contain interesting facts relating to the churches and chapels themselves. *(See Tabular Statement.)*

I have also applied for, and obtained as readily, returns from the teachers in the borough, whose schools are not connected with churches

H

or chapels, giving a total of 1834 scholars in attendance at these last-mentioned schools.

The returns, altogether, shew the following results, viz. :—

		Total.
Scholars in attendance at day schools in connection with churches and chapels	1633	
Scholars in attendance at day schools *not* in connection with churches or chapels	1834	3467
Sunday school scholars	3143	
Gratuitous Sunday school teachers	344	

You have thus brought before you, for future use, educational statistics of importance, in such an analyzed shape, as may be safely referred to, whenever occasion may require. The collection of them has been attended with considerable trouble, but I shall be amply rewarded if, by any exertions of mine, I have contributed in this way, by a disclosure of facts, towards the creation of an increased or a renewed interest in the education of the people, amongst whom and their children, there is unhappily to be found, a lamentable amount of culpable ignorance, notwithstanding the schoolmaster has been for so long a time abroad.   For the existence of this ignorance there are many causes, which, if it came within my province, could easily be explained ; but one of the most mischievous of them certainly is, the sinful indifference of parents to the education of their children, and their wicked neglect of the facilities for improvement in that direction, which are afforded through the medium of our numerous schools.   It is society which suffers from this—for ignorance is undeniably one of the great sources of crime, in the removal of which it is the duty of us all, and likewise our interest, most zealously to assist.

South Shields, until the 6th of April, 1848, formed a portion of the port of Newcastle-upon-Tyne, but on that day South Shields and North Shields, after many former efforts, on the part chiefly of the latter, were constituted a distinct port, by the name of " The Port of Shields," the line of demarcation between the two ports of Shields and Newcastle having been drawn from the lower end of Jarrow quay on the south side of the river, to Hayhole-point on the north side, a division which seems to be, not unreasonably, complained of by North Shields, as not being coextensive with its municipal and Parliamentary boundaries.

North Shields, on the division of the port, became possessed of an independent Custom House—a reward, I had almost said, for her long and persevering efforts to obtain it.

South Shields has also obtained a Custom House, but it is subservient (perhaps as a punishment for her supineness) to that of the sister borough of Tynemouth.

. As a matter of pride, this is displeasing enough to South Shields; but since the granting of the recent additional Customs' facilities, I am not aware of any substantial loss or grievance which she sustains from the arrangement. Whether on the completion of Jarrow docks, within our borough, the necessity for an independent Custom House, at South Shields, may arise and force itself upon the authorities, is more than I can venture to predict; but, however that may be, I consider it an imperative duty, which every South Shields citizen owes to his borough, to contribute, by all the means in his power, to the obtaining of this desirable object, by the registration of his ships and the transaction of his business at the Custom House of his own town, it being certain, that so long as North Shields retains her present superiority as regards duties which pass through the Customs, so long will she preserve the distinction which is derived from the possession of an independent Custom House. By the amount of its Customs' duties, chiefly, is the importance of a port viewed by the Customs' authorities at head quarters, and by that will the relative importance and claims of the two boroughs be at all times considered and decided.

I have extracted the following particulars from the Shipping Returns, made to the House of Commons, on the motion of our member, Mr. Ingham, who has laudably procured a yearly continuation of those previously obtained by his predecessor, Mr. Wawn. The extracts are purposely confined to the ports of Newcastle, Shields, Sunderland, Hartlepool, and Stockton. I have placed them in juxta-position, with this express object, that here and elsewhere, they may be compared with each other, and judged of as to the trade carried on in each; a comparison which the ports of Shields and Newcastle may safely undergo, without detriment to their high positions. But it is always necessary to keep in mind, that to arrive at the real import-ance of the Tyne, and the trading communities on its banks, the numbers and registered tonnage of vessels, the entrances and clear-ances inwards and outwards, shipments and exports, for the ports of *Shields and Newcastle*, must be formed into an *aggregate*, and *then* compared with the neighbouring and other ports of the kingdom.

Number and tonnage of *sailing* vessels *registered* at the following ports, distinguishing those under, and those above, 50 tons register, on the 31st December, 1855. Also, a similar return of *steam* vessels, and their tonnage :—

	SAILING VESSELS REGISTERED.				STEAM VESSELS REGISTERED.			
	Of and under 50 tons.		Above 50 tons.		Of and under 50 tons.		Above 50 tons.	
	Vessels.	Tons.	Vessels.	Tons.	Vessels.	Tons.	Vessels.	Tons.
Newcastle	108	2961	466	126,937	73	1221	24	7687
Shields	21	660	858	237,838	95	1878	10	968
Sunderland	91	2760	851	226,230	43	752	7	3582
Hartlepool	2	30	172	36,753	2	52	5	1849
Stockton	14	394	129	27,441	21	462	2	278

Number and tonnage of vessels that entered and cleared *coastways* at the following ports (including their repeated voyages), distinguishing British from Foreign vessels, and steam from sailing vessels, between the 31st day of December, 1854, and the 31st day of December, 1855 :—

	SAILING VESSELS.							
	INWARDS.				OUTWARDS.			
	British		Foreign.		British.		Foreign.	
	Vessels.	Tonnage.	Vessels.	Tonnage.	Vessels.	Tonnage.	Vessels.	Tonnage.
{ Newcastle	1826	157,488	76	10,620	10,121	1,380,381	2	178
{ Shields ..	395	42,946	46	12,407	1,209	122,458	—	—
Sunderland	1381	232,453	16	2,244	11,028	1,358,463	3	194
Hartlepool..	313	23,903	8	626	5,614	737,332	4	253
Stockton ..	376	31,281	2	216	1,520	135,774	—	—
	STEAM VESSELS.							
{ Newcastle	433	91,026	—	—	556	118,123	—	—
{ Shields ..	3	54	—	—	19	1,678	1	550
Sunderland	4	59	—	—	67	16,040	—	—
Hartlepool..	7	115	—	—	62	26,042	—	—
Stockton ..	43	9,208	—	—	47	9,503	—	—

Number and tonnage of vessels that entered and cleared from and to the *Colonies* (including their repeated voyages), distinguishing steam from sailing vessels, between the 31st December, 1854, and the 31st December, 1855 ; further distinguishing British from Foreign vessels :—

	SAILING VESSELS.							
{ Newcastle	64	13,676	14	2,366	270	56,271	56	18,938
{ Shields ..	39	13,226	2	985	26	10,430	4	1,893
Sunderland	112	26,517	14	3,723	162	36,528	2	773
Hartlepool..	19	3,509	6	732	74	17,652	21	8,012
Stockton ..	14	3,404	5	1,305	5	566	1	166
	STEAM VESSELS.							
{ Newcastle	—	—	—	—	1	13	—	—
{ Shields ..	—	—	—	—	1	462	—	—
Sunderland	—	—	—	—	—	—	—	—
Hartlepool..	—	—	—	—	—	—	—	—
Stockton ..	—	—	—	—	—	—	—	—

Number and tonnage of vessels that entered and cleared from and to *Foreign ports* (including their repeated voyages), distinguishing steam from sailing vessels, and British from Foreign vessels, between the 31st December, 1854, and the 31st December, 1855 :

	SAILING VESSELS.							
	INWARDS.				OUTWARDS.			
	British.		Foreign.		British.		Foreign.	
	Vessels.	Tonnage.	Vessels.	Tonnage.	Vessels.	Tonnage.	Vessels.	Tonnage.
{ Newcastle	1339	216,843	2352	341,451	2676	547,535	3412	505,583
{ Shields ..	902	189,993	405	41,243	473	84.677	418	39,340
Sunderland	1045	181,507	938	89,463	1278	252,677	1109	117,068
Hartlepool..	690	126,140	777	87,761	795	157,501	1340	158,476
Stockton ..	282	45,383	233	23,334	286	46,739	305	33,710

	STEAM VESSELS.							
{ Newcastle	67	21,554	—	—	72	22,588	1	25
{ Shields ..	—	—	—	—	13	1,535	—	—
Sunderland	1	407	—	—	2	704	1	257
Hartlepool..	55	19,835	1	235	53	19,443	—	—
Stockton ..	—	—	—	—	—	—	—	—

Aggregate number and tonnage of vessels entered and cleared (including their repeated voyages), in the *coasting, Colonial,* and *Foreign* trades, in the year 1855, distinguishing British from Foreign vessels :—

{ Newcastle	3729	500,587	2442	354,437	13,696	2,124,911	3471	524,724
{ Shields ..	1339	246,219	453	54,635	1,741	221,240	423	41,783
Sunderland	2543	440,943	968	95,430	12,537	1,664,511	1115	118,292
Hartlepool..	1084	173,502	792	89,354	6,598	957,970	1365	166,741
Stockton ..	715	89,276	240	24,855	1,858	192,582	306	33,876

I have also, with the same object, made the following extracts as regards coals, cinders, culm, &c., from a return made to the House of Commons, on the the the 6th March, 1856, viz.:—

No. I.—An account of the quantities of coals, cinders, and culm, and patent fuel, *shipped* at the following ports, *coastways, to other ports of the United Kingdom :*—

Ports from which shipped.	COALS, CINDERS, AND CULM.								PATENT FUEL.	
	1854.				1855.					
	Coals.	Cndrs.	Culm.	Total.	Coals.	Cndrs.	Culm.	Total.	1854.	1855.
	Tons.	Tons.	Tons.	Tons.	Tons.	Tons.	Tons.	Tons.	Tons.	Tns.
{ Newcastle ..	2,138,311	9,765	—	2,148,076	2,014,760	7,599	—	2,022,359	6,811	5,419
{ Shields	225,763	—	—	225,763	164,339	52	—	164,391	—	—
Sunderland ..	2,068,198	247	—	2,068,445	1,942,060	801	—	1,942,861	—	—
Stockton	198,002	14,524	—	212,526	141,454	751	—	142,205	15,120	2,460
Hartlepool ..	1,264,366	4,217	—	1,268,583	1,137,178	1,571	—	1,138,749	—	—

No. II.—An account of the *quantities* and *declared value* of coals, cinders, and culm, and patent fuel, *exported*, from the following ports, *to Foreign Countries* and *British Settlements abroad* :—

Ports from which shipped.	1854.									
	QUANTITIES EXPORTED.					DECLARED VALUE THEREOF.				
	Coals.	Cinders.	Culm.	Total.	Patnt. Fuel.	Coals.	Cndrs.	Culm.	Total.	Patnt. Fuel.
	Tons.	Tons.	Tons.	Tons.	Tons.	£.	£.	£.	£.	£.
{ Newcastle....	1,345,456	74,065	—	1,419,521	451	593,221	62,855	—	656,076	288
{ Shields	178,267	15,936	—	194,203	—	78,052	13,222	—	91,274	—
Sunderland	479,271	26,177	—	505,448	—	163,280	19,467	—	182,747	—
Stockton	62,976	23,336	—	86,312	105	27,890	17,019	—	44,909	63
Hartlepool	375,680	34,100	—	409,780	—	143,913	26,139	—	170,052	—

Ports from which shipped.	1855.									
{ Newcastle....	1,417,640	102,784	—	1,520,424	1042	635,271	86,123	—	721,394	966
{ Shields	168,433	2,086	—	170,519	50	75,892	1,692	—	77,584	27
Sunderland	542,163	28,165	—	570,328	—	196,221	21,961	—	218,182	—
Stockton	74,525	17,980	—	92,505	—	33,009	15,891	—	48,900	—
Hartlepool......	428,579	40,501	—	469,080	—	164,791	33,944	—	198,736	—

No. III.—An account of the quantities of coals and patent fuel brought *coastways*, and by *inland navigation*, and *land carriage*, into the port of London, during the year 1855, comparing the same with the quantities during the year 1854 :—

	Coals.		Patent Fuel.	
	1854.	1855.	1854.	1855.
	Tons.	Tons.	Tons.	Tons.
Coastways	3,399,561	3,016,868	40,289	30,788
By inland navigation and *land carriage* .... }	979,171	1,162,487	—	—
Total	4,378,732	4,179,355	40,289	30,788

Shewing an *increase*, in one year, of 183,316 tons in the quantity of coals brought by inland navigation and *land carriage* into the port of London, and a *decrease* of 382,693 tons in the quantity of coals brought *coastways* into that port: two disheartening facts in connection with each other, which are too significant to require note or comment from me. They most assuredly are not an agreeable or promising ingredient of our *Future*.

The formation of an extensive *Cemetery* of sixteen acres, in a most convenient and proper locality, and which will be so laid out as to meet and satisfy the conscientious scruples of Churchmen and Dissenters, gives satisfaction to all. The state of St. Hilda's churchyard had long been a subject of offence to the inhabitants, and the time had come when such a state of objectionable intramural interments could no longer be suffered to continue. That particular graveyard was closed finally on the 1st January last, without the slightest chance of being reopened; and Holy Trinity is under orders for closing on the 1st July next. In the mean time the united Burial Board of South Shields and Westoe is using every exertion to be in readiness to supply the want which will be created when Saint Stephen's churchyard will be the only one left open within the Borough.

Whoever has visited, as I have lately done, a country churchyard,

> "Beneath whose rugged elms, that yew-tree's shade,
> Where heaves the turf in many a mouldering heap,
> Each in his narrow cell for ever laid,
> The rude forefathers of the hamlet sleep:"

must have been struck with the peaceful character of the scene, and compared it, as I did, with the rank and crowded graveyards of his own city. It is right beyond all doubt that intramural burying grounds when they become offensive should be closed, and I rejoice with the inhabitants of this borough at the certainty which exists as to the closing of those of Saint Hilda and Holy Trinity.

What can be done to improve the unsightly appearance of the former will be a matter for serious consideration, for it is an object of a nature to impress a stranger, on his first arrival by railway, most unfavorably with our town; and we know how difficult, and frequently impossible it is, to remove impressions of an unfavorable kind, when once they are formed.

The Baths and Wash-houses in John Street, Cuthbert Street, were erected by the Corporation in 1854, with a kind consideration for the comforts of the working classes. They have more than answered expectation; and are now being considerably extended in the washing department, in order to supply the demands of the people for washing accommodation. They are under the management of a corporate committee, with Alderman Matthew Stainton as chairman; and of a master and matron, who give satisfaction, in the persons of Mr. and Mrs. Atkinson.

The Common Lodging Houses are under the inspection of Mr. Hedington, the superintendent of our borough police; and their sanitary condition is carefully attended to by him.

The Races used to be held annually on the sands, on Whitsun-Monday, Tuesday, and Wednesday; and were at one period more respectably patronized than any other leather plate races in the north of England. They are now under orders to be discontinued in consequence of the riotous proceedings, attended with loss of life, which took place at them last year. With the exception of the publicans and their customers, all had ceased to take an interest in them, and it is well, when we consider the circumstances under which they were abolished, that they can be looked upon now only as things of the *past*.

A Lecture at and concerning South Shields by me, without mention of the Church Leasehold Tenure—that incubus, which has been such a bar to our advancement—would be somewhat like the play of Hamlet, with the principal character of Hamlet omitted. It is not, however, my intention, after all that has been said, and the volumes which have been written, in explanation of the tenure, its ancient origin, continuation for centuries, and present position, to attempt in a space which is unavoidably circumscribed, a repetition which would be deserving of a lecture itself, on a subject so immensely important. It is better that I should briefly content myself with a warning to the Lessees against that fatal confidence which still relies for safety on the good faith of the Lessors, and with an exhortation, no longer to calculate on the system of renewal, but to rescue themselves from the dangers of eventual confiscation, by the conversion of their leaseholds into freeholds, through means of that which is commonly known as *Enfranchisement.* They may rest assured, that the question is no longer one of renewal, but of enfranchisement; and bitter will be the unavailing reflection if, through misplaced confidence, the opportunity for the latter be stupidly disregarded and lost. In anticipation of this, for it has long been foreseen, I have, since my first examination before the Commons' Committee, in 1838, been almost unceasingly engaged in endeavours to obtain for the Lessees that justice which, in my conscience, I believe them to be entitled; and I still adhere to the opinion which I boldly declared in my examination before the Royal Commissioners, in 1849, that to deprive the Lessees of their benefit of renewal, under any pretence whatever, would be an act of gross injustice and spoliation. In opposition to any such dishonest deprivation, I have never hesitated to lift up my voice in indignant remonstrance, and it is to me a matter of the most heartfelt satisfaction that, frequently under discouraging circumstances, but always without flinching, I have, to the best of my ability, for nearly twenty years, been a resolute defender of the claims of the Lessees, and an uncompromising supporter of their rights and interests. But it is by their own deeds, and not by my words, that anything approaching to a rescue can now be effected; and I say to the Lessees, therefore, with all the solemnity which is engendered by a knowledge of their danger, —Enfranchise! Enfranchise! Enfranchise!

In addition to the charities before enumerated, by which our town is blessed and honoured, it seems to be necessary briefly to particularize the following, which are of long standing, viz.:—

The old Charity School, which was established in and has been supported since 1769 by legacies, donations, and benefactions, bequeathed and bestowed by Christopher Maughan, Ann Aubone, Lord Crewes' Trustees, Henry Wilkinson, Lockwood Brodrick, Ralph Redhead, and the other benevolent individuals, whose names are recorded in Saint Hilda's Church. Its educational arrangements will be found in the Tabular Statement which is comprised in this lecture, and its affairs are managed by the Incumbent of Saint Hilda and four other Trustees, who derive their appointment from the benefactors, subscribers to the charity, or their representatives.   An annual meeting is held on the 1st of May, notice whereof is previously given in Saint Hilda's Church, at which the form of electing trustees is gone through; but as, in fact, the meeting is seldom attended except by those who acted in the preceding year, the same persons are generally reelected. The funds are vested in the trustees, and the annual income of the school is about £100.   The school house is leasehold under the Dean and Chapter of Durham.   The scholars are appointed by the trustees, to whom recommendations are sent by the original subscribers or their representatives, orphans being always preferred.   None are admitted under 7 years of age, or are allowed to remain beyond the age of 14. The boys are taught reading, writing, and arithmetic, and the girls reading, writing, and needlework, the schoolmistress being allowed the profits arising from the work, for her own benefit.

Glazonby's Charity which was created by the will of Margaret Glazonby, of Corbridge, widow, bearing date the 21st of March, 1810, whereby she bequeathed £200 to be paid to five or more persons of reputed integrity, inhabitants of the chapelry of Saint Hilda, who should be nominated and chosen at a public vestry meeting for that purpose, upon trust, to place the same out at interest, or in the public funds, and to pay, apply, and dispose of the interest or dividends thereof towards the education and clothing of poor children belonging to the charity school in South Shields, in such manner as the trustees should think proper; it being provided that whenever two or more of the trustees should happen to die, proper persons to succed them in the trust should, from time to time, be elected and chosen at a public vestry meeting, to be held for that purpose as aforesaid, and so often as a vacancy should happen.

On the 28th of August, 1848, Christopher Bainbridge being then the only surviving trustee, James Wardle Roxby, Robert Dawson, Thomas Forsyth, and Thomas Wallis, were elected trustees, at a vestry meeting, in the place of George Townsend Fox, Joseph Bulmer, James Kirkley, and Jeremiah Archer, deceased.   Christopher Bainbridge, James Wardle Roxby, and Thomas Wallis have since departed this life, thereby causing three vacancies in the trust, which now have to be filled up according to the will.

Hood's Charity, created under the will of William Hood, mariner, bearing date the 30th August, 1788, whereby he gave and bequeathed to the curate and churchwardens, for the time being, of the chapelry of Saint Hilda, £20 *upon trust*, to place the same out at interest, and at their discretion to distribute the same, on the first day of every year, amongst the poor people belonging to the chapelry.

The Court Leet and Baron of the Dean and Chapter of Durham,

I

as Lords of the Manor of Westoe, is also deserving of notice. It is for the recovery of petty debts, before a barrister as judge and a jury, once a year, in the Town Hall; Mr. Andrew Stoddart being the manor bailiff, by whom summonses are granted and executions issued. Presentments for nuisances, encroachments, &c., used formerly to be made with great ceremony by the jury on these occasions, but the greater and better defined powers of the South Shields Improvement Act have rendered unneccessary the continuance of an interference, which received little or no attention from parties presented. William Grey, Esq., is the talented and highly respected judge who presides over the proceedings of the court, and by him justice is feelingly administered with an impartial care, which obtains for him the confidence of those whose humble differences have to be decided in his court.

South Shields was first visited by *asiatic cholera* in 1832, and its dreadful visits have been since repeated in 1834, 1848, 1849, and 1853. May it never again be looked upon in this borough otherwise than as a thing of the *Past*, and may we be spared, by the goodness of the Almighty, from a repetition of the horrors of so terrible an infliction. It was during those visitations that the Reverend James Carr, the truly christian minister of Saint Hilda's parish, with a disregard for his own life and a contempt of danger which were beyond all praise, distinguished himself by a courageous attention to the bodily and spiritual wants of his afflicted parishioners, which won for him universal admiration.

"Afraid not for any terror by night, nor for the arrow that flieth by day;
"For the pestilence that walketh in darkness; nor for the sickness that destroyeth in the noonday;"

He was unceasing in the discharge of all those dangerous duties, which so well became his holy calling. High and low, rich and poor, alike received his unremitting attention; and, amidst the haunts of death and the dangers of contagion—in the mansions of the rich, and the hovels of the poor—he was ever to be found in willing attendance upon the temporal wants of all who required his aid, or by an administration of the consolations of religion, smoothing the passage to the grave of some heavily afflicted sufferer. Happily, "the path of duty" proved to be the "path of safety."

"A thousand shall fall beside thee, and ten thousand at thy right hand; but it shall not come nigh thee."

And so, under the divine protection, it proved in the case of our excellent friend, who still survives to receive from us, even until now, a grateful continuance of the sense we entertain of his never-to-be-forgotten services.

In affectionate acknowledgment of services so meritorious, the Reverend Gentleman was gratified by the presentation of various valuable tokens in silver and gold, the nature and object of which, will be best explained by the respective inscriptions which appear thereon, as follow :—

"This salver, with seventy-five sovereigns, was presented to the Reverend James Carr, perpetual curate of South Shields, by his *parishioners*, as a tribute of respect and esteem for his unwearied exertions and christian sympathy during the two awful visitations of cholera, with which the town and neighbourhood were afflicted. 1835."

"This salver, together with a Pocket Communion Service, was presented to the Reverend James Carr, by the *working classes* of South Shields, as a testimony of their gratitude for his unwearied exertions in visiting the poor and afflicted, during two awful visitations of the cholera. 1835."

"From the scholars of the national school, Westoe, to the Reverend James Carr, as a token of regard. 1834."

The latter was inscribed on a handsome gold ring, the interesting gift of 500 children; and all the gifts were accompanied by appropriate addresses, (that of the working classes being signed by 1239 working men) expressive of the feelings of gratitude, and warm attachment of the donors, towards their reverend friend.

It was on the 20th July, 1831, that Mr. Carr, was appointed to the living of Saint Hilda, on the death of the Reverend William Maugham, and on the 14th of the following month, that he was formally read in. This appointment has proved a happy one for South Shields, amongst all classes of the inhabitants of which, he has been eminently successful, by his prudent, mild, and conciliatory conduct, in the preservation of a peaceful and kindly understanding amongst those whom religious differences might otherwise have kept at an unfriendly or, perhaps, a hostile distance. By his wise suggestions and indefatigable exertions, the wide spread chapelry of Saint Hilda, with a population too numerous, by thousands, for one ecclesiastical district, has been divided into three, as set forth in my Tabular Statement, viz., those of Saint Hilda, Holy Trinity and Saint Stephen, with a separate church and incumbent for each, and the spiritual wants of the church-going population, have thus been provided for by ample church accommodation, while the parochial duty of every description has been effectually discharged by means of the extensive change.

Although these the important, long, and peculiar services of Mr. Carr, render just the special allusion, which I have considered it my imperative duty thus gladly to make, I would not by any means pass by the merits of the incumbents of Holy Trinity and Saint Stephen, or of the numerous other zealous and hard working ministers of Christ's Gospel within this borough; I know that both in and out of their churches, chapels, and schools, no exertions are spared by any of them, and that in the preaching of God's Word, the dissemination of gospel truths, the visiting of the sick, and the discharge of all other requisite duties, the people are benefited to an extent, most gratifying to all who have at heart their religous and moral improvement. But this I also know, that much, notwithstanding, remains to be done, for habits of intoxication and neglect of the sabbath prevail within our bounds, to a fearful extent, while by profane swearing of the most offensive description, the ears of the well disposed are openly offended, in our streets and public thorougfares, not only by men but by young

70

and thoughtless boys. I call the attention of all my reverend friends, dissenters as well as churchmen, to this most wicked and offensive state of things, and I pray most earnestly for a blessing upon all such endeavours as they may see fit to use, for the cure and prevention of the two crying sins, which I have thought it my duty thus prominently to bring under their notice and consideration.

One hundred and forty years ago, *Westoe Common Fields*, then consisting of one great and three lesser fields, and containing by estimation 484 acres, were held by certain parties in undivided fourths, under leases granted by the Dean and Chapter of Durham, for 21 years each. Disputes having arisen out of the common occupancy, and it being considered by some of the parties interested, that a division of the grounds would tend much to the improvement thereof, proceedings in the Court of Chancery at Durham were instituted, and by a decree of that Court, it was ordered that the parties should forthwith proceed to a division of the "Westoe Common Fields;" and for the better settling and ascertaining the shares of the several persons concerned, in proportion to their several farmholds, it was further ordered that a commission should be forthwith issued, directed to certain commisioners therein named, with power for the making of the division. A commision for the purposes aforsaid was issued accordingly bearing date the 1st December, 1715, and by an award made thereunder, on the 25th of February, 1716, under the hands and seals of the commissioners, Thomas Hilton, Thomas Garth, Anthony Young, and John Huntley, they divided, apportioned, allotted, set out, and boundered the same lauds in question, in manner following, that is to say:—

This is now the Bent House Farm and Bents. *Unto* Adam Bentley, and Barbara his wife for their farmhold right in the said Westoe Common Fields, 160 acres of ground, parcel of the said Common fields, as the same was dowled out, and *boundering* upon the Sea on the east, the lands of Nicholas Burdon, called Shields Heugh on the north, the ground belonging the township of Harton on the south, and the ground thereby allotted to George Harle on the west; *to hold* unto the said Adam Bentley and Barbara his wife, and the executors, adminatrators, and assigns of the said Barbara, for such term and interest as they had in the said undivided part of the premises. The fee simple and inheritance thereof to be and remain to the Dean and Chapter and their successors, to be held and enjoyed in severalty.

This is the Farm now under lease to Robt. Ingham, Esq. *Unto* George Harle for his farmhold right, in the said Westoe Common Fields, 105 acres of ground, parcel of the said common Fields, viz., 103 acres. parcel thereof, *boundering* upon the grounds thereby allotted to the said Adam Bentley and Barbara his wife, on the east, the said ground of Nicholas Burdon, called Shields Heugh, and some grounds called Fowler's Closes on the north, part of the town of Westoe, and the grounds belonging to the township of Harton on the south, and part of the grounds thereby allotted to Robert Adamson for his leasehold interest in the premises, the said Fowler's Closes, and an inclosed piece of ground thereinafter mentioned, to be also allotted to the said George Harle, called the Cow Night Fold on the west, as the same was then dowled out. *And unto* the said George Harle, an inclosed piece of ground, called the Cow Night Fold, parcel of the said Common Fields, containing 2 acres of ground, to be the residue of the said 105 acres of ground, as allotted to him as aforesaid: *to hold* unto the said George Harle, his executors, administrators, and assigns, for such term and estate as he had in his undivided part of the premises. The fee and

71

inheritance of the said George Harle's allotment to be held and enjoyed in severalty by the Dean and Chapter.

This is the Farm now under lease to the Rev. Robt. Green, of Newcastle-upon-Tyne.
 Unto the said Robert Adamson, for his *leasehold* farmhold right in the said Westoe Common Fields, 109 acres of ground, parcel of the said Common Fields, viz., 69 acres, parcel of the said 109 acres, *boundering* on the said George Harle's allotment on the east, on Fowler's closes aforesaid, on an inclosed piece of ground called the New Close, thereinafter mentioned, to be also allotted to the said Robert Adamson, on the north, the town of Westoe aforesaid on the south, and the grounds thereby allotted to Mary and Robert Eden on the west, as the same was then dowled out. *And unto* the said Robert Adamson. an inclosed piece of ground called the New Close, parcel of the said Common Field, containing 40 acres or thereabouts, to be the residue of the said 109 acres, so allotted to him as aforesaid: *to hold* unto the said Robert Adamson, his executors, administrators, and assigns, for all such term and estate for years, as the said Robert Adamson had in his said *leasehold* undivided part of the premises. The fee and inheritance of the said leasehold allotment to be and remain to the Dean and Chapter and their successors, to be held and enjoyed in severalty.

The property of the late Mrs. Green, at Laygate, upon which Brunswick Street, Green Street, Adelaide St., &c., are built.
 Unto the said Robert Adamson, for his *freehold* tenement in the said Common Fields, all that piece or parcel of ground, as it was then fenced out, called the *Ox Night Fold*, parcel of the said premises, containing 17 acres or thereabouts, together with the mines and quarries, and their royalties therein; *to hold* to the said Robert Adamson, his heirs and assigns, for ever in severalty.

This is the Farm now under lease to the exors. of the late T. Forrest, Esq., deceased, upon trust.
 Unto Mary Eden and Robert Eden, in trust for the said Robert Eden, his executors, administrators, and assigns, for their farmhold right in the said Westoe Common Fields, 93 acres of ground, parcel of the said Common Fields, viz., 85 acres and 1 rood thereof *boundering* upon part of the ground thereby allotted unto the said Robert Adamson on the east, on the other part of the grounds thereby allotted unto the said Robert Adamson, and an inclosed piece of ground called the Horse Close, thereinafter mentioned to be also allotted unto the said Mary and Robert Eden, and the said Ox Night Fold, thereby allotted to the said Robert Adamson, for his freehold, on the north, and the lane leading from Westoe aforesaid to West Pans on the south, the same lane and the said Ox Night Fold on the west, as the same was then dowled out. *And unto* the said Mary and Robert Eden, in trust, as aforesaid, an inclosed piece of ground called the Horse Close, parcel of the said premises, containing 7 acres and 3 roods, to be the residue of the said 93 acres so allotted to them as aforesaid; *to hold* unto the said Mary and Robert Eden, in trust for the said Robert Eden, and to the executors, administrators, and assigns of the said Robert Eden, for all such term and interest as they or either of them respectively had in or to their said undivided part of the said premises. The fee and inheritance thereof to be held and enjoyed in severalty by the Dean and Chapter and their successors.

Several *private* occupation *ways* were also awarded and set out by particular description, and in various directions, through the allotments in question—regulations as to certain bounder fences were made—liberty was given to the said Adam Bentley and Barbara, his wife, and the owners and occupiers of their said allotments, in case of necessity by reason of drought, to water their cattle at the springs or pools in the said George Harle's allotment called Emmimoor Pool—and all the said parties and the owners and occupiers of their several allotments, at all times thereafter, were to have liberty to work and win all such stones, as they or any of them should have occasion for, for the use of the said grounds, as well leasehold as freehold, in the limestone quarries, called *Caston Quarries*, thereby allotted to the said Mary and Robert Eden, without paying any damages either for the working or loading thereof, only spreading the rubbish occasioned by such working, and leaving the land level and not in heaps.

It is much to be regretted, that no plan accompanies the award, for it would have been particularly useful in the present day in throwing light upon the *ways* which are set out as *private*, by the award. It is more than probable that a plan would be used in the making of the division, but none is referred to by the award, and ineffectual search has been made for it in the Archives of the Court of Chancery, at Durham.

And now, though like Moses of old, I may view from some modern Pisgah, that promised land, over to which I myself may not be permitted to pass, it becomes my duty, nevertheless, to attempt to shadow forth, however difficult it may be, the position of South Shields as connected with its

FUTURE !

The facts which I have already detailed do, indeed, themselves indicate it, without any imaginary or prophetic picture.

The Docks at Jarrow Slake—that great element of our coming and increasing prosperity—will, when finished, contain nearly 500 vessels. The magnificent public railways, with their various ramifications, that terminate in these docks, connect them, and consequently South Shields, with all the midland counties, with the manufacturing county of Lancaster, and with Scotland. Within a radius of 120 miles the manufacturing, mineral, and other produce of England and Scotland will find the most convenient port of shipment for the Baltic and Europe generally at South Shields, there being at present from the Tyne nearly 200 ships per week, on an average, sailing for foreign countries, chiefly in Europe,—exceeding those of the Thames itself, and amounting to more than all the other ports on the east coast united, from Harwich to Edinburgh, and upwards of three times as many as Hull and Grimsby together.

Merchants will discover it to be their interest to go to the port where ships will be always found without detention, and the Tyne is the nearest for all the Scotch produce, south of the Forth and Clyde, having an European destination.

The increase of tonnage inwards and outwards, to and from the Tyne last year, was about 1000 tons a day, in which South Shields largely participated.

The railway distance to South Shields from all the districts to the extreme verge of the west coast, is not more than 120 miles, and goods carried by the railways will cost considerably less, at the present rates, than 10s. per ton ; as a proof of which, the railways are now carrying coals from Wigan, in Lancashire, to London, a distance of about 200 miles, at a rate less than the amount I now specify.

This amount is nothing on the valuable goods to be transmitted, and will not be affected at all by the minor ports of Hull, Grimsby, and Hartlepool, or any of the eastern ports, the difference caused by the distance being so trifling that to the latter named port it would amount only to about 7*d.* per ton, with all the inconvenience and loss of being obliged to rewarehouse, until vessels were ready for sea; while so abundant are the foreign going vessels at South Shields, that the warehouses there are the ships themselves.

Eventually, in addition to the coals, iron, lead, and extensive manufactured articles of Durham and Northumberland, there will be drawn, by the South Shields facilities of shipment, at the Jarrow docks, the products of Yorkshire and Lancashire, and the valuable coals, minerals, and principal manufactured produce of all the southern counties of Scotland. Much will depend upon the railway facilities; but these the dock proprietors will be sure to give or obtain, for their interests and those of the railway proprietors may be looked upon as identical.

The Docks, at Hayhole, will also administer to the advance of South Shields, by a wise foresight and adequate araangements.

Such will be the extension of trade at Hayhole and of the Tyne, of which South Shields is the chief seaport town, that scarcely another Session of Parliament can pass over without an application for a dock at Coble Dean, which will help to concentrate on the Tyne business of truly national importance. And the time, perhaps, may not be very far distant when Mr. Mather's project, or some modification of it, for a harbour of refuge and sea dock, will have to be carried out between the South Pier and Trow Rocks, in anticipation of which the following resolution stands recorded, at the instance of Mr. Mather, in the minute book of proceedings of the Tyne Improvement Commission :—

"That it be an instruction to the Piers' Committee, that a strong barrier of rock at the Trow Rocks, be left fronting the north, of not less than six feet above the level of high water mark, so that any future operation to form sea docks between the South Pier and the Trow Rocks may be completely secured."

Within the period of the present generation, it is not improbable that much that I have presumed to predict may come to pass. But even should we stand unmoved at the value of our position, and the importance of our interests, the pressure from without will have impelled us onward.

With such an increase as I thus anticipate, through the medium of the Jarrow docks, and the substantial improvement of the bar and harbour, by means of the piers, it is easy to foresee the impetus which will be given to all our trade. The town itself will extend in almost every direction. Population will rapidly continue to increase—streets and houses will spring up to meet the requirements of that population— not as of old, but wide, convenient, and such as are demanded by our sanitary regulations. Cleanliness and health will be cared for by a perfect system of underground sewerage. By the enfranchisement of property, much of this would be greatly facilitated; and while merchants and brokers will be constrained to establish themselves amongst us, all should be preparing for the advancement in position which I have thus briefly ventured to foreshow. A new Town Hall, suitable for all the municipal and public purposes of the borough, and a public quay, will surely be supplied. The adaptation of our splendid sea beach for bathing purposes, should not be overlooked. And while all this has reference to the living, the extramural cemetery, which is already arranged for, shews that the dead are likewise remembered. Depend upon it, my friends, that South Shields has before it prospects of future greatness and increasing prosperity, far surpassing that of its earlier days; and it behoves every one amongst us to assist by all the means in his power, in the development of our great resources. Much, but not all, will depend upon ourselves, and as we are told from the highest authority, how good and joyful a thing it is for brethren to dwell together in amity, let me exhort you to unite and join together in the promotion of all such measures as may be considered necessary for our public advantage. Many occasions will occur in which this union will prove strength, and I mistake very much the disposition of my fellow-townsmen if, by any disunion or lukewarmness of theirs, the progress of South Shields towards the goal which it has to reach will be prevented or retarded. While Sunderland, with natural capabilities far inferior, indeed, to those of South Shields, is a proof of what can be accomplished by the energy of a *people*, Seaham harbour is a wonderful instance of what can be effected by a single *individual*—the truly noble and lamented Marquis of Londonderry. Hartlepool and Grimsby have likewise worked out their own elevation. All of them are stimulants by which we should be excited to the adoption of measures in aid of the vastly superior advantages of our own local position, and are, also, reproaches to the slumbering remissness of those to whom the destinies of the Tyne were, until recently, intrusted.

And now, having exhausted you, I fear, with much that has been unavoidably dry, if not altogether uninteresting, I conclude with an expression of my cordial thanks for the attentive hearing with which you have favoured me, an apology for the unreasonable detention to which I have subjected you, and a heartfelt good wish for the smoky old town, whose *Past, Present,* and *Future* I have thus imperfectly portrayed.

"If I forget thee, O Jerusalem : let my right hand forget her cunning."
"If I do not remember thee, let my tongue cleave to the roof of my mouth : yea, if I prefer not Jerusalem in my mirth."

FINIS.

PRINTED BY H. HEWISON, MARKET PLACE, SOUTH SHIELDS.

—The remains of Mr Thomas Salmon, late Town Clerk of South Shields, were interred in the South Shields cemetery. In accordance with the wishes of the Mayor and Town Council there was almost an entire suspension of business in the town and the greater proportion of the shops in the Market Place, King Street, and Fowler Street were closed from 12 till 3. The cortege was headed by a body of constables and a Volunteer Corps. The chief mourners were the five sons of the deceased, Mr John Salmon, Mr George Salmon, Rev. Gordon Salmon, Rev. R. Ingham Salmon, and Mr Thomas Salmon; also the Rev. H. B. Boulby, son-in-law. The members of the Corporation, the Board of Guardians, and the Pilotage Board followed, the rear being brought up by the Freemasons and other friendly societies.

2/6/1871

—At a meeting of the South Shields Board of Guardians Mr J. Salmon was unanimously elected clerk and also superintendent registrar in succession to his father, the late Thomas Salmon.

15/6/1871

—At a meeting of the South Shields Town Council a motion empowering the Market Place and Quay Committee to purchase the house and offices of the late Town Clerk, Mr Thomas Salmon, in the Market Place, was carried by 15 votes to 13. = July 5th 1871 =

—At a meeting of the South Shields Town Council Mr Joseph Mason Moore was elected Town Clerk in succession to the late Thomas Salmon by 16 votes to 6 for Mr T. G. Mabane and 5 for Mr Duncan. 5/9/1871.

—Mrs Salmon, widow of the late Town Clerk of South Shields and joint secretary of the Ingham Infirmary, presented a portrait of that gentleman for preservation in the Infirmary when erected. July 13 1871

Mrs. Salmon's maiden name was Hannah Marshall She was the daughter of George Marshall of Westoe, a Shields shipowner

* At St John's Paddington, on April 21st 1858, George second son of Thomas Salmon, esq, of South Shields, to Harriett Isabella, younger daut. of the late John Kinnersley Hopper, esq, of Cambridge Sq. Hyde Park, London. Gent's Mag. 1858. p665.

Shields, after a short illness, Thomas Salmon, first Town Clerk of South Shields, aged 77. He was the youngest of two sons of Mr John Salmon, of Wellington Street, South Shields, shipowner. He was born in that street on the 26th May, 1794, was educated up to a certain point, much after the fashion of South Shields in that day, first at the elementary school of Mr Tate, the parish clerk of St. Hilda's, in East Street. Marked Place, in the house afterwards known as the Central Hall; and afterwards at the superior academy of the late Charles Johnson, in Lower Thames Street, from whence he was removed to the Durham Grammar School, where he remained for three years and upwards, under the mastership of the Rev. James Britton. He there made the acquaintance of R. Ingham, with whom he maintained an unbroken friendship for sixty years, his brother having also been a medical pupil under Mr Ingham's father, Dr William Ingham, of Newcastle-upon-Tyne. On leaving school, he was articled as a law clerk in Newcastle-upon-Tyne, with Mr Walter Heron, then the Under-Sheriff of that place, and upon his decease a year later, with Mr Thomas Carr. On completing his articles he became the managing common law clerk

in the office of a rising solicitor in Chancery-yard, London, where he continued for two years and a quarter. In 1817 Mr Salmon settled down in South Shields. The following are a few of the public matters in which he was actively and prominently engaged:—The South Shields Improvement Act of 1829, the Parliamentary Reform Bill of 1832, and the successful proceedings for the insertion therein of South Shields as a Parliamentary borough; the Brandling Railway Act of 1836, for the junction of South Shields, Sunderland, and Gateshead; the defence for many years of the important interests of the Church leaseholders of South Shields and neighbourhood; the inquiry and proceedings of 1854 on the supply of water to South Shields; the Sunderland and South Shields Water Works Act of 1852; the Royal Charter of 3rd September, 1850, for the Municipal Incorporation of South Shields, when he was appointed town clerk. He also took part in the Tyne Improvement struggle; the South Shields Improvement Act of 1851; the creation of a public cemetery, the struggle connected with the Tyne Pilotage Order Confirmation Act of 1865; the creation of South Shields a separate port with an independent Custom House; and the establishment of a separate Local Marine Board. Mr Salmon

of charity and in other public business. Possessed of considerable literary taste and of a keen love of the classics, he was author of several publications of great merit, amongst which was a local history of South Shields, "The Story of the Shields Lifeboat," "South Shields Custom House and its Claims for Independence," and "St. Hilda's Church; its Pews and Sittings." The confidence and good opinion of the public were evinced by the offices which he held in the borough, for he was Town Clerk, Clerk to the South Shields Poor Law Union, Clerk to the Burial Board, Superintendent Registrar for the Union, and Vestry Clerk. He was also a Tyne Pilotage Commissioner, a vice-president of the Mechanics' Institution, and a director of the Savings Bank. In 1865, Mr Salmon was presented with a magnificent testimonial as a token of esteem and respect for his eminent services in connection with public matters and for his constant attention to the interests of South Shields. Mr Salmon's last public services were in connection with the election of School Boards at South Shields and Jarrow. Deceased leaves a widow and large family, all of whom are in good positions in life. May 25. 1871 —

SOUTH SHIELDS:

ITS PAST, PRESENT, AND FUTURE

BEING A

DECENNIAL SUPPLEMENT

TO THE

TOWN CLERK'S PUBLISHED LECTURE

OF 1856.

BY THOMAS SALMON.

"Thus shall you something of our Borough know."

SOUTH SHIELDS:

PRINTED AND PUBLISHED BY H. HEWISON, MARKET PLACE.

1866.

78 ¼

SOUTH SHIELDS WORTHIES.

June 5.—The death of Mr. Thomas Salmon, the Town Clerk of South Shields, at the ripe age of 77, is an event that should not pass unnoticed. Mr. Salmon belonged to one of the old families of that seaport known as the Bank Top and Westoe quality, families distinguished by singular force of character and very considerable ability. Few of the members of these old houses remain; but those who do have made a mark—Dr. Heath, of Newcastle, Mr. Ingham, Q.C., Mr. Richard Shortridge, the Rev. Robert Green, and Mr. Geo. Marshall, of London, are amongst them. The late Dr. Winterbottom, the late Nicholas Fairles, and others also belonged to the old stock of Tyneside magnates. They were all of the Church and King kind; but it is a remarkable thing that the upper middle classes of South Shields at that time sustained a higher standard of literary taste, read and wrote more books, interested themselves more in promoting objects of national interest, such as the lifeboat movement, etc., and were more inventive than their successors. They were amongst the first who carried out extensive improvements in graving docks and other similar works. They had, likewise, fine dramatic taste; and were able to introduce Kean, Kemble, the elder Matthews, and other celebrities to the boards of the old theatre on the Bank Top, of which Stephen Kemble was manager for many years, and which over a long period was the property of his daughter, Mrs. Arkwright, the wife of the descendant of the famous Lancashire inventor. Mr. Salmon was a gentleman of unflagging industry; a thorough South Shields man, and South Shields behaved kindly to him, for he was not only Town Clerk, but Vestry Clerk, Clerk to the Board of Guardians, Clerk to the Burial Board, Clerk to the Assessment Committee, and Superintendent Registrar. All the duties he performed and performed well, besides carrying on his private practice, with marvellously little assistance.

When the Whigs brought in the Reform Bill forty years ago, South Shields was left out in the cold, and it was mainly through him and others who pressed the claims of the borough to be enfranchised that it was subsequently made a parliamentary borough. ✳1871.

◇◇◇◇◇◇◇◇◇◇◇◇◇◇◇◇◇◇◇◇◇◇◇◇◇◇◇◇◇◇◇

SOUTH SHIELDS SUBSCRIPTION LIBRARY.—The annual meeting of the members of this institution took place in the Library Room, on Tuesday, the 12th inst., when the following gentlemen were elected officers, for the ensuing year—viz. President, J. W. Roxby, Esq.; Treasurer, G. T. Fox, Esq., Committee, Messrs. R. Dawson, T. Salmon, H. Anderson, J. Clay, W. A. Swinburne, J. Toshach, W. Anderson, E. Bell, J. Eden, W. K. Eddowes, and J. Robinson. *February 12, 1839.*

SOUTH SHIELDS :

ITS PAST, PRESENT, AND FUTURE

BEING A

DECENNIAL SUPPLEMENT

TO THE

TOWN CLERK'S PUBLISHED LECTURE

OF 1856.

BY THOMAS SALMON.

—◦◦—

" Thus shall you something of our Borough know."

—◦◦—

SOUTH SHIELDS:
PRINTED AND PUBLISHED BY H. HEWISON, MARKET PLACE.

1866.

TABLE OF CONTENTS.

A DECENNIAL SUPPLEMENT

TO

"SOUTH SHIELDS, ITS PAST, PRESENT, AND FUTURE."

"I mind it weel, in early date,
When I was beardless, young, and blate,
E'en then, a wish, I mind its power,
    Shall strongly heave my breast,
That I for auld South Shields' sake,
Some useful Plan or Book could make,
    Or sing a Sang at least."

When I publicly delivered my unpretending but successful Lecture on " SOUTH SHIELDS, ITS PAST, PRESENT, AND FUTURE," to a crowded audience in the Central Hall, on the 9th of April, 1856, I formed to myself a secret resolution to continue it at intervals by way of *Supplement,* so long as my earthly sojourn was permitted here with unimpaired mental faculties. Ten years have since elapsed with surprising swiftness, and I now proceed to carry out my determination, an older, if not a better man, with some fear and much trembling, by bringing under public notice, the many important events and occurrences which have taken place in quick succession, during that period, in, or having reference to, South Shields ; not because

"'Tis pleasant sure to see one's name in print,
A book being a book, although there's nothing in't ;"

but simply because I consider him to be

"The wisest and the happiest man,
Who in his sphere does all the good he can."

Before however attempting to do so, I shall not be deterred by a probable accusation of senseless vanity, if I venture as one who has officially and otherwise, engaged the attention of the South Shields public, for almost half a century, to record and leave behind me the leading circumstances of my active life, in order that they may become known from my own authority to all those, who as fellow inhabitants of South Shields, may be considered entitled to the information, and more particularly in the hope that as incentives to a life of sobriety, industry, and active usefulness, they may be beneficial to my younger friends of the rising generation.

Thus then I proceed—

The youngest of the two only sons (I had no sister) of John Salmon, of Wellington Street, South Shields, Shipowner, I was born in that Street, on the 26th of May, 1794, and was educated up to a certain point, much after the fashion of South Shields in that day, first at the elementary School in East Street, Market Place, of Mr. Tate, the Parish Clerk of Saint Hilda, in the house now, as altered, known as the Central Hall; and afterwards at the superior academy of the late Charles Johnson, in Lower Thames Street, from whence I was wisely removed at a proper age by my father, with his characteristic far-seeing sagacity, to the Durham Grammar School, where I remained for three years and upwards, under the mastership of the Rev. James Britton, associating with the sons of gentlemen, and receiving that classical knowledge which has since been the source to me of much advantage and gratification. I there made the acquaintance of Robert Ingham, our beloved neighbour and deservedly popular member, with whose unbroken friendship for sixty years I have ever since been honored, my brother having been a medical pupil under his eminent father, the late William Ingham, Esq., of Newcastle upon Tyne, who by universal consent occupied at that time the highest professional position and reputation in the North of England. "The great good man," who

> "For noblest cause displays,
> What many labors taught, and many days."

The Durham Grammar School has reason to feel proud of the public career and subsequent elevation, of many of the youths, some of them contemporaries of mine, who received education within its old walls, of whom the following selected few may deservedly here be made prominent, the pride no doubt of the venerable Dr. Britton, in the ripe old age which he lived to attain, and of his worthy successors in the mastership, by whom the character of the School has been successfully and ably sustained, amongst whom, tho' last not least, the present head master, Dr. Holden, stands eminently conspicuous. Of my old master it truly may be said

> "Long had he lived, and much he loved to trace,
> His former pupils, now a lordly race,
> Whom when he saw rich robes and furs bedeck,
> He marked the pride which once he strove to check."

The distinguished worthies in after life to whom I have alluded as Durham Scholars, are *Henry Viscount Hardinge,* Governor General of India, Field Marshal and Commander in Chief; *Sir Charles Grey,* M.P., Privy Councillor, Governor of Jamaica, and Chief Justice of Bengal; *Sir Robert Ker Porter,* Artist and Author; *Prideaux John Selby,* Author of British Birds; *Nathaniel Ellison,* District Commissioner in Bankruptcy; *Sir Roderick Impey Murchison,* Bart., F. R. S., and Vice-President of the Royal Geographical Society;

Noel Thomas Ellison, Scholar of C. C. C. Oxford, 1st Class in Classics, Fellow and Tutor of Balliol, and twice Public Examiner; *Richard Burdon Sanderson*, Fellow of Oriel College, Oxford, English Verse Prize, and 1st Class; *Edward Bannerman Ramsey*, Dean of Edinburgh, *Robert Ingham*, M.P., M.A., and F.G.S., Queen's Counsel, Recorder of Berwick, and Attorney General for the County Palatine of Durham; *John Graham*, Bishop of Chester; *William Blanshard*, Recorder of Doncaster and County Court Judge; *Thomas Colpitts Granger*, M.P., Queen's Counsel, and Recorder of Hull; *William Clayton Walters*, the eminent Conveyancer; *Rowland Burdon*, Chairman of the Durham Quarter Sessions; *Henry Manisty*, Queen's Counsel; *James Losh*, County Court Judge; *John Hodgson Hinde*, M.P., *Thomas Emmerson Headlam*, Q.C., M.P., and Judge Advocate General; *Henry Bond Bowlby*, open Scholar and Fellow of Wadham College, Oxford; *Henry Trstram*, Master of the Hospital and Vicar of Greatham, and Author of Travels in Algeria and the Holy Land; and lastly *John Mitchison*, open Scholar of Pembroke College, Oxford, 1st Class in Classics (Moderations,) 1st Class Classics, B.A. Examination, 1st Class Natural Science, Fellow of Pembroke, and now Head Master of the Cathedral School, Canterbury; to which formidable and creditable list might be added Classmen, Senior Optimes, Wranglers, Fellows, Tutors, and Scholars of Colleges, Archdeacons, Canons, Commissioners, Authors, Public Examiners, Classical, and other Prizemen, the enumeration of whom is unnecessary, and would be tedious, my object in bringing under notice the distinguished character of the Durham Grammar School, "past and present," having been gained by the selection of well known names of distinguished excellence already given.

On leaving the Grammar School I was articled at once in the usual manner, for five years as a Law Clerk in Newcastle-upon-Tyne,

> "Him a keen old practitioner admits,
> To write five years and exercise his wits."

And there I served the first year with Mr. Walter Heron, "a fine old English Gentleman," then the Under Sheriff of that Town and County, and upon his decease, the four last years with Mr. Thomas Carr, a very able man, who ranked conspicuously high in a Profession, which in that great northern metropolis, could ever boast of members not only celebrated for legal acquirements, but for high professional integrity and conduct, educated habits, and gentlemanly demeanour, which are not always attributes of a profession to which I myself have the honor to belong, or indeed of any other.

> "There are who living by the legal pen,
> Are held in honor—honorable men."

But there are others if Crabbe is to be believed,

> "Who to contention as to trade are led,
> To whom dispute and strife are bliss and bread."

I need not say that with the latter, if any such there be, I never did or could hold sympathy.

At the expiration of my clerkship at Newcastle I became the managing Common Law Clerk, to the well known firm of Bell and Brodrick, Bow Church Yard, London, where I continued for two years and a quarter, to my great advantage and experience, hard worked enough, but certainly not to death.

> " Run if you like, but try to keep your breath,
> Work like a man, but don't be worked to death."

Very sound advice and worthy of attention, not only by those who *run*, but by those who *work*.

In 1817 I made a mistake in a worldly point of view, if some of my friends have judged correctly, by casting aside offers with a more flatter-ing prospect, and settling quietly down in South Shields as a country practitioner, but so much happiness and so many blessings have arisen out of it, that I never regretted the step which I took, and I now in all probability will end my days not amongst those " who knew not Joseph," but here where I began, in my own native Shields, in continued possession of that public regard which my townsmen have unequivocally shewn and expressed by their recent public acknowledgment, and the circum-stances attending it, the introduction of which in its proper place on a subsequent page as a matter of local history, can be neither vain nor presumptuous on my part after the full publicity which has been given to it. I have certainly a right to feel proud of the almost universality of the compliment, for

> " When by a generous public's kind acclaim,
> That dearest meed is granted—honest fame,
> What breast is dead to heavenly virtue's glow,
> But heaven impression'd with the grateful throe."

And the value of the gift to which I thus at present make passing allusion was immeasurably enchanced by the ready contributions of the cheerful donors. It will remain I trust in the possession of my descendants for many generations, reminding them not only of the high estimation in which their ancestor was held by those who knew him best, but of the considerate mode by which the inhabitants of South Shields conveyed to him their sense of the public services which they believed him to have rendered. May those who succeed me be actuated by the same unselfish zeal for its welfare, advancement, and prosperity as I have been, and verily they also in due time will have their reward. As to the public matters in which I have been actively and prominently engaged during the last half century their name is legion, but they may be briefly enumerated as follows :—

The South Shields Improvement Act of 1829.

The Parliamentary Reform Bill of 1832, and the successful pro-ceedings for the insertion therein of South Shields as a Parliamentary Borough.

The Brandling Railway Act of 1836, for the Junction of South Shields, Sunderland, and Gateshead.

The vigorous defence for many years of the important interests of the Church Leaseholders of this Town and Neighbourhood.

The Investigation and Proceedings of 1839 into the causes of Accidents in Coal Mines.

The inquiry and proceedings of 1845 on the supply of Water to South Shields; followed by

The Sunderland and South Shields Water Works Act of 1852.

The Royal Charter of 3rd September, 1850, for the Municipal Incorporation of South Shields.

The separate commission of the Peace for this Borough.

The Tyne Improvement struggle of 1850.

The South Shields Improvement Act of 1853.

The South Shields Improvement Amendment Act of 1861.

The creation of a Public Cemetery.

The defence and protection of the rights in Family Vaults, in the Church Yards of Saint Hilda and Holy Trinity, when they were closed by order in Council.

The struggle and proceedings connected with the Tyne Pilotage Order Confirmation Act of 1865.

The creation of South Shields a separate Port with an Independent Custom House.

And the establishment therein of a separate Local Marine Board.

It being unnecessary here to enumerate my many other services of a public nature, in connection with Meetings, Lectures, Addresses, Deputations to London and elsewhere, Balls, Soirees, Dinners, Tea Drinkings, Bazaars, Institutes, and such like, in aid of which their promoters will do me the justice to admit, that they ever found me a willing coadjutor.

My acknowledged publications of a literary kind may be easily specified as follows, viz. :—

A local history of South Shields, under the title of "South Shields, its Past, Present, and Future."

To which this *Supplement* may now be added.

A story of a Shields Life Boat, as a contributor to the South Shields Amateur Magazine.

South Shields Custom House and its claims for Independence, and Saint Hilda's Church, its Pews and Sittings.

To which in addition have been spread over a by-gone period of many years, numerous serious and humorous productions in prose and verse, at times of election and other excitements, which at the moment attracted attention, but are now almost, if not altogether forgotten. Two of them however under the adopted name and signature of " Thomas Place," may be considered worthy of rescue from that oblivion which has overtaken the rest, and I therefore now republish them with this somewhat curious anecdote, that so great was the curiosity of the late Dr. Winterbottom to acquire a knowledge of their then anonymous author, that he actually offered £5 as a reward to any one who could make that disclosure, information which I hardly need say the venerable Doctor obtained for nothing, with much surprise and many thanks on his part, for he had suspected many, and never dreamt of me. They appeared in the heat of the first bitterly contested election for this Borough, when Ingham, Palmer, Gowan, and Russell Bowlby were candidates, and party spirit ran very high, but much of the point and sarcasm, which at the time were apparent enough and easily understood, will now be as a sealed book to many.

SOUTH SHIELDS ELECTION.

"The South Shields Independent Election Committee," appointed at Mr. Lackland's School Room, on the 23rd inst., have the satisfaction to acquaint the "Independent and worthy Voters of South Shields and Westoe," that the THIRD Person of "unquestionable Reform Principles," to whom they alluded in their "Notice to the Electors" of the 27th inst., is MR. THOMAS PLACE, Sand Merchant, a Resident in this Borough, possessing every requisite Qualification for the high office to which he aspires. They refer the Electors to his subjoined expose of his Political Principles, which are such as to entitle him to their support. It is his intention to "solicit their suffrages, in the course of a short period."

TO THE ELECTORS OF SOUTH SHIELDS AND WESTOE.

"Here's to Budgets, Bags, and Walletts!
Here's to all the wand'ring Train!
Here's our ragged Brats and Callets!
One and all cry out—Amen!"

GENTLEMEN,—A Requisition, *neither numerously nor respectably signed*, having been presented to me from the "South Shields Independent Election Committee," I offer no apology for thus, at the "Twelfth Hour," presenting myself as a Candidate for the distinguished honor of presenting myself as a candidate for the distinguished honor of representing you in Parliament.

Although no man has *made more noise*, or *declared himself more publicly in your streets*, than I have done, yet as the two honorable Gentlemen who have preceded me, have thought proper to make an avowal of their "leading sentiments," in compliance with an inconvenient "Custom," which "would be more honored in the Breach than the Observance," I follow their example, not doubting but that such avowal will secure me the support of, at least, those who are as poor and destitute as myself.

I am neither a Whig nor a Tory, but a staunch Radical Reformer. Having nothing to lose myself, and being of opinion that "Honesty is the best policy," I willingly and *without subjecting myself to a charge of inconsistency*, pledge myself "upon all occasions," and by "all the means in my power," to support such measures as will conduce to a general and equal division of property amongst the people, myself of course being included. Not being a *Landowner*, I disinterestedly say, "No Corn Laws;" not being a *Fundholder*, "Rob the National Creditor;" and not being a holder of Church Property, *as Lessee* or otherwise, "down with the Church." In short, not being possessed of one Sixpence in the world, I say, Liberty and Equality—Robbery and Spoliation.

"A Fig for those by Law protected,
Liberty's a glorious Feast,
Courts for Cowards were erected,
Churches built to please the Priest."

I also am a friend to " Civil and Religious Liberty, in its most expansive range ;" for as Falstaff says, " An' I have not forgotten what the inside of a church is made of, I am a peppercorn, a brewer's horse: the inside of a church! company, villanous company, hath been the spoil of me."

Although I am well known to my private friends as a rank free trader, yet, with a view to obtain the support of the shipping interest, I avow myself an enemy to free trade. The Shipowners (who are not I hope, aware of the contempt with which I have always treated and spoken of them,) will, however excuse me if I make an *exception* in favor of the " Sand Trade," now fearfully depreciated, the perfect freedom of which I shall ever advocate in my " Place" in the House of Commons. This exception will probable expose me to an opposition from Mr. Anderson, the owner of the sand Bents; but I cannot, consistently with my own interest, alter my pledge in this respect

I pledge myself to introduce into Parliament a Bill for preventing Cruelty to " Asses" most sincerely assuring the members of the Committee, that nothing *personal* is intended to *them*, by this allusion to my four-footed friends.

Friendly at all periods of my life to *receipts* rather than to *payments*, I will vote against all taxes whatever, except a property tax, because I have *no property* of my own liable to such a tax—a disinterestedness on my part which cannot but be duly appreciated by the Electors.

As to Negro Slavery, Triennial Parliaments, and all such like humbugs, I don't care how the devil I vote. This is, perhaps, more candid than polite ; " but shall I tell you a lie ? I do despise a liar, as I do despise one that is false, or as I despise one that is not true "

These, Gentlemen, are my political sentiments, which, I am proud to declare, have met with the approbation of the " South Shields Independent Election Committee." If there are other points, upon which any elector is desirous of obtaining further information, he will have an opportunity of questioning me in the course of my canvass.

It is my intention to wait upon you on Wednesday, to " solicit your support," in the mean time

I am, Gentlemen,

Your most obedient and faithful Servant,

THOMAS PLACE-

July 30*th*, 1832.

N.B.—Mr. Place's Committee, consisting of Mr. James Gibson, Mr. John Waugh Mr. William Parker, and other *well known* and *influential* individuals, will sit daily at the Poor House, where all communications on the subject of the Election are requested to be addressed.

TO THE INDEPENDENT ELECTORS OF THE BOROUGH OF SOUTH SHIELDS.

" I do begin to perceive, that I am made an Ass."

GENTLEMEN,—Called by the requisition of " The South Shields Independent Election Committee," from the " calm, humble walk in life, in which I had been contented and happy, to assert the independence of your infant Borough," I patriotically obeyed the call, hesitating not to sacrifice my own private interests, and the lucrative trade in which I was engaged, for your welfare, and the public advantage. Nothing having since occurred to remove this good understanding, you may judge with what feelings of astonishment and indignation I noticed an Address from Mr. Mather, as the Chairman of that very Committee, introducing and recommending a MR. GOWAN,—" the friend of Hume,—the friend of his Country," as a Candidate for the suffrages of the Electors of this Borough, at the approaching Election, and making no more allusion to me, than if I were " tho veriest varlet, that ever chewed with a tooth." If my political principles had in any respect differed from those of Mr. Gowan, I would not have complained, but that gentlemen cannot be a more determined supporter of " Triennial

Parliaments," "Vote by Ballot," "Cheap and intelligible Law," and the "Repeal of the Taxes on Knowledge," or a more "stern opponent" of the "Corn Monopoly," "the East India Monopoly," "the Corporation Monopoly," "the Church Monopoly," "the System of Impressment," and "Slavery," than I am. If moreover, I had refused to pull down the Church,—rob the National Creditor,—ruin the Landowner,—and reduce the Shipowner to beggary, I am bound to confess, the Committee would have been perfectly justified in turning their backs upon me as a renegade hostile to the accomplishment of these their great objects, but I have made no such refusal, being on the contrary, as fully prepared now, as I was at the time of the presentation of the requisition, cheerfully and zealously to perform my pledges on all these points. In real, downright radicalism, I will yield to no man, not even to Mr. Gowan himself, or his friends of "The South Shields Independent Election Committee." Why then am I discarded, and thrown like a noxious weed away, my principles as approved of by the Committee, being unchanged and unchangeable?

> ————"What should be in that Gowan
> Why should that name be sounded more than mine
> Write them together, mine is as fair a name ;
> Sound them, it doth become the mouth as well ;
> Weigh them, it is as heavy."

But Falstaff truly says, "there is nothing but roguery to be found in villanous man ;" and verily I am a living instance of the correctness of the maxim. Deeply wounded by the undeserved ill-treatment I have received,—insulted by open enemies and deceived by pretended friends,

I RESIGN THE CONTEST,

So far the "machinations of the wicked" have prevailed, but let not the Gadolas,—the Lack*lands*,—and the Lack*votes* of the Committee, exult over a fallen foe, for by "yonder blessed Moon I swear," if they do not "purge, leave off sack, and live cleanly as gentlemen should do,"

> "An I have not Ballads made on them all,
> And sung to filthy tunes, let a cup of Sack be my Poison :
> When a jest was so forward, and a-foot too,—
> I hate it."

It now only remains to say the painful word—FAREWELL! At the outset of the contest, I certainly looked forward to a very different termination, having been taught to suppose that the "proud situation of the first representative of our maiden borough," was within my grasp. It was however observed to me. by my friend MR. THOMAS DAY, that "There's many a slip, between the cup and the lip," and I find from the result, that his *characteristic shrewdness*, had not escaped him, in making this trite, though perfectly correct observation.

In the words of one of my honorable opponents, (which I take leave to quote,) "Your interests are mine, and though defeated as a candidate, it will be well for me as an Elector. I should indeed be ungrateful for years of happiness spent amongst you, if I could doubt your friendly feelings ; and let me but preserve these, and it matters little, whatever else may be lost to me."

And now my kind friends and fellow townsmen, "Good Night, and Joy be wi' ye a'!"

> "Who will not sing, "God save the King,"
> Shall hang as high's the steeple;
> But while we sing, " God save the King,"
> We'll ne'er forget the people."

I have the honor to subscribe myself,

Gentlemen, your ever faithful Servant,

THOMAS PLACE.

August 16th, 1832.

N.B.—All persons having any claims upon Mr. Place, in reference to the Election, are requested to forward the same to his Committee at the Poor House, addressed to

to Mr. John Waugh, the Chairman, by whom an order for payment on the Overseers
for South Shields and Westoe Townships, will be immediately made, Mr. Place, holding
to the old proverb, " short accounts make long friends."

The confidence and good opinion of the Public are evinced by the
situations which I officially hold in the Borough, for I am Town Clerk,
Clerk to the Local Board of Health, Clerk to the South Shields Poor
Law Union, Clerk to the Burial Board, Clerk to the Union Assessment,
Committee, and Honorary Vestry Clerk of Saint Hilda.

I am likewise a Tyne Pilotage Commissioner, by the honorable
appointment of the Board of Trade, a Vice-President of the South
Shields Literary, Mechanical, and Scientific Institution, a Director of
the Saving's Bank, and a member of Saint Hilda's Ancient Vestry, as
my father was before me.

My father died on the 20th September, 1831, in the 90th year of
his age, and my mother on the 29th February, 1844, aged 78½ years.
They and my brother lie buried in the enclosed Family Burial Ground,
at the North East Corner of Saint Hilda's Church Yard, and as it cannot again be opened for any future interments, a new resting place
will have to be found for me and mine in the Public Cemetery, where
so many of my neighbours have gone before me.

" Yes! they are gone, and we are going all;
Like flowers we wither, and like leaves we fall."

But enough of myself, and now to other matters of more real consequence, the first of which being

SOUTH SHIELDS A SEPARATE PORT WITH AN INDEPENDENT CUSTOM HOUSE.

By the Pamphlet which I published under the authority of the Town
Council in 1864, on "South Shields Custom House and its claims for
Independence," I brought under notice the circumstances attending
the severance of the Port of Tyne in 1847, the serfdom in Custom
House matters to which South Shields then became subjected, the
vexatious continuance of that humiliating thraldom, and the incon-
trovertible claims which our important Municipal and Parliamentary
Borough possessed for emancipation and total independence.

In carrying that out I introduced without stint or curtailment those
numerous and somewhat lengthy documents, which were the growth
of circumstances, and which chronologically told their own lucid tale, in
explanation of the facts, complaints, grievances, and demands which
they set forth from 1847, and they were accompanied when necessary
with proper elucidatory observations.

That Pamphlet, to the persual of which I refer my readers, renders
it only necessary for me to *continue* the history to its satisfactory close,
and that I do in the spirit of a victor, who has lived to see the accomplishment in 1865, of his own encouraging prophecy.

"Magna est Veritas et prevalebit."

For truth did prevail when the demands of South Shields were conceded by the grant to her of independence in all that relates to her Custom House Establishment, the same as that of which North Shields and Newcastle had long been the lucky possessors.

The course of procedure suggested by the Pamphlet was followed, and the following is a copy of the memorial with its concentrated facts, from the Town Council to the Treasury as it was presented and supported by an influential deputation.

To the Right Honorable the Lords Commissioners of her Majesty's Treasury.

The Memorial of the Mayor, Aldermen, and Burgesses of the Borough of South Shields, in the County of Durham.

HUMBLY SHEWETH—

That in renewing their application on behalf of the Borough of South Shields, for a grant to it of such free and absolute independence in all that relates to its Custom House Establishment, as that of which the Boroughs of Tynemouth and Newcastle have long being the possessors on the Tyne, your memorialists have felt it convenient to make a methodical arrangement of all the proceedings before your Lordships and otherwise which have taken place since 1847 to the present time, and they refer your Lordships, with confidence, to the full printed statement of their case containing as it does all necessary statistics and particulars which accompanies this memorial, and which may be considered as forming a component and very material portion of it.

That in so doing, your memorialists have satisfaction in bringing under the notice of your Lordships, a fact so important in connection with this application, as an increase of eighty ships with cargoes, reported inwards, from Foreign Ports, and of nearly £5,000 in the Customs' Revenue at South Shields, which has taken place during the past year, an increase which was foretold on our former application, and a continuation of which is now so confidently anticipated for the future.

That your memorialists have furthur satisfaction in reminding your Lordships of the following Table, compiled from authority, which contains facts and particulars sufficient of themselves to settle and secure at once the independence of South Shields showing as they do its superior claims over a very large proportion of the existing Ports now favored with independence—claims so superior as to make it a subject for wonder and dissatisfaction, why South Shields should be made an exception to that independent position which has been obtained by others of immeasurably inferior pretensions, standing proudly and pre-eminently thus, as South Shields does, in comparison with them, viz.—:

	With less superior claims than South Shields.	With more superior claims than South Shields.
Population	102	22
Revenue on direct Importation	77	47
Total Revenue	69	55
Light Dues Collected	75	49
Vessels with Cargoes, outwards	66	58
Vessels with Cargoes, inwards	92	32
Number of Vessels Registered	102	23
Tonnage of Vessels Registered	119	6

These are the statistical results of the Trade and Business of the various Ports for the year 1862, compared with those of South Shields for the year 1863, and the large increase of the business at South Shields for the year 1864, already referred to, would contrast to that extent still more in favor of South Shields. In fact, the increase of the business at South Shields alone during the latter year, exceeds in those respects the business done at 70 Ports in the one case, and 48 Ports in the other case, of the 124 Ports of the United Kingdom of Great Britain and Ireland.

That by the printed statement before referred to, your memorialists are enabled to restrict themselves to a recapitulation on the present occasion, of those unanswerable claims for Customs' independence, which are truly put forth by South Shields, and universally admitted by all to whom its locality, capabilities, and circumstances, as in comparison with the other two Boroughs of the Tyne, are known.

And therefore, your memorialists content themselves with prominently setting them forth as briefly and as clearly as follow, viz. :—

1.—The existence of South Shields as an independent parliamentary and municipal Borough, of such magnitude and importance as is proved by the statistics hereinbefore referred to, and with a population, according to the census of 1861, of 35,239.

2.—Its complete separation from North Shields, by the broad navigable River Tyne, as shewn by the explanatory Plan of South Shields and North Shields, with the River running between, which is hereunto annexed, and to which the attention of your Lordships is specially and earnestly requested.

3.—Its situation in the County of Durham, North Shields being located in that of Northumberland, and its preferable claims to the name of the Port of South Shields ; North Shields being only a Township in the parliamentary and municipal Borough of Tynemouth.

4.—Its superiority in all those requirements and qualifications which ought to be considered in a question of Custom House independence.

5.—The facility with which South Shields can be separated from North Shields, so as to form two distinct Ports—greater, in fact, than that with which the division was effected in 1848, between Newcastle and Shields.

6.—The manifest injustice of withholding from South Shields that perfect independence to which its superiority over so many inferior independent Ports, is shewn triumphantly by the comparative Table incorporated herewith.

7.—The existence of South Shields already, as a distinct Port for Ship Registration purposes.

8.—The extraordinary injustice and inconsistency of the present objectionable arrangement of the Port of Shields, by which merchants and others who have now a splendid recently erected Custom House, every way suitable, in their own Town of South Shields, where also Ship registration business is transacted, are under any necessity whatever, to cross the Tyne, from one County to another, for the purpose of transacting business at North Shields, which ought to be accomplished at their own South Shields' Custom House.

9.—The right of South Shields to be independently represented on all public questions affecting the general interests of the River Tyne, through its own Custom House, and not through the medium of the Custom Houses of rival towns, directly interested in promoting their own advancement, to the detriment of the interests of South Shields.

10.—The simple and undeniable right of South Shields to be placed, at once, on an equal footing with the other two Custom Houses of the Tyne, and to the consequent possession of an equally independent name and position.

11.—The satisfactory and approved accommodation already afforded by the new Custom House Building, specially erected at great cost, for the business of the Customs and of the Mercantile Marine Shipping Department, for both of which purposes it is now occupied, and used as Tenants by the Commissioners of Customs, and by the Tr̶i̶n̶i̶t̶y̶ ̶H̶o̶u̶s̶e̶,̶ ̶u̶n̶d̶er the sanction of the Board of Trade.

12.—The opening out of the Tyne Docks, within its boundaries, and the growing extension of the trade of South Shields, which calls for its entire freedom from all unnecessary trammels; and the further increase thereof which may be confidently expected, and which demands that South Shields shall have all the advantages of an independent Port and Custom House Establishment, and be freed from that galling sense of injustice and injury to its trade, which is at present correctly entertained by its inhabitants.

13.—The absence of any substantial cost or trouble, in the effecting of the proposed change.

That fortified by this summary of claims of their own, so just and irresistible, your memorialists are saved the unpleasantness of asking for interference with the position and trade of the other two towns of the Tyne, further than the placing of South Shields on a footing of perfect equality with them in regard to entire independence, and the conduct of official business, holding that the true design of all fiscal arrangements is not unnecessarily to cramp and interfere with, but to afford every proper facility, consistent with a due regard to the safety of the revenue, for the development of trade and the transaction of business.

In conclusion, your memorialists pray your Lordships to do justice to South Shields, by raising it to an equal status, in Custom House matters, with its neighbouring rivals of Newcastle and North Shields, by extending to it all the advantages of a distinct Port and independent Custom House Establishment; whereby South Shields and North Shields will then be placed in no other position towards each other, and to Newcastle, than that of friendly rivalry, having for its object the production of effects and benefits advantageous to the best interests of the entirety of that noble River the Tyne, in the welfare and prosperity of which they are all so equally and so largely interested.

And your Memorialists will ever pray, &c.

Given under the Common Corporate Seal of the Borough of South Shields,
this 16th day of March, 1865.

(Signed),
WILLIAM JAMES, Mayor.

(Countersigned),
THOMAS SALMON, Town Clerk.

The not idle interval of five months which elapsed between the presentation of the memorial, and the official answer of the Treasury was most anxious and tantalizing, for South Shields had opponents in high places and elsewhere, so formidable as to render necessary the exercise of the utmost watchfulness and exertions on her part, and well and prudently was she protected during the whole of that eventful period by her faithful friends, amongst whom her own wise, attentive, and influential member, Mr. Ingham, was ever conspicious in the front ranks, answering opposing arguments, reassuring fainting friends, and proving himself in every respect worthy of that unbounded confidence which he has ever possessed, as the representative of his first Parliamentary love, the Borough of South Shields, in his unflinching and constant attachment to which he has never wavered.

The decision of the Treasury was made at last, and on the 29th of August, 1865, a day which ought ever to be memorable in the annals of South Shields, it was announced by the following communication to William James, Esq., our then highly respected Mayor.

TREASURY CHAMBERS,

29th August, 1865.

SIR,

The Lords Commissioners of Her Majesty's Treasury, having had before them a memorial dated the 19th March last, signed by you on behalf of the Corporation and Burgesses of South Shields, praying that South Shields may become an independent Port, I am directed by their Lordships to state, that having communicated with the Commissioners of Customs, and having given the subject full consideration, they have felt that there are not sufficient grounds for longer refusing their sanction to South Shields becoming in name, as it is already in effect, a separate Port, and that they signified this a short time ago to the Commissioners' of Customs, directing them at the same time to consider and report a proper boundary for the Port.

I am to add that their Lordships, having now received a report from the Commissioners of Customs on the subject, have been pleased to issue the necessary warrants constituting South Shields a separate Port and declaring the limits, commencing at Souter Point, the Northern Limit of the Port of Sunderland, extending along the Coast of Durham to the entrance of the Tyne, from thence along the mid-channel of the said River to a point in mid-stream, opposite the East end of Jarrow Quay, and comprising so much of the said River as is Southward of such limits.

I am, Sir,

Your obedient Servant,

GEO. A. HAMILTON.

W. JAMES, Esq.,

Mayor, of South Shields.

This was followed up by the following orders of the Treasury, whereby the limits of the respective Ports and Legal Quays of South Shields and North Shields, were severally and satisfactorily defined.

PORT OF SOUTH SHIELDS—LIMITS OF PORT AND LEGAL QUAYS.

We the undersigned Lords Commissioners of Her Majesty's Treasury, do hereby under the authority of the Custom's Consolidation Act, 1853, appoint South Shields to be a Port in that part of the United Kingdom called England, and we do hereby declare that the limit of the said Port shall commence at Souter Point in the County of Durham, being the Northern limit of the Port of Sunderland, and shall extend from thence along the coast of the said County, to the entrance of the River Tyne, from thence along mid-channel of the said River, to a point in mid-stream opposite to the Eastern end of Jarrow Quay, and comprising so much of the said River Tyne as is southward of such limits, and that the limits of the said Port of South Shields, shall extend seaward a distance of three miles from low water mark of the Coast of the said County, and shall include all Islands, Bays, Harbours, Rivers, and Creeks within the said limits.

And we the said Lords Commissioners do hereby appoint the following places within the said Port of South Shields, to be legal Quays, for the lading and unlading of goods, and do declare the bounds and extent of such Quays to be as follows—that is to say.

All that open place, quay, or wharf, called Cookson's Quay, situate near Ferry Street, South Shields, in the County of Durham, and being in length from East to West, six hundred and sixty feet, and in breadth thirty two feet or thereabouts.

Also all those open places, quays, or wharfs, surrounding the Dock, known by the name of the Tyne Dock and the Timber Pond, belonging to and adjoining the said Dock on the North West side thereof, both of which are situate on the South side of the River Tyne, in the County of Durham, and commencing at the North

East corner of the said Dock, at a distance of four hundred and twenty feet from the entrance lock of the said Dock, and thence proceeding round the said Dock and Timber Pond, to the North West side of the said entrance lock, and extending uniformly in width sixty feet from the edge of the said Dock and Pond, and including all landing places and jetties within the said Dock.

Also all that open place, quay, or wharf at South Shields aforesaid, called the Corporation Quay, situate at the Mill Dam, and immediately bounding upon an open inlet of the River Tyne, called the Mill Dam Dock, being in length from the River Tyne aforesaid to Brewery Lane, two hundred and seventy feet or thereabouts, and in breadth sixteen feet or thereabouts.

And also all that other open place, quay, or wharf at South Shields aforesaid, situate near Brewery Lane aforesaid, and being in length from North to South, fronting the River Tyne aforesaid, seventy five feet or thereabouts, and in breadth at the North end thereof twenty five feet, and at the South end thereof sixteen feet or thereabouts

Whitehall Treasury Chambers, the 16th day of September, 1865.

(Signed,)

W. P. ADAM,
LUKE WHITE.

A true copy, Custom House, Shields, 23rd Sept., 1865,

R. S. Kilgour, Collector.

PORT OF NORTH SHIELDS—LIMITS OF PORT AND LEGAL QUAYS

We the undersigned Lords Commissioners of Her Majesty's Treasury, do hereby under the authority of the Custom's Consolidation Act, 1853, appoint North Shields to be a Port in that part of the United Kingdom called England, and we do hereby declare that the limits of the said Port shall commence at Seaton Point, about one mile North of the River Aln, in the County of Northumberland, (being the Southern limits of the Port of Berwick,) and shall extend from thence along the Coast of the said County, to the entrance of the River Tyne, from thence along the mid-channel of the said River to the Eastern end of Whitehill Point in the said County, comprising so much of the said River as is Northward of mid-stream between the said entrance and Eastern end of Whitehill Point, and that the limits of the said Port of North Shields shall extend seaward a distance of three miles from low water mark of the Coast of the said County, and shall include all Islands, Bays, Harbours, Rivers, and Creeks within the said limits.

And we the said Lords Commissioners, do hereby appoint the following places within the said Port of North Shields, to be legal quays for the lading and unlading of goods, and do declare the bounds and extent of such Quays respectively to be as follows—that is to say.

All that open place, quay, or wharf called Northumberland Wharf, situate near the head of Clive Street, North Shields, and being in length from East to West, two hundred and nineteen feet, and in breadth twenty one feet or thereabouts.

And also that open place, quay, or wharf called "The Shields Steam Shipping Wharf," at North Shields aforesaid, being in length from East to West on the River front forty feet, and in breadth from North to South twenty feet, bounded at the East end by Shepherd's Quay, and at the West end by Elder's Quay.

And we, the said Lords Commissioners, do hereby under the authority of the said Act, annul all former limits of the Port of Shields, and all former legal quays set out and appointed within the same.

Whitehall Treasury Chambers, the 16th day of September, 1865,

(Signed,) } W. P. ADAM,
LUKE WHITE.

True Copy, Custom House, Shields, 23rd September, 1865,

R. S. KILGOUR, Collector.

15

These happy results were not arrived at without a desperate resistance on the part of Newcastle upon Tyne, which through the instrumentality not only of its Town Council and Chamber of Commerce, in which Gateshead was included, but (tell it not in Gath, proclaim it not in the streets of Ascalon,) of the River Tyne Improvement Commissioners, (at the extraordinary, I had almost said unnatural, instigation of a representative in that commission, of the Harbour Town of North Shields,) brought every possible influence to bear upon the Government for a restoration of the "*status ante bellum*," with the intention, not only of bringing us back to the unjust Custom House system and arrangements of 1847, whereby South Shields and North Shields were in a state of vassalage to Newcastle, but of inflicting upon South Shields a speedy loss of that highly prized independence as a separate port, which she had hardly fought for and recently obtained. The Lords of the Treasury, as was to be expected, preserved their consistency by steadfastly adhering to their well considered determination in favor of South Shields, and South Shields retained the position which had been allotted to her as a separate Port of the Tyne, not from the unfair exercise of any favor or influence on her behalf, but simply because she had made out a case of right and justice, which could not without manifest injustice be longer resisted. The jesuitical attempt for a Trinity in Unity, under the plausible pretext of a " Port of Tyne," was signally set at nought with its cunning pretences of " aggregate statistics," and instead of a " Port of Tyne," which meant Newcastle sole supremacy, and Shields inferiority, the Tyne remained divided, as I trust it ever will, into the separate Port of Newcastle (upon Tyne,) the separate Port of South Shields (upon Tyne,) and the separate Port of North Shields (upon Tyne,) to the entire satisfaction of the people of those two latter Boroughs, but to the disappointment of Newcastle, and of those short sighted few, who had been weakly induced to sacrifice the Harbour Towns to the pretensions and selfish monolopy of their ancient taskmaster, and modern rival at the head of the river, who must now rest content with those objectionable coal dues, and other remaining advantages which she still continues, fortunately for herself, to possess. The River however now is *free*, and of it we can joyfully and triumphantly sing,

"River! O River! thou roamest *free*,
From the mountain height to the fresh blue sea!
Free thyself, but with silver chain
Linking each chain of land and main,
River! O River! upon thy Tide,
Full many a freighted bark doth ride."

The following is the reply of the Treasury to the memorial of the Newcastle and Gateshead Chamber of Commerce.

TREASURY CHAMBERS,

January 20th, 1865.

SIR,

The Lords Commissioners of Her Majesty's Treasury, have had under their attentive consideration, the memorial of the Newcastle upon Tyne and Gateshead Chamber of Commerce, and their Lordships direct me to state that they are not prepared to adopt the suggestion contained therein, that the several Ports on the River Tyne shall be consolidated under the general title of " Port of Tyne." The arrangement recently made with regard to the Ports on the Tyne, will in no way disturb the interests of the Port of Newcastle, as laid down by this Board in the year 1848, nor is there any intention of curtailing the privileges which the Merchants of Newcastle and Gateshead have heretofore enjoyed. I am to add that with regard to the appearance in the public accounts of the statistics of the whole River Tyne, that although the returns of the Trade and Tonnage of the three Ports in that River will be rendered separately in the usual manner, yet still it will always be in the power of persons desirous of shewing the whole trade of the Tyne, to complete such a return themselves from the separate official documents.

I am, Sir,

Your obedient servant,

H. CHILDERS,

Secretary, &c., &c.

And now assurance having been thus made doubly sure, by this further proof of the steady adherence of the Lords of the Treasury to South Shields, and its newly acquired independence as a separate Port, "our brows" may indeed in perfect safety be said to be

" Bound with victorious wreaths,
And all the clouds that lowr'd upon our *Port*,
In the deep bosom of the ocean buried."

Mr. James Blaikie received the well deserved appointment of first Collector of Customs for the new Port of South Shields, to the entire satisfaction of the whole of its shipping and mercantile community, to whom his high fiscal attainments, Custom House experiences, promptitude in the discharge of his collectorship duties, and courteous manners, had universally endeared him. Under his vigilant superintendence the newly acquired rights of South Shields as a Port will neither be jeopardized nor infringed upon, and I leave him to the undisturbed enjoyment of his responsible situation, with my own personal congratulations on his merited advancement.

THE PUBLIC DINNER TO R. INGHAM, ESQ., M.P.

As arising out of these free Port and Custom House Triumphs on the part of South Shields and her champions, the public dinner and address to Mr. Ingham, and the testimonial to myself, naturally present themselves in close connection together, and as a faithful local historian I must record them here. They both originated at meetings held respectively on the 23rd and 30th of August last, at the former of which Mr. Ingham and I were publicly thanked for services in our several capacities; and at the latter a public dinner and address to Mr. Ingham

were determined on, expressive of the great satisfaction of the inhabitants with his conduct as their representative, and in acknowledgment of the many important services rendered by him to the Borough,
and at the same time a subscription was ordered to be entered into,
with a view to the presentation to me of a public testimonial, in
recognition of my long and (what were pleased to be designated)
"valuable services, gratuitously rendered to the Town on many important occasions." Of these the public dinner to Mr. Ingham is
entitled to undoubted precedence. It came off in the spacious Hall of
the Mechanics' Institute, on the 2nd of November, 1865, and was
attended in a manner which did honor alike to our popular member,
and to his well contented constituents by whom the noble room was
filled. The Mayor, William James, Esq., occupied the chair, wearing
the gold chain of office, and Mr. Alderman Glover and my willing self
had the honor to officiate as vice-chairmen. The proceedings were of
a nature most gratifying to all, affording another confirmatory proof,
if any were wanting, that

> "Not from gray hairs *authority* doth flow,
> Nor from bald heads, nor from a wrinkled brow;
> But our past life, when virtuously spent,
> Must to our age those happy fruits present."

The address itself was beautifully illuminated on parchment, and in
justice to Mr. Ingham, and to the Inhabitants of South Shields, whose
sentiments were so truthfully and feelingly expressed thereby, its full
insertion is provided for here.

TO ROBERT INGHAM, ESQUIRE, OF WESTOE, THE REPRESENTATIVE
IN PARLIAMENT OF THE BOROUGH OF SOUTH SHIELDS.

BELOVED AND RESPECTED SIR,

The interval between the termination of the last Parliament, and the meeting of
its approaching successor, to which you have again been independently returned with
universal consent and approval, has been taken advantage of by your constituents,
as a convenient opportunity for conveying to you by this their address, their well
merited thanks for the past, their heartfelt congratulations on the unopposed renewal
of your Parliamentary connexion with the Borough, and their encouraging assurance
of the confidence with which their important interests have been again entrusted to
your wise, successful, and statesmanlike watchfulness and care.

For this confidence so justly obtained, you are indebted to the judicious and
attentive discharge of your Parliamentary and other duties, since the passing of the
Reform Bill in 1832, and the Borough has indeed proud cause for thankfulness in the
reflection, that while neighbouring Boroughs have been disturbed and vexed from
time to time by bitter contests arising from the candidature of strangers, South Shields,
by the happy circumstances of your elevated resident position, unblemished character,
and undoubted capabilities, has been preserved in peace from those local feuds and
bitter estrangements, which are the usual concomitants of political divisions.

But great as the advantages are which have thus arisen from your Parliamentary
connexion with the Borough of South Shields, there are others of a different complexion and character, which its Inhabitants have derived from your residence
amongst them education has been encouraged, charities promoted, and religious dis-
sensions assuaged, by your own enlarged and Christian example—literary, scientific,
and social institutions have found in you, irrespective of class or sect, a liberal and

an enlightened patron—the poor, in many of their humble difficulties, have felt the benefits of your wise and experienced advice—while all the classes of our people have been brought to look upon you with affectionate attachment and confidence, as a well tried neighbour and a sure friend, freely joining and participating with them as inhabitants of one common town, in all that was beneficial, instructive, improving, and advancing.

Well may we pray to Almighty God, that all those benefits and advantages which we have thus imperfectly pourtrayed, may long be secured to us as a community, by the blessing of your continued health and citizenship amongst us; and that identified as you so completely are with South Shields, its inhabitants and institutions, that day may be far distant, when in sorrowful submission to that lot which is common to all, we shall be deprived of your accustomed presence and co-operation, in all that concerns our welfare and improvement, by that inevitable separation which is at once the cause of earthly sorrow, and of everlasting hope.

Signed on behalf of the Inhabitants of South Shields, this 2nd day of November, 1865,

WILLIAM JAMES, Mayor.

The *dinner* having thus been so agreeably and satisfactorily disposed of, the *plate* became at liberty, and this brings me to

THE SALMON TESTIMONIAL,

Which next demands attention as a matter of public interest. It was raised with the utmost facility and without pressure, from the willing contributions of my neighbours and friends, amounting to the munificent sum of £260, and consisted of the following silver articles, viz. a massive tea tray, a beautiful tea kettle and stand, and four substantial corner dishes, convertible into eight when required for the dinner table. The inscription upon all of them was this :—

"Presented by the friends of Thomas Salmon, Esquire, Town Clerk of the Borough of South Shields, as a token of respect and esteem, and as a Testimonial for his eminent services in connexion with many important public matters, and for his constant and watchful attention to the interests of his native Town."

DECEMBER, 1865.

The presentation was made in the following happy terms on the 1st of January, 1866, by Mr. Alderman Glover, in a manner which certainly could not in any way be excelled, and the Town Hall was filled with an influential assemblage, the Mayor wearing the robes and gold chain of office presiding. The bells of Saint Hilda's Church rang a merry peal on the occasion, and its flag was hoisted on the old Steeple in kind compliment to me as Town and Vestry Clerk.

"Those bells, those bells, those well known bells,
How many a tale their music tells,
Of youth and home—and that sweet time,
When last I heard their soothing chime."

Mr. Mayor, ladies, and gentlemen—I have been requested by the committee to present this testimonial to Mr. Salmon, the town clerk of this borough, as an acknowledgment of long and valuable services. Some short time ago on the attainment of our Independent Custom House a meeting was publicly called, when it was unanimously determined to give our much respected member, Mr. Ingham, a public dinner and present him with an address. That deserved compliment has been already paid to Mr. Ingham, who has so long, so faithfully, and so independently represented this town in parliament. He can say what few members of parliament can say, that he has never asked a privilege for the borough he represents which he has not obtained—a fact which testifies at once to the justice of our claims, and to his influence and perseverance in parliament. It is therefore not remarkable that, at the recent dinner given to him, a great honor was shewn to him, whether we consider the large number who were present, or the number of public men who regretted their absence. At the same meeting it was resolved that the long and numerous services of the Town Clerk should be acknowledged in a substantial manner by a testimonial—a testimonial, I may now take leave to say, such as has never been presented to any individual in this borough. This testimonial, ladies and gentlemen, is now before you, the expression of your esteem and liberality. It would not be easy for me, well as I know the Town Clerk, to say all that there is in Mr. Salmon and his services which make me glad that he has received this testimonial. Mr. Salmon, like all our pleasantest and best friends, is something which we cannot define, but which we all understand. He is one of the best institutions of the town. Like the Cross in the Market-place, or like the lifeboat, central, important, always ready. The great services of a public man are, perhaps after all, his least services; it is his daily life; his elastic step; his familiar look and style; his voice; his ready pen; aye, if you like it, his ready temper. It is these that make up more than the occasional services. It is the possession of qualities like these, and the disposition to turn them to public account, which makes a man respected and important. But Mr. Salmon's occasional services have been most important. I cannot in the course of my short address, attempt to mention these. They are so well known to you all that it will be quite unnecessary for me to enlarge upon them. There is, however, the matter of the Custom House that deserves prominence and mention. We had for some time seen that while we wanted a suitable place for the transaction of custom house business, it was in vain for us to go either to the Treasury or the Board of Customs, claiming our independence; and, in a generous spirit of liberality, the Town Council wisely determined to build a new Custom House, which is at once an honor and ornament to the town. And shortly after this, the battle for our independence began, and a good share of the honor of the victory obtained is due to the energy and ability of the Town Clerk. He published at the request of the Corporation a pamphlet, containing statistics carefully drawn up, memorials and arguments boldly and fearlessly stated, which stimulated and gave fresh life and energy to every one connected with the Borough. The Corporation again appointed a deputation to wait upon the Lords of Her Majesty's Treasury. That deputation went to London, were introduced to Mr. F. Peel by Mr. Ingham, who stated the claims of South Shields to be placed on an equality with neighbouring Boroughs, in a clear and emphatic manner, that seemed to carry conviction; and after some delay, ended, as we are all aware, with the Government granting us our just and righteous claims. And the success of that measure has already far surpassed the expectations of its most sanguine friends. Thus it will be seen that in all public questions in regard to which he was interested, Mr. Salmon has worked with energy; he has not spared himself by night or by day, seeming to be amply repaid by the gratitude and kindness of his fellow townsmen. One of Mr. Salmon's principal virtues is that he is a real local man. Mr. Salmon has always talked, and sometimes lectured, as a Shields man. Who does not remember his famous lecture, since become a book, on "South Shields, its Past, Present, and Future?" He may be called the historian of the place. He at times abused it, no doubt, but it was for the love he bore it, and because it did not rise and progress so fast as he wished it. I am not a believer in testimonials as a rule, but every rule has its exceptions, and I believe it is good for men and for towns sometimes to resign themselves to the occasional impulses of their favor and gratitude, and to say to an old servant and an old friend, "Thank you, let us give you a proof of our gratitude, that will be a pleasure to us, and will not be unpleasing to you and to your children after you." I think the whole town concurs in what we are doing to day. It should not be all the same with a man when he gets to, I wont say old, but the good age of Mr. Salmon, whether he has done well or ill, been active or indolent, selfish or public spirited, the good, the highest and the best good which a man does, he cannot and should not be rewarded for it. But we may occasionally and exceptionally testify our regard for good services by a testimonial to the men who do them. Such a procedure is calculated to impress young men, and others, with the nobleness of living usefully, temperately, and withal publicly.

> "Tell me not in mournful numbers,
>   Life is but an empty dream,
> For the soul is dead that slumbers,
>   And things are not what they seem,
> Lives of great men all remind us
>   We can make our lives sublime,
> And departing leave behind us,
>   Footprints on the sands of time;
> Footprints that perhaps another
>   Sailing o'er life's solemn main,
> A forlorn and shipwrecked brother
>   Seeing, shall take heart again."

Such words express the character of Mr. Salmon's life. I am not going to flatter Mr. Salmon, or to say he is faultless; he would not and you would not like me the better if I did. This testimonial is from his native town, from the inhabitants of his native place, and this after all is the testing place for a man; where he was born; where he has been tried; where he has done his life work; where he has had his ups and downs; and gone through evil and good report. To go through all this, and survive to a ripe age, respected and still a useful man, still a public man, is no small credit. Turning to Mr. Salmon, Mr. Ald. Glover said:—I have great pleasure, Mr. Salmon, in presenting you with this magnificent testimonial. You will receive it, I feel assured, with pleasure and gratitude. It comes from all classes and parts of your native town, and from a few who take a deep interest in our prosperity, and represents the esteem of men of every class, of every church, and of every shade of political opinion. The very harmony of the sentiment it expresses is a virtue and a pleasure. I am sure this testimonial will be highly prized by you and your family. I have now only to wish you many long years of health and usefulness, many returns of this blessed Christmas time. Long may your happy home and the festive gatherings of this season enjoy the light of your countenance, and the sound of your voice. As a family, long may you continue unbroken, and at last be found—

" No wanderer lost, a family in heaven."

In the name of the subscribers, I have to ask your acceptance of these various articles of plate. It is a satisfaction to them to know there is no lack of heirs by whom they will be transmitted to future generations.

The reply I take from the newspaper report, as follows :—

Mr. Salmon said that his first duty was to thank the Mayor, as chief magistrate of the borough, for presiding on that occasion, and next to thank those kind friends of the committee who had taken so very active a part in originating and bringing the subject matter of that meeting to so satisfactory a conclusion. Their exertions had been very indefatigable, and a very pleasing part of the address delivered to him by their friend, Mr. Ald. Glover, was that wherein he spoke of the spontaneous nature of the contributions which had been given. He [Mr. Salmon] could assure them that it would have lessened the pleasure which he derived from the receipt of that splendid testimonial, if he, for one moment, supposed that those who had contributed to it had done so through interest or by importunity. His desire was that the testimonial should be the spontaneous gift of the inhabitants of that town. They knew him best, he having lived among them all his life, and they knew whether he was or was not deserving of any public acknowledgment of his services at their hands, and the reply which they had given was most satisfactory. His next duty was to thank Mr. Ald. Glover for the very handsome address, in which he had been pleased to present the testimonial. It was very gratifying to him, [Mr. Salmon] as it would be to those of his family by whom he had the pleasure of being surrounded that day, to hear the manner in which Mr. Ald. Glover had been pleased on behalf of the town, to express himself regarding him [Mr. Salmon]. He need not tell them that in the profession to which he had the honor to belong a man was sure, from the peculiar nature of it, to give offence to some ; and even in the discharge of duties by a public officer he did not always succeed in making friends. He therefore thought that he had just cause for an honest feeling of pride, when he was enabled to stand before them that day, after an experience of him of nearly half a century, for the purpose of receiving at their generous hands the splendid acknowledgment of his public services or which they believed him deserving, and which they were that day placing in his possession. He assured them that he gratefully thanked them from the bottom of his heart, and he scarcely need say that their present kindness would be an incentive for further exertions on his part on behalf of his well beloved native town; though they must bear in mind that independent ports, custom houses, and marine boards were not to be fought for every day, nor must they weep, as Alexander was said to have done, when he found no more worlds to conquer, because they had no more independence to fight for and win. All that they had now to do was to work out their newly acquired independence as a Port, to the advantage of the town, which possessed many capabilities by which it might be raised to a very high elevation. There were two kinds of honors usually bestowed upon a public man in acknowledgment of services rendered; one during his life time; the other after his death. Now he certainly considered the first to be the most satisfactory. And they had happily for him adopted it in his case, though the Greeks did not in the case of Homer,

> "Seven Grecian cities strove for Homer dead,
> Through which the living Homer begged his bread."

Homer according to his [Mr. Salmon's] view of the case, would rather have preferred present to those posthumous honors, which he, doubtless, received as the author of the Iliad and the Odyssey. But Greeks had always had a queer way of doing things. It might, perhaps, have been expected by some that he should make some particular allusion to the various public works in which he had been engaged in the cause of South Shields, and which had produced that demonstration in his favor, but he purposely avoided wearying them with the long particulars, for he might inform them that he was at present engaged in the preparation of a supplement to his little publication of 1856, on "South Shields, its Past, Present, and Future," which would contai nthe events of the last ten years; and he intended to introduce those very particulars "after what flourish his nature would." It was, in fact his intention to keep up the history of South Shields so long as he lived. As to the articles themselves they were indeed most splendid, doing credit to the taste and skill of Mr. Bell and his correspondent. He assured them that it added greatly to the pleasure of their reception by him to know that they were procured by a worthy townsman of their own. The articles seemed to him to divide themselves, into three distinct classes, as their friend the Rev. Mr. Chester would say. First. There was the *open* expansive salver, so emblematic of the *open* generous nature of his fellow townsmen, and their liberality towards him. Secondly. There was the elegant tea kettle and stand, reminding him so happily of his female friends of the borough, with whom he had spent so many happy evenings in their ball rooms during the last fifty years, presiding over them and contributing by all the means in his power to their amusement and comfort. And Thirdly. There were the table dishes, so emblematic of those tempting corporate entertainments with the turtle soup and other accompaniments which were *supposed* to fall to the lot of those lucky individuals who entered within those municipal walls. He said *supposed*, for the dinners were, indeed, *more mythical* than real! And now he was done. He thanked them for their kindness in honoring him with their presence there on that memorable occasion. And he earnestly prayed that the commencing new year would be a happy and a prosperous one to them and all of theirs.

Other gentlemen then took part in the vote of thanks and other formal proceedings which remained to be done, but it might be considered uncourteous and almost disrespectful, if I were to withhold from insertion here, as a very important part of the proceedings, the reply of my *family* to the compliment paid to me their head, which on the considerate suggestion of the Mayor, was then made through the medium of my son, the Rev. Robert Ingham Salmon, and I do it the more readily in consequence of its unavoidable omission at the time from the published report of the proceedings, which were otherwise sufficiently lengthy.

Mr. Mayor, Ladies, and Gentlemen,

I regard the words which have just fallen from the Mayor, in the light of a challenge, which it would be discourteous and unchivalrous to pass by in silence, and yet I confess it is with extreme reluctance that I take up the gauntlet, and venture to address you on the present most gratifying occasion. I say, I rise with reluctance, because I have ever deeply been impressed with a sense of the propriety of a great Roman writer's observations to the effect, unless my school boy memory betrays me, that young men ought to remain silent in the presence of their seniors, and account it their honor and their privilege to reverence their elders with the homage of a silent respect. It is with diffidence that I speak also, because I fear lest, rising unprepared, through any inadvertence of language or undesigned omission, I should appear to detract from the importance or mar the impressiveness of this meeting.

I need hardly say what intense satisfaction I, in common with the other members of our family, have derived from the present ceremony, what gratification we have had in listening to every portion of the admirable address with which Mr. Glover accompanied the act of presentation. I was glad to see the address was a written one, because in the written words of men we generally have a truer expression of their real thoughts than we can gain in the words which find birth in the excitement of the moment. And I rejoice to think Mr. Glover said neither more nor less about my father than he really felt and meant. Among much that was gratifying in what Mr. Glover said, I know not that any part of his address afforded me so much pleasure as the significant remark, that it was not in the extraordinary or exceptional occasions when men are enabled to achieve great things, but rather in the punctual and conscientious discharge of ordinary duties, in the little and some would call the insignificant details, which form the routine of common daily life, that we are to look for the only or the most reliable expression of real character and true genuine worth. It is a reflection which appeals with no small emphasis to one whose duty it is to dwell on, and give utterance to such thoughts. It is indeed the common little details of the weary, working, week-day life, which give the whole color, love, and complexion to a man's character. These are the elements which constitute the true self, not the brilliant achievement or flashy exploit, but the thorough going unostentatious performance of common duties. I rejoiced in this sentiment, because it is one that must at once approve itself to the hearts of all here present, as the expression of the profound truth, that in the experiences of daily life, in the allurements to lusts, the excitements to worthless pleasures, the incentives to holiness, and the dissuasives from sin, which meet us on the common high road of life, we find the elements which compose and mould the character, and have the opportunities for deciding whether ours shall be the calm peacefulness and rest, and happiness of Him whose name we bear, or the restlessness and agitation which a troubled world has to offer.

You, my friends and fellow townsmen, know and can speak of my father's public services, his more prominent and now locally patriotic exploits. I know and can speak of those little acts which form the staple of daily life, and really make the man what he is. I have viewed him from the stand point of a closer intimacy; I can speak as a son of a father, and as a son who is proud of his father, and I hope, while I feel a just pride in my father as a public man, and rejoice in seeing him honored this day by grateful fellow townsmen, now assembled to bear testimony to the value of his public services, and to express their sense of his well merited deserts, I can yet, in the happy memories and ineffaceable associations which cluster round the family hearth, where the father can unbosom to his nearest and dearest, find cause for a still deeper and truer joy. If his public acts have deservedly won for him this magnificent tribute of your esteem and love which I see before me, I trust in the tenor of his daily life at home, no less, if not more than abroad, there are tokens of a yet higher and nobler future reward; and while I rejoice that my father feels a pride, an honest proper pride, as he casts his eye upon this substantial proof of your esteem and regard and appreciation of his work, I rejoice yet more in the belief that he holds those enviable honors second to the grander, the truer, the more enduring reward which is laid up in store for those who love *Him*.

As I look around me now, I am half ashamed of having ever sheltered so unworthy a thought in my breast, and yet I am bound to confess that often in days gone by, when I have returned to my home from the distant sphere of my own special work, and have thought of my father's many and great public services, yet could not lay my hand upon any public acknowledgment, recognition, or testimonial expressive of his fellow townsmen's appreciation of them, I have been tempted to endorse bitterly the sentiments which I think fell from Mr. Glover's lips, that the worthiest men never receive testimonials, and in the spirit of a sour Cynic to exclaim,

> "I've heard of hearts unkind, kind deeds
> With coldness oft returning."

But this day with this splendid, massive yet graceful tribute before me, and so many faces expressive of good will and kindly feeling, and honest appreciation around me, I am constrained from my heart's depth to add the remaining couplet of the poet,

> "Alas! the gratitude of men,
> Has oftener left me mourning."

You will not thank me if I spoil your new year's day dinner, I must not therefore detain you longer, and it remains for me now simply in the name of our family, to thank you one and all for the honor you have this day done our father, and us through him, and to wish you all, with an honest, hearty English goodwill, a really and an earnestly happy new year.

So the proceedings at the Town Hall terminated, and they and the many kind friends who took part in them will ever live in the grateful remembrance of me and mine. I may however before advancing to other less personal subjects, briefly remark that besides this memorable *public* acknowledgment, I have from time to time been gratified by the receipt of others of a *private* nature, which are highly prized by me, and which I thus acknowledge, viz.:

A Silver Snuff Box with this inscription,

> "From a grateful Client to Thomas Salmon, Esq., in memory of his Integrity, Disinterestedness, and Ability, 24th February, 1831."

A Massive Silver Inkstand,

> "From R. I. to T. S., 1841."

A Silver Salver, the inscription upon which tells its own gratifying tale,

> "Presented to Thomas Salmon, Esq., by the Workmen of the Plate and Crown Glass Works, South Shields, in testimony of their gratitude for his valuable professional services gratuitously rendered them, 1849."

A Silver Salver with this inscription,

> "From Mrs. Roxby to Thomas Salmon, Esq., in remembrance of Thos. Forrest, Esq., born 1766, died 1852."

And a pair of Gold Spectacles,

> "To Thomas Salmon, Esq., by an old Friend, 1862."

The value of the foregoing gifts remains in my estimation almost wholly undiminished, for though in the reproachful words of sweet Ophelia to her princely lover of Denmark,

> "To the noble mind.
> Rich gifts wax poor, when givers prove unkind,"

From few, very few only of the contributors whose liberality was so recently extended to me, has any act of unkindness since proceeded, and the possession of the gifts remains therefore only partially disturbed by the recollection of that which is perhaps undeserving even of this passing attention.

My portrait in the Town Hall was placed there by the voluntary gift to the Corporation of ex-Alderman James Young; and the bust of me is indebted for its position there to the kindly feeling and liberality of Thomas William Rowe, F.S.A., our talented local sculptor, from whose studio it proceeded, and by whom it was presented to the Town Council.

QUOTATIONS.

Somebody was once uncharitable enough to say, that the man who would make a pun would pick a pocket, though Byron and Goldsmith were of a different opinion, as we may fairly surmise, from what the former wrote, as follows :—

> " For ever foremost in the ranks of fun,
> The laughing herald of the harmless *pun*."

And the latter thus,

> " Rare compound of oddity, frolic, and fun,
> Who relished a joke, and rejoiced in a *pun*."

My own belief being, that a man may be a punster without being a pickpocket.

The quoter fares little better than the punster with some people, amongst whom Young may be reckoned,

> " Some for renown on scraps of learning dote,
> And think they grow immortal as they *quote*,
> To patch work learn'd *quotations* are allied,
> But strive to make our poverty our pride."

And likewise Prior,

> " He ranged his tropes and preached up patience,
> Backing his opinions with *quotations*."

To this latter charge I myself plead guilty, for I envy the *puns* of a witty North Shields Neighbour of mine who is also learned in the law, and I glory in the *quotations* which I myself bring forward in illustration and support of my own opinions, for that is in reality the chief utility of *quotations*, and it is for that reason that I have introduced them so bountifully into my own humble productions, the spirit and weight of which latter I conceive to be thereby considerably enhanced. In following this up, it is however sometimes difficult to discover a quotation suitable for your purpose, and this became so serious to the late Sir Walter Scott, that in the preparation of his numerous novels and works of fiction, he fairly abandoned the troublesome search for real extracts from the works of others, and actually manufactured appropriate headings for his own chapters from time to time as he required them, purposely misleading the inquisitively curious, by giving some imaginary authority for that which the industrious baronet so solemnly indorsed.   My readers must not suspect me of similar frauds !

THE OLD THEATRE IN WELLINGTON STREET.

> " See the players well bestowed,
> For they are the abstract and brief chronicles of the time,"

Was the order given by Hamlet to Polonius; and when the latter

in reply engages " to use them according to their deserts," the well
known answer of the Prince was given, " Odds bodikin, man, much
better ; use every man after his desert, and who shall escape whipping."

The Theatre in which the players were " bestowed" at South Shields,
perhaps at that time " according to their deserts," and in which up to
this time, they made " their exits and their entrances, one man in his
time playing many parts," was erected 75 years ago in Wellington
Street, and first opened to the public in 1791.   Plain and ugly as the
building was and still is, and inconveniently situate as it became when
the Town gradually extended itself Southward and Westward, Wellington Street was for many years the principal Street in which shipowners
"most did congregate," and the Theatre was as well supported as
provincial theatres usually are.   It was visited from time to time by
the Metropolitan Stars, in their periodical orbits through the provinces,
and I am unfortunately old enough to remember the crowded performances therein of William Henry West Betty, the young Roscius,
Emery, Incledon, Bannister, Liston, Fawcett, Matthews, Stephen and
Charles Kemble, T. P. Cooke, Mrs. Kemble, Misses DeCamp, Mellon,
Kelly, Duncan, Smith, and Mrs. Glover, all tragedians or comedians
of well remembered name and repute.   What the future fate of the
old building, with all the interesting reminiscences connected with it
may be, I know not, but as

" Two stars keep not their motion in one sphere,"

So it may be supposed that this our Borough will not

" Brook a double reign"

Of Theatres, in which case as the *old* are expected in the natural order
of decay, to give place to the *young*, so the old Theatre will yield to
the superiority of the new one as a place of public amusement, and this
brings me to the next pleasing subject of my work, which is

THE NEW THEATRE IN KING STREET.

In spite of the broad and well known assertion, " that all the world's a
stage, and all the men and women merely players," this Theatre has
just been erected by the " South Shields Theatre Company, (Limited),"
to whom the play going portion of the community are greatly beholden
for the supply of a long felt desideratum occasioned by the inconvenient
situation, and other defects of the old Wellington Street Play House.
It stands on the North side of King Street, in one of the most central
and populous positions in the town, for an erection of this kind, and
will, I sincerely hope, be productive of all those advantages to the
spirited company and the lovers of theatricals, which are looked for
from it.   It is a very chaste and beautiful building of the Italian order
of architecture, with an imposing facade in front, and has a portico in the
centre of four coupled columns surmounted by a pediment and pilasters

to correspond, there being for purposes of revenue, two shops underneath, and a spacious entrance in the centre from King Street to the boxes and pit. Extending backwards as the building does from King Street to Union Alley, a distance of 114 feet, the gallery, although next to King Street, is judiciously approached from an entrance in Union Alley, by means of a stone staircase and fire proof passages. The entire area of the building is 733 superficial yards, and there is accommodation for an audience of 1750, of which the boxes will hold 300, the pit 500 seated and 200 standing, and the gallery 700 seated and 50 standing. There is a large saloon on a level with the boxes, and a ladies' retiring room, with all requisite conveniences.

The work was fairly submitted to public competition, and although many designs of merit were sent in, Mr. T. M. Clemence, of this Town, and Mr. J. C. Phipps, of Bath, were the successful competing architects for the work, and were jointly appointed to carry it out, which they have done in a manner which leaves nothing to be desired on the part of the public, and more especially of those who take pleasure in theatrical amusements. Artistically and tastefully has their work been done, and confidently may they appeal to the South Shields Theatre in King Street as proof, if proof be required from any quarter, of their capability for a work to be executed in any distant or other locality, of a nature similar to that which has been accomplished here.

A district so populous as that of South Shields, with a modern theatre, such as that which I have described, should command at all times a theatrical company of no ordinary pretensions, and this I doubt not will be secured for the public by those who are interested in the success of the undertaking. But the "troop dramatic," for our theatre must be very different from that so graphically described by Crabbe, for I can then venture to promise and predict, on the part of the play goers of South Shields, that,

"He who plays the King shall be welcome, his Majesty shall have tribute of me, the adventurous knight shall use his foil and target, the lover shall not sigh gratis, the humorous man shall end his days in peace, the clown shall make those laugh whose lungs are tickled o' the sere, and the lady shall say her mind freely, or the blank verse shall halt fort."

THE FACTION FIGHTS OF THE PANNERS AND FISHERS.

In the school days of Sir Walter Scott, at the high school in Edinburgh, we are told that a dangerous mode of fighting in parties or factions, scottice *bickers*, was permitted in the streets of Edinburgh, to the great danger of the youthful parties concerned ; that these parties were generally formed from the quarters of the town in which the combatants resided, those of a particular square or district fighting against those of an adjoining one ; but that those fights were in fact only a rough mode of play without malice or illwill of any kind towards the opposite party, although maintained with great vigour with stones at a distance, and with sticks and fisticuffs when one party dared to charge, and the other stood their ground.

As it was at Edinburgh then, so it was at South Shields in the days of my boyhood, for the latter had its faction fights as well as the former, as gallantly fought, with as little illwill, and much after the same daring, fearless fashion. The *Fishers* of the low part of the town, fought against the *Panners* of the high part, the sons of the upper classes being mingled with the other classes in the contests, the missiles used being not smooth stones from the brook such as those with which David slew Goliath, but stones of all sorts and sizes, gathered from the hills or battle grounds of the respective belligerents. The two youthful armies were usually separated from each other by a chasm in the hill, used as a road by the carts employed in the conveyance of ballast from ships discharging at Fairless' crane, to the place of deposit, and when the charges were made the combatants rushed down from their encampment on one hill, across the ravine and up the other hill to the opposite encampment, with shouts and threats ; the hats taken on such occasions being ruthlessly sacrificed and destroyed as warlike spoils. The cutting through of this memorable battle field by the Stanhope and Tyne Railway of necessity caused a discontinuance of those civil wars,

"Now civil wounds are stopp'd, peace lives again,
That she may long live here, God say—Amen."

The boys of the present day having no knowledge of the hard fought battles of their fathers and grandfathers, on Fairless' and sometimes on Harding's hill, the former being the stronghold of the *Fishers*, while the latter was the impregnable position of the *Panners*. Slings were never used.

It is melancholy to reflect upon the fate in after life of many of those my gallant fellow combatants, of whom I can scarcely now call to mind a survivor. Some would die in the forced naval service of the country, during the revolutionary and Buonapartean wars ; others would perish by shipwreck in the merchant service ; to pestilence and disease in foreign lands many would succumb ; while by natural causes and decay, not a few would be cut off in their own native land ;

"Such have I seen in life, and much deplore,
So many dying—that I see no more,
Some shewn by records where I grieve to trace,
How death has triumph'd in so short a space."

OUR BOROUGH ELECTIONS.

Mr. Ingham was the borough's first love in 1832, and although she jilted him in 1841, and took to her bosom a child of her own, in the person of John Twizell Wawn, who served us well, she returned to her allegiance in 1852, and again elected Mr. Ingham. As his liberality in politics has "grown with his growth, and strengthened with his strength," until it has acquired the comeliness and perfection of the full grown man, there can be no doubt that the politics of our present member are in accordance with those of the great majority of the electors, and that he will therefore continue to represent South Shields in Parliament without opposition, so long as by his health and strength he is permitted to do so with advantage to his constituents. The following are the particulars of the various elections from the first to the last.

VOTES.

1832—ROBERT INGHAM, Westoe, (Returned) 205
GEORGE PALMER, London 108
WILLIAM GOWAN, London........................ 104
RUSSELL BOWLBY, South Shields.................. 2
1835—ROBERT INGHAM, (Returned)...................... 273
RUSSELL BOWLBY 128
1837—ROBERT INGHAM, (Returned without opposition) ....
1841—JOHN TWIZELL WAWN, West Boldon, (Returned).. 240
ROBERT INGHAM 207
GEORGE FYLER, London 34
1847—JOHN TWIZELL WAWN, (Returned) 333
WILLIAM WHATELEY, London.................... 176
1852—ROBERT INGHAM, (Returned).................... 430
HON. HENRY THOMAS LIDDELL, Eslington 249
1857—ROBERT INGHAM, (Returned without opposition) ....
1859—ROBERT INGHAM, (Returned) 506
JOHN TWIZELL WAWN........................ 300
1865—ROBERT INGHAM, (Returned without opposition) ....

In the year 1832, the number of Parliamentary voters on the registered list for the borough, including duplicates or persons registered in both the townships of South Shields and Westoe, was 540;—In 1856, 1073;—And in 1865, 1211. Shewing an increase between 1832 and 1865, of 671; And between 1856 and 1865, of 138.

OUR VOLUNTEERS.

It was so far back as April, 1795, that the patriotic heart stirring song of "the Dumfries Volunteers" was first written and sung, and from it I make the following appropriate extract,

"Does haughty Gaul invasion threat?
Then let tho loons beware, Sir,
There's wooden walls upon our seas,
And Volunteers on shore, Sir,
The Nith shall run to Corsincon,
And Criffel sink in Solway,
Ere we permit a foreign foe,
On British ground to rally!

And it is gratifying to be able to record, that whilst South Shields has made the most remarkable progress in every direction since the Volunteer rising alluded to in the song, it has not receded in the loyalty and patriotism of its inhabitants. Now, as then, when the Nation feeling intensely the indignity of the constant panics of threatened invasion, to which its insular position rendered it peculiarly liable, rose and asserted itself, our town was not slow in furnishing its little contingent of Volunteers to that noble citizen army, the moral influence of which has been to place England on such a pedestal of security as to render her inaccessible to foreign menace, or internal fears.

Before however entering upon the subject of our local corps, it may not be uninteresting to give a short history of the force from its commencement to the present time. In the Spring of 1859, General Peel, the then Secretary for War, issued two circulars to the Lieutenants of Counties; the first announcing the readiness of the Government, who saw the wisdom of complying with the wish of the nation, to accept the services of Volunteer corps; and the second containing the principles, upon which it was proposed to act in doing so. It appears to have been then, the intention to limit the formation of corps to independent companies, which should occasion no cost whatever to the public. At the end of June, 1859, when a new Government came into office, there were thirteen corps, (including the 1st Middlesex, and the 1st Devon, which had been formed several years previously,) eleven having been raised under the new rules. From that period, numerous applications from corps formed under the original circular, were received in rapid succession. It was then deemed advisable to aid as far as possible, the development of what promised to be in time a very powerful aid to the standing army, and first, a grant of 20, and afterwards of 100 per cent. of rifles was made, and the original idea of separate companies only abandoned for consolidated and administrative battalions. As this force gradually assumed the proportions of an army, it then became necessary to have the Volunteers properly drilled, and the first step was to supply the corps with adjutants and drill instructors from the line and militia, they providing every thing else.

In 1863, the government acting upon the report of a Royal Commission, appointed to inquire into the necessities of the force, made permanent provision for its maintenance and efficiency, by a capitation grant of thirty shillings to each efficient Volunteer. In the same year a comprehensive bill, consolidating and amending the Volunteer acts was passed by Parliament, and a code of regulations, having the force of law, framed in accordance with it. At this period the citizen army may be said to have passed through its probationary stage, and to have taken its permanent place among the institutions of the country. It has since improved in strength and efficiency, the last returns shewing a muster roll of 170,615 trained men, in addition to a very large number who have been drilled and will be forthcoming in case of emergency. This large army is composed substantially of Artillery, and Rifles, with a few corps of Engineers, and Mounted Rifles.

The preceding being a brief outline of the history of the organization of the Volunteer Army, I will now relate the part which South Shields took in the movement. In the winter of 1859-60, when its importance was generally recognized, and every town and hamlet was occupied with the task of raising its band of Volunteers, a public meeting was held in the Central Hall, at which, after a few energetic and patriotic speeches, it was resolved to form a corps of Riflemen. Many names were then enrolled, and the business being taken up with spirit, in a few weeks almost as many members were enlisted as sufficed for the formation of two companies. Before however, the required number was reached, some of the members being of opinion that rifles were not the proper arm for a maritime town, withdrew their names, and proceeded to form an Artillery Corps, and success soon rewarded their efforts. No time was lost in commencing the work of training, and a spacious loft near the Mill Dam, and a drill instructor from Tynemouth, having been obtained, it was carried on with vigour. A feeling of rivalry stimulated the exertions of the members of each corps, and the necessary point of efficiency being in time arrived at, they held meetings, at which names of members were agreed upon for recommendation to the Lord Lieutenant for commissions. The following were the first appointments,

ARTILLERY.
CAPTAIN .... James Cochran Stevenson
FIRST LIEUTENANT...... Thomas Bell Barker
SECOND LIEUTENANT .... Joseph Logan Thompson
HON. ASSISTANT SURGEON Joseph Frain

RIFLES.
CAPTAIN .... John Williamson
LIEUTENANT .... Charles W. Anderson
ENSIGN .... Robert Blagdon Dawson
HON. ASSISTANT SURGEON.. Richard Baty Ridley

Each corps rapidly increased in strength, and the loft being required for other purposes, a large drill shed was erected in Chapter Row, at the expense of Captain Stevenson, and two 32 pounder guns obtained from Woolwich, one of which was placed in position for practice at a sea target, and the other used for the drill under cover.

The work now proceeded with energy, and the two arms soon manifested signs of considerable efficiency, the rifles being chiefly active little fellows, and the artillerymen remarkable for their fine athletic appearance. In course of time the former increased their establishment by an additional company, and the latter by a battery. No event of importance took place until the beginning of the year 1864, when for obvious reasons, it was deemed expedient to amalgamate the two corps, and this difficult measure was effected with great judgment and good feeling, the result being four tolerably strong batteries of Artillery, and the well merited promotion of Captain Stevenson to the rank of Major. A natural feeling of irritation on the part of the Riflemen, at having to part with their favourite Enfields, prevailed for a short time, but it soon subsided, and they all ere long worked together in perfect harmony. They have not relaxed their efforts, and the corps is now the most distinguished in the county, having carried off all the prizes (save 1½) of the association at Hartlepool in the year 1864, and earned general admiration by the spirit they displayed in putting in an appearance at Shoeburyness, at the first meeting of the National Artillery Association last year, when they and the Sheffield men were the only detachments from the North of England, and their most soldierly appearance, and remarkable dexterity in the handling of the guns when there.

They have also taken a part in all the county reviews; and at each inspection of the corps, have received the favorable report of the Field Officer. As a South Shields man, I am exceedingly proud of its local defenders; feeling perfectly assured that in the improbable event of the oft-threatened invasion taking place, they will be found in the front ranks, courageously ready to "do or die" in defence of their Queen, their Country, and its Laws.—

The present Officers of the Corps are : —

MAJOR.
JAMES COCHRAN STEVENSON.

CAPTAINS.

JOHN WILLIAMSON,   HENRY WILSON,
CHARLES WILLIAM ANDERSON,   CUTHBERT YOUNG.

FIRST LIEUTENANTS.

THOMAS BELL BARKER,   JOSEPH LOGAN THOMPSON,
ROBERT BLAGDON DAWSON,   JOHN SALMON.

SECOND LIEUTENANTS.

ARCHIBALD STEVENSON,   JOSEPH RICHARDSON,
ISAAC TWEDDELL,   WM. J. DAWSON.

SURGEON.   HON. CHAPLAIN.
JOSEPH FRAIN.   REV. THOMAS HENRY CHESTER.

A few willing words relating to Major Stevenson, the Commander, and I have done, for his influence, his talents, his time, and his purse, have all been bestowed in the organization, advancement, and present efficiency of the third Durham Artillery Volunteers; and he is truly deserving of the thanks of his townsmen for benefits of so public and even national importance. To him our town is mainly indebted for the honour it derives both near and at a distance, from its gallant band of well-disciplined Volunteers, and I comply with what I believe to be the universal feeling,when I adopt the means afforded by this favourable opportunity, of not only recording my own private acknowledgment, but that of the South Shields public, of the obligations under which we are placed by those spirited services, to which I have had such sincere and disinterested satisfaction in making allusion.

"O well done! I commend your pains,
For every one of us shares in the gains."

THE CORPORATION QUAY.

Following the wise and prudent course of 1861, with respect to the Corporation Quay, which enabled them by their Improvement Act of 1853, to become possessed of the Town Hall, Markets, Fairs, and Tolls, in the manner I have already explained the Corporation went to Parliament, and on the 17th of May, 1861, obtained "The South Shields Improvement Amendment Act, 1861," under the title of "An Act to enable the Mayor, Aldermen, and Burgesses of South Shields to maintain a Quay there, and for other purposes," the chief contents of which, with all possible brevity, consistent with so very important a subject, I proceed to set forth.

Its explanatory recitals are, *inter alia*, as follows, and I introduce them fully, on account of the important information which they convey, viz :

That by the Tyne Improvement Act, 1850, it was enacted, that when the Mayor, Aldermen, and Burgesses of South Shields, should have opened within the Borough, a Quay of not less than 100 yards in length for the use of the public, subject to the payment of Quay dues thereat to the parties erecting such Quay, the goods, wares, and merchandise, loaded thereat, should thenceforth be exempted from the payment of *one half* of the Dues described in the said Act as Import Dues.

That a Quay of more than 100 yards in length had been constructed on the banks of the Tyne, and was then the property of the North Eastern Railway Company.

That the said Company were willing to sell, and the Corporation to buy such Quay, and to open the same for the use of the public, on payment of such dues as were thereinafter mentioned; and that the said Corporation were also desirous of using for quay purposes, certain land adjoining to the said quay, and then vested in them, and of enlarging the said quay on the landward side, with a view of making the same more commodious for the public; and for that purpose to take compulsory powers for the purchase of lands and divers buildings adjoining the said quay.

That it was expedient that all necessary powers should be conferred on the said Corporation for making such purchases as aforesaid, and for raising the necessary funds therefor.

That in pursuance of the powers conferred by the South Shields Improvement Act, 1853, the Corporation had purchased the building called the Town Hall, with its Appurtenances, standing in the centre of the Market Place, and the right of holding markets and fairs in the borough, and of taking tolls for such markets and fairs.

That it was provided by the said South Shields Improvement Act, that it should be lawful for the Corporation to maintain and improve, or alter, as they should think fit, the existing market or markets, and also to establish, erect, and maintain stalls, standing sheds, booths, shambles, and proper conveniences within the said Market Place, for the sale of cattle and animals; and of provisions, goods, wares, and merchandises, and other marketable commodities; and to alter or enlarge the said Town Hall, and to enclose and incorporate therewith, the open space of ground floor beneath it, or otherwise to improve it, or pull it down and erect a building for a Town Hall in lieu thereof, more suitable and convenient for municipal and public purposes, and to furnish and fit up the Town Hall, and any offices, committee or other rooms and apartments therein, with all necessary furniture and fittings, and to repair and reinstate the same from time to time as they should see fit; and powers of raising money for the above purposes, therein-after called "Town Purposes," to an extent not exceeding £6000, were vested in the Corporation.

That no improvements had been made in the said Town Hall, in pursuance of the said Act, and it was for the advantage of the public that the whole thereof should be taken down and a new one erected on another site in the Market Place; but doubts had arisen whether such change of site was allowed by the said Act.

That by the 41st section of the South Shields Improvement Act, it is provided that the surplus of the stallages, rents, and tolls to be levied under provisions of that Act in respect of the said Markets and Fairs, after providing for the payment of the interest of the monies borrowed, and for the expenses therein mentioned, should be allowed to accumulate as a sinking fund to be applied by the Corporation in paying off the principal monies to be borrowed as therein mentioned, and subject thereto, that it should be lawful for the Corporation either to lower the stallages, rents, and tolls, to such an extent as would reduce the

36

stallages, rents, and tolls to be levied and raised in respect of the said markets and fairs, to the annual amount (as near as might be) of the expenses of the maintenance, repair, working and management respectively of the said Town Hall, and market buildings, markets and fairs, or to appropriate and apply the same wholly or in part towards the extension and improvement of the said markets and fairs; and in and towards providing suitable works and conveniencies connected therewith; and that it was expedient that power should be given to the Corporation to apply the said surplus in aid of the General District Rate, levied by the Corporation.

And that doubts had arisen as to the operation of certain sections of "The Local Government Act, 1858," on the provisions relating to the borrowing of money contained in the said South Shields Improvement Act, and it was expedient that such doubts should be removed.

It was therefore enacted as follows, amongst other merely formal provisions which it is unnecessary to trouble my readers with.

CLAUSE 1 —This act may be cited for all purposes as " the South Shields Improvement Act, 1861

2.—The Corporation, acting by the Council of the Borough, shall carry this act into execution.

3.—"The Lands Clauses Consolidation Act, 1845," and "the Lands Clauses Consolidation Acts, Amendment Act, 1860," shall be incorporated with and form part of this act.

4.—Whereas plans and sections of the said quay and works to be purchased, and plans of the lands proposed to be taken compulsory for purposes aforesaid, together with a book of reference to such plans, have been deposited at &c. Be it enacted that subject to the provisions of this act, and in accordance with the plans and sections (deposited), the Corporation may purchase the said quay, belonging to the said North Eastern Railway Company, and for the purpose of enlarging the same, or the approaches thereto, or works connected therewith, may purchase, take, and use such of the said lands as they may think expedient for such purposes.

5.—Rights of the Crown reserved.

6.—The quay hereinafter referred to in this act is as follows:—A quay in the said Borough, bounded by the River Tyne on the north, by the Mill Dam Dock on the East, by Brewery Lane in part, and by dwelling houses abutting on East Holborn Street, on the other part, on the South, and by Messrs. Cookson and Cuthberts' Bottle Works on the West; with approaches, wharfs, shipping and landing places, stairs, slips, sheds, cranes, warehouses, sluices, works, and conveniences connected therewith.

7.—If the Corporation shall hereafter widen such quay on the River side, with the consent of the Tyne Improvement Commissioners, the enlargement of such quay, produced by such widening, shall be deemed to be part of the quay hereinafter referred to in this act.

8.—Before commencing works, below high water mark, the Corporation to deposit plans with Admiralty, and works to be constructed under their approval.

9.—Admiralty may direct local survey.

10.—Admiralty may restore abandoned works at cost of Corporation.

11.—The Corporation may maintain the quay, and may alter, improve, take down, and rebuild the buildings, erections and works now on the quay and lands, and erect other buildings and works thereon.

12.—Mode of rectification of errors and omissions in the plans.

13 —True copies of plans &c., to be received as evidence.

14.—Incorporation of certain clauses of " The Harbours, Docks, and Piers' Clauses Act, 1847."

And in the construction thereof the word "Pier" shall mean " Quay," and

" Harbour Master" shall mean " Quay Master," and à vessel shall be deemed to be within the limits of the quay when moored at, or approaching near the quay for the purpose of mooring thereat ; and goods shall be deemed within the limits of the quay when they are lying on any part of the quay and lands hereby authorized to be purchased, and inasmuch as the quay hereby authorized to be purchased, is already completed and fit for the purpose for which it is intended, no certificate of the Chairman of Quarter Sessions shall be required as evidence of its completion or fitness, but such quay shall for the purposes of " the Harbours, Docks and Piers' Clauses Act, 1847," be deemed to be complete and fit immediately after the same is taken possession of by the Corporation.

15.—As to recovery of penalties, damages, &c.

16.—Compulsory purchase of lands limited to 3 years.

17.—Appointment and removal of Quay Masters, Meters, Weighers, and other Officers for the purposes of the Act, so far as they relate to the quay.

18.—The Corporation may, subject to the superintendence and control of the Tyne Improvement Commissioners, from time to time, dredge, deepen, and remove the bed of the River Tyne in front of the quay.

19.—Every person who shall throw or put any rubbish into the River Tyne, in front of the quay, shall for every such offence be liable to a penalty not exceeding £5.

20.—Powers of Quay Master not to interfere with those of the Harbour Master.

21.—The quay shall not be deemed to be a legal quay for the shipping and unshipping of goods, until the same has been approved of by the Commissioners of Her Majesty's Treasury, and the Commissioners of Her Majesty's Customs respectively for the purpose, and such quay, and the use thereof, shall be subject to all the same rules, regulations, and restrictions to which legal quays are, or may be by law subject.

22.—As soon as the quay hereby authorised to be purchased, is taken possession of by the Corporation, the goods landed at the quay shall, subject nevertheless to the payment to the Corporation of the rates by this Act, authorized to be taken by them, be exempted from the payment of one half of the dues in " The River Tyne Improvement Act, 1850," described as the import dues.

23.—The Corporation shall at all reasonable hours allow the Tyne Improvement Commissioners and their servants, to inspect the books and accounts of the Corporation, relating to goods landed at the quay, liable to the said import dues.

24.—The Corporation from time to time may demise on such terms and conditions, and to such persons as they think fit, any of the said warehouses, and other buildings, works, and conveniences purchased by them under the authority of this Act, and any of the said lands vested in them as aforesaid, and not required for the purposes of the quay, for any term not exceeding 21 years.

25 —Rates to be taken according to schedules A and B, for vessels using the quay, and for goods shipped or unshipped, received or delivered, upon or from the quay.

26.—Exemption of vessels in Her Majesty's Service, &c. from rates.

27.—Additional rate for vessels using the quay beyond 8 days.

28.—Rates for weighing machines, cranes, mooring posts, &c.

29.—The Corporation shall keep a separate account of all rates and dues specified in the *Schedules to this Act*, and levied by them under the authority of this Act, and of all rents and other monies received by them pursuant thereto.

30.—The Corporation, *for Quay purposes*, including under that term the purchase and maintenance of the Quay, with all such approaches and works as aforesaid, the purchase of the lands hereinbefore authorized to be taken, and the constructing and doing all such other works and things in relation to the Quay as hereinbefore mentioned, may from time to time *borrow on the security of the General District Rate* leviable by them any sums of money not exceeding in the whole the sum of *twenty thousand pounds* ; and, in the event of any part of such money being paid off otherwise than by the Sinking Fund, may re-borrow the same, and so *toties quoties ;* and the Corporation may mortgage the above-mentioned rate to the persons, bodies corporate or companies who may lend such money, or to their nominees, as a security for the repayment of the money so borrowed, with interest for the same.

31.—For the purposes of such mortgages as aforesaid the provisions of " The Commissioners Clauses Act, 1847," with respect to mortgages to be executed by the Commissioners, shall be incorporated with this Act.

32.—The Corporation may, *in addition* to the sum of *six thousand pounds* hereinbefore mentioned to have been authorized to be borrowed by them for *town purposes*, borrow a further sum of *four thousand pounds*, to be raised in the same manner, upon the same securities, and to be applied for the like purposes.

33.—Provided always, that all mortgages and other charges on the said rate hereinbefore authorized to be mortgaged, which at the time of the passing of this Act are in force, shall, during the continuance thereof, have priority over all mortgages granted thereon under this Act.

34.—It shall be lawful for the respective mortgagees of any of such rates as aforesaid to enforce the payment of the arrears of principal and interest due to them respectively on their respective mortgages by the appointment of a Receiver, and the amount to authorize a requisition for a Receiver shall be five hundred pounds.

35.—*In addition* to any other security which the Corporation are by this Act authorized to give for monies borrowed for Quay purposes, they may *mortgage the Quay*, with the erections and buildings now thereon, or which may heieafter be erected thereon, and the lands hereinbefore authorized to be taken, and the several rates, rents, and dues by this Act authorized to be taken in respect of such Quay, erections, and buildings ; and any mortgages so made may be in such form as may be agreed upon between the Corporation and the lenders of the monies, and may contain powers for the mortgagees to sell the property mortgaged or any part thereof, or to appoint a receiver of the income arising therefrom.

36 —There shall be a *Sinking Fund* for paying off the sums borrowed under this Act, and the sum to be set apart and appropriated as such Sinking Fund shall in every year be not less than *one-fortieth* part of the aggregate amount of the monies from time to time so borrowed : Provided always, that it shall not be lawful for the Corporation to reborrow any sum or sums of money paid off by means of the Sinking Fund.

37.—All rates, rents, tolls, or monies leviable by the Corporation in respect of the *Quay* shall be applied as follows, (that is to say,)—

(1.) In payment of any interest due on principal monies borrowed for *Quay purposes.*

(2.) In providing the *Sinking Fund* by this Act directed to be provided in respect of such monies.

(3.) In payment of the expenditure incident to the maintenance, repair, improvement and management of the *Quay.*

and the *surplus,* if any, shall go in aid of the General District Rates.

38.—The Corporation may build a New Town Hall on such part of the market place as they think fit, and may pull down the present Town Hall, and use the site thereof for the purposes of markets within the Borough, or for such other purposes as they think fit.

39.—The Corporation may purchase by agreement any lands required for the purposes of building the said New Town Hall, or enlarging or improving the said market place.

40.—The Corporation may erect on the *ground floor* of the *Town Hall* built by them *shops,* to be let by the Corporation for any period not exceeding seven years, to such persons as may be willing to rent the same for the purpose of carrying on therein any business which the Corporation may approve of.

41.—All the provisions of this Act relating to a *Town Hall,*, markets or fairs shall be deemed to be in addition to the powers conferred by the said " South Shields Improvement Act," in relation to the same subject matters, and shall be construed as if they were inserted in the said " South Shields Improvement Act "

42.—The Corporation, acting by the Council, may appoint out of the body of the Council from time to time such and so many *Committees,* consisting of such number of persons as they think fit, for all or any of the purposes of this Act, which in the discretion of the Council would be better regulated and managed by means of such Committees : Provided always, that the acts of every such Committee shall, in case the Council shall so order, but not otherwise, be submitted to the Council for their approval ; but no expenditure or payment, or contract to pay or expend any sum of money, made by such Committee. shall be lawful or valid when such sum exceeds the sum of fifty pounds, unless such Committee has been authorized by the Council to make such expenditure, payment or contract, or unless, if not so authorized, such expenditure, payment or contract has, after the same has been made, been approved of by the Council.

43.—Every Committee so appointed may meet from time to time, and may adjourn from place to place, as they may think proper, for carrying into effect the purposes of their appointment, but no business shall be transacted at any meeting of such Committee unless the quorum of members (if any) fixed by the Council, and, if no quorum be fixed, unless three members be present; and at the first meeting of every such Committee, one of the members shall be appointed Chairman of the Committee, and all questions shall be determined by a majority of votes of the members present, and in case of an equal division of votes, the Chairman shall have a casting vote in addition to his vote as Chairman of the Committee.

44.—The forty-first Section of "The South Shields Improvement Act, 1853," shall be *repealed*, and *in lieu thereof* it shall be enacted as follows:—The stallages, rents, and tolls to be levied under the provisions of this Act, in respect of the said markets and fairs, shall be applied by the Corporation in manner hereinafter mentioned (that is to say,) in the first place, in the payment of the annual interest of monies borrowed for the purchase of, or for purposes connected with, the Town Hall and market buildings, and markets and fairs in the Borough, and due and owing under the authority of this Act; and in the second place, in payment of the expenditure incident to the maintenance, repair, and management of the Town Hall and market buildings, markets and fairs in the Borough, and the repair of the market place pavement; and the surplus, if any, shall be allowed to accumulate as a sinking fund, which shall be applied by the Corporation in and towards paying off the principal monies so to be borrowed as aforesaid; and when, and so soon as the whole of the money so to be borrowed as aforesaid shall have been paid off and discharged, it shall be lawful for the Corporation either to lower the said stallages, rents, and tolls to such an extent as will reduce the stallages, rents, and toll to be levied and raised in respect of the said markets and fairs to the annual amount (as near as may be) of the expenses of the maintenance, repair, working and management respectively of the said Town Hall and market buildings, markets, and fairs, or to appropriate and apply the same wholly or in part in and towards the extension and improvement of the said markets and fairs, and in and towards providing suitable works and conveniences connected therewith, or in aid of the General District Rate.

45.—For the purpose of removing the doubts that have arisen as to the construction and operation of "The Local Government Act, 1858," with reference to certain provisions of "The South Shields Improvement Act, 1853:" Be it enacted, That all the borrowing and mortgaging powers contained and enacted by reference to "The Public Health Act, 1848," or otherwise in and by the said "South Shields Improvement Act, 1853," as amended by this Act, shall not be deemed to have been in any way repealed or affected by "The Local Government Act, 1858," or any provisions therein contained, except that in all cases in which the sanction, consent, direction or approval of the General Board of Health is rendered requisite in and by the said "South Shields Improvement Act, 1853," to the due exercise of any of the powers vested thereby in the South Shields Corporation as the Local Board of Health, such powers or any of them shall and may henceforth be exercised with and under the sanction, consent, direction or approval of one of Her Majesty's Principal Secretaries of State, in lieu of the sanction, consent, direction or approval of the General Board of Health mentioned in the said "Public Health Act, 1848."

46, 47, 48, & 49. Except as by this Act expressly provided, the existing rights, &c., of the Dean and Chapter of Durham, the Tyne Improvement Commissioners, the mayor, aldermen, and burgesses of the Borough of Newcastle-upon-Tyne, and the Corporation of the Master, Pilots and Seamen of the Trinity House, Newcastle-upon-Tyne, and the members thereof, are reserved.

50.—Provides for the expenses of the Act.

Then follow the Schedules to the Act, viz:—

SCHEDULE A.

Rates on Shipping, outward and inward.

SCHEDULE B.

Rates or dues on goods, package duty, (in addition,) and dues for the use of sheds.

The intentions of the Improvement Acts with respect to the pulling down of the old *Town Hall* and the erection of a new one remain unperformed, for it still stands where it did, in the centre of the Market Place, in all its pristine originality ; the open space beneath it remains unenclosed, and no "market stalls, standing sheds, booths, shambles, or other conveniencies" have been erected by the Corporation for the use and accommodation of the frequenters of the Markets.

Not so have the intentions of the Acts been disregarded with respect to the quay and the erections thereon of the North Eastern Railway Company, for they have become the property of the Corporation by purchase at the price of £10,000, it not having yet been found necessary to enlarge the quay on the landward side, nor on that of the river. The Corporation being already the owners of the narrow portion of quay, immediately adjoining the Mill Dam Dock, and lying between it and the quay of the North Eastern Railway Company, the entirety of the two quay properties mentioned in the Act and now forming one compact united quay, became indisputably vested in the Corporation, as sole owners for the use of the public, and certain convenient parts of them have since become legal quays, by approval of the Commissioners of Customs and Her Majesty's Treasury, for the shipping and unshipping of goods.

The Corporation Quay, as I delight to designate it,

"Yon is our quay ; in front our river shows
Hoys, pinks, and sloops ; brigs, brigantines, and snows."

is midway between the Eastern and Western River Side Termini of South Shields and has two water frontages. That which faces the River is 330 feet in length, and the Corporation are certain at some future period to extend it riverward, so as to make it a deep water quay. In the mean time the advantages to trade already derived from the corporate possession of the quay and its appurtenances have been all that could be wished for, and the passenger traffic is truly astonishing. In this quay alone there is indeed a prosperous "future" connected with our town.

Of the new Custom House Building itself, standing proudly on the quay, in conspicuous view from the ever busy River, little need be said, for all its merits and those also of Clemence, its skilful Architect, and Rowe, its talented Sculptor, have been truthfully and willingly set forth in my Custom House Pamphlet, and to that it is necessary for me now only to refer. It affords every requisite accommodation as a South Shields Custom House, for the Tyne Pilotage Board, the South Shields Local Marine Board, and the South Shields Shipping Offices ; all the business connected with the four being conveniently transacted therein. And by its commanding business like appearance on all sides, impresses strangers with a favourable opinion, not only of itself as a public erection, but of the spirit and judgment of those by whom it was provided in prophetic anticipation of those commercial and other

T. M. Clemence Arch.ᵗ

CUSTOM HOUSE SOUTH SHIELDS.

Lambert. lith. Newcastle.

requirements which loomed in the distance, and which by their actual possession, have since added so greatly to the name, position, and consequence of South Shields as a seaport town of shipping, manufacturing. and trading importance.

EXTENSION OF LIMITS AND THE TYNE DOCKS.

The South Shields Improvement Act, 1853, was passed on the 8th of July, 1853, whereby it was (*inter alia*) enacted as follows by Section 4,

"That this Act shall extend to, and comprise the *whole* of the Borough, *except* that portion of the same, which lies to the Westward of the hedge upon the East side of Boldon Lane, and to the Westward of a straight line drawn from the Northern extremity of the said hedge, to the mouth of the River Don at low water; *provided* nevertheless, that in case the town of South Shields shall become connected with the village of East Jarrow, which is situate within the portion of the Borough hereinbefore excepted from the operation of this Act, *or in the event of a Public Dock being constructed in Jarrow Slake in the Borough*, it shall be lawful for the Corporation *after. the expiration of three years from the completion* of such continuous line of buildings, *or of such Public Dock*, such completion to be certified by two Justices, *to extend the limits of this Act to the whole of the Borough*, in manner hereinafter mentioned. *Provided always*, that a line of buildings from the West side of Boldon Lane to East Jarrow, shall be deemed continuous notwithstanding any openings for branch streets or public roads."

And by Section 5,

"That after the expiration of three years from such completion, the Council may at any meeting, of which special notice shall be given, resolve that the limits of this Act shall be *extended* to the whole of the Borough; but such resolution shall have no effect until the same shall have been confirmed at a subsequent meeting, held not sooner than four weeks after the preceding meeting, and which subsequent meeting shall have been advertised once at least in each of the weeks intervening between the two meetings, in some newspaper circulating within the limits of this Act, and of which special notice in writing has been given to each member of the Council; and from, and after such confirmation, the limits of this Act shall extend to, and comprise the whole of the Borough, and this Act shall be read and constructed as if the limits of the Act had been hereby made co-extensive with the Borough."

The Tyne Docks were made and completed under the provisions of the "Jarrow Dock and Railway Act, 1854," and its Incorporated Acts, and were formally opened for business with great ceremony, on the 3rd of March, 1859, amidst the public rejoicings of assembled thousands, the event having moreover been celebrated by large public dinners at South Shields and Newcastle-upon-Tyne, the Mayor of South Shields, John Williamson, Esq., presiding as chairman at the former, and Mr. Thompson, the chairman of the company, at the latter. They have continued uninterruptedly open ever since, and are possessed of all the means and appliances necessary for the enormous business which is carried on therein.

The water area of the Dock is 50 acres, and of the basin 10 acres, and there is a timber pond of 5 acres, with entrance Locks, coal and coke shipping jetties, spouts where the largest description of ships can be loaded afloat, commodious goods warehouses, hydraulic and steam travelling cranes, shears, ballast apparatus and tramways. In short every requisite convenience and accommodation which might be looked for in a public Dock capable of containing 500 Ships, and connected by Railways with all parts of the kingdom.

After the expiration of three years from the completion and opening of the Dock as aforesaid, the Corporation of South Shields, took steps to extend the limits of the "South Shields Improvement Act, 1853," to the whole of the Borough; and for that purpose, all the requirements of the 4th and 5th sections of that Act were carefully and correctly complied with, so as to make those limits co-extensive with the Borough. Previous to the effecting of this, a *part* only of the Docks had been within the limits of "The South Shields Improvement Act, 1853," but by the extension of those limits the *whole* of the Docks were brought within the limits, and consequently became subject to general and special district rates, leviable within the Borough. They were so rated accordingly, and then and not before, the Dock Company, thinking perhaps

> " He either fears his fate too much,
>   Or his deserts are small,
> Who dares not put it to the touch,
>   To win or lose it all."

brought forward their most extraordinary objection that the Docks were not *public* Docks within the meaning of the 4th section of the Act, and consequently that all the steps taken by the Corporation were null and void, and the Docks not properly assessed. By arrangement between the Town Clerk and the Solicitors for the Dock Company, the Company appealed *pro forma* to the Court of Quarter Sessions against the rate, and a special case was obtained for the determination of the Court of Queen's Bench; all technicalities on both sides being wisely waived, leaving for the decision of the court the simple question whether the Tyne Docks were or were not Public Docks within the meaning of the Act. Whatever doubt the Dock Company might really have entertained on the point, the Corporation never had any; and the result proved that the latter were right, for when the special case was ripe for argument before the Judges of the Court of Queen's Bench, the Dock Company suddenly abandoned their opposition, on the very threshold of the Court, submitted to the extension of limits, paid the costs, and then the rate, so that nothing could have been more triumphantly successful on the part of the Corporation, than the way in which the matter terminated.

The co-extension of limits thus submitted to and secured, is valuable and important as regards rating and otherwise, for nothing would have been more inconvenient and ridiculous than the continuance of a boundary by which one part of the Docks would have been assessable to the rates of the Corporation, and the other part exempt from them altogether, while other disadvantages would constantly have arisen from so confused and objectionable a state of affairs.

By these vast and mighty Tyne Docks on one side of the river, where once the rank and slimy Slake alone lay festering beneath the burning sun, and by those other noble Docks so appropriately termed "Northumberland" almost opposite, with the commercial fleets not only of England but of the world, in safety congregating therein, we have proofs of that modern energy, skill, and capital, which in connexion with our advancing trade and improving river, have kept pace with Sunderland, Seaham, Hartlepool, Middlesborough, and Stockton; and if not altogether convinced by what I have adduced, we have only to bring under the vision of those who doubt, the magnificent works of Jarrow's Chemical Company, and the busy manufactories of which East Jarrow may well feel proud. To which may be added, if permitted to pass beyond the boundaries of our own advancing borough, the extraordinary Cyclopean works at busy Jarrow, of Palmer's princely Company, who are living instances amongst many which abound upon the Tyne of the mighty things which may be accomplished by ability, industry, judgment, integrity, and well-directed perseverance.

> "Near these a crew industrious, in the Docks,
> Rear for the sea, those castles on the stocks;
> See! the long keel, which soon the waves must hide,
> See! the strong ribs which form the roomy side;
> Bolts yielding slowly to the sturdiest stroke,
> And planks which curve and bend within the smoke.
> Around the whole rise cloudy wreaths, and far
> Bear the warm pungence of o'er-boiling tar."

THE TOWN HALL, MARKETS, FAIRS, AND TOLLS.

Although not prepared with an affirmative answer to the simple inquiry asked,

> "Can measured lines these various buildings show,
> The town hall, markets, fairs, or Chapter Row?"

I may nevertheless venture to explain without the "aid of fancy," that in the year 1855, The South Shields Corporation with that watchful attention to the interests of the Borough, which it must be admitted has characterised it since our municipal incorporation in

1850, purchased of the Dean and Chapter of Durham, for the very moderate price of £500, the building in the Market-place, well known as the town hall, together with the important and profitable right of holding markets and fairs, and of levying tolls, they having previously obtained powers for that purpose, under the Improvement Act of 1853, The building still stands proudly in the centre, externally unaltered as it was built a century ago, but internally fitted up in good style for the meetings of the council and its various committees, and the busy markets and fairs outside actually produced last year to the Corporation a gross revenue of £377 2s. 4d., all of which, with the valuable addition of the town hall building itself, the Corporation became possessed of for their £500. Their constituents, the burgesses, may form their own estimate of the value of the bargain.

The Magistrates' court used to be held in the town hall, which was also in former days occupied as a school room.

The only lock-up for prisoners was then the cell under the Eastern steps leading up to the town hall.

The premises now occupied by Messrs. Kirkley and Fenwick, were the first erections in the Market Place.

The judicious purchase, pulling down, and entire removal of St. Hilda's old parsonage house by the Corporation in the year 1862, by which the Market Place was enlarged and an unsightly excrescence removed, was another sagacious improvement effected by the Corporation with the late Incumbent upon fair terms and with every proper assistance from him, and the widening of Church Row in connection therewith, forms a component part all ready prepared, of the improvements looked for from the expected conversion of Messrs. R. W. Swinburne and Co's., unsightly, triangular piece of ground in front of their works, to purposes which will be alike advantageous to the public and to them.

The Dean and Chapter reserved to themselves on the sale of the town hall, the use of it for the holding of their Courts Leet, and the transaction of such of their business as Lord of the Manor of Westoe, as had usually been transacted by them therein.

A crowded and a busy *market* of vast convenience to the inhabitants is held in the Market Place on the Saturday in each week; and may be held on such other days, and during such hours as the Corporation may from time to time appoint. But a market is not to be held on Christmas Day, or Good Friday, or on any day appointed for a public fast or thanksgiving.

The *fairs* are held on the days on which they have been usually held; but when any such day is Sunday, or a day appointed for a public fast or thanksgiving, on such day, not being more than six days before or after the usual day, as the Corporation shall think fit and appoint.

Under the head of "Corporation Quay," will be found such of the provisions of "The South Shields Improvement Amendment Act, 1861," as relate to the town hall, and the markets, fairs, and tolls.

In no direction has advancement shown itself more forcibly than in these markets since the first was held at South Shields, on the 17th of October, 1770. The *fairs* with all their temptations could always command a merry assemblage of the old and young; but the *markets* could only of late years boast of the numerous "buyers and sellers" by which they are now steadily frequented. Unsheltered as they are, and totally unprotected from the weather, and the "pelting of the pitiless storm," this can be attributed to the force of their own intrinsic usefulness and value, as a place of public traffic, purchase, and sale.

It was so far back as the year 1259, that by an order made between the Town of Newcastle and the prior and convent of Durham, among other things it was stipulated, that the tenants of the latter at South Shields should have liberty to bake and brew for themselves only, but not for the use of strangers! Whatever our situation as tenants under the Dean and Chapter of Durham, may still be, we are happily at liberty to bake and brew without leave or licence from Newcastle, not only for ourselves but for strangers, our emancipation being so much further complete as to enable us to lie down and rest under the shadow of our own vine and our own fig tree (if we had any,) none rising up against us to make us afraid.

THE TYNE CONSERVANCY.

During the last ten years to which I am restricted, the Tyne Improvement Commissioners have been watchfully alive to the requirements of their position, and legislation, with all its costly consequences, has from time to time been industriously invoked to their aid and assistance. As it was however with the *intended* paving of a certain vulgar place, the very naming of which would be little short of treason to "ears polite," so has it abortively been with some of the legislative intentions of the Commissioners, for

"With much cry and little woo,
As the deil said when he shore the sow,"

The construction of Docks at Coble Dene has, unhappily for South Shields and perhaps for North Shields also, not been accomplished; and the Tynemouth Dock at the Low Lights, with its high sounding "basins, locks, entrances, approaches, and other works and conveniencies," still remains an unperformed subject of doubtful expediency and cautious accomplishment. At the same time it must be admitted, that while the Western River Improvements connected with the removal and re-construction of Newcastle Bridge, and from thence upwards to Hedwin Streams have been steadily kept in view, all proper attention has at the same time been bestowed by the Commissioners and their able officers, upon the other more important division of the river lying Eastward of Newcastle, between it and the sea, embracing the piers both South and North, the deepening of the bar, dredging, the removal of shoals and sandbanks, the erection of river walls, the laying down of moorings, and the performance of other works of various descriptions, " *de omnibus rebus, et quibusdam aliis,*" with a result so successful and encouraging as to give confidence even to the sceptical and timid when they doubted the correctness of the views, and the prudence of the acts of the Commissioners, proved as they not only have been by the success of their active operations, but by their cautious refrenation from works of a doubtful character, until by time and their completion the results of other works in progress which may be termed experimental, shall have been fully ascertained and tried upon our broad and noble river, of which it may in truth be said

> " With ceaseless motion comes and goes the tide,
> *Flowing,* it fills the channel vast and wide;
> Then back to sea, with strong majestic sweep,
> It rolls, in *ebb* yet terrible and deep."

Into the particulars of the River Tyne Improvement Acts of 1850 and 1852, it is unnecessary here to enter, for they were sufficiently set forth in my former work. They were followed on the 27th July, 1857, by "An Act to amend and enlarge the provisions of the acts relating to the River Tyne, and to enable the Tyne Improvement Commissioners to construct Docks at Coble Dene, and certain works for the improvement of such river, and for other purposes."

The works which the Commissioners were authorised by that act to execute within the limited space of seven years, comprised the following, that is to say,

   1st. The improving of the navigation of the river from Hay Hole Point to Coble Dene.

   2nd. The making and maintaining of Coble Dene Docks.

   3rd. The making and maintaining of a Junction Channel or communication between Coble Dene Docks and the Northumberland Docks.

The Coble Dene Docks and Junction Channel were never made, and by the expiration of the seven years, the powers granted for executing them ceased, and cannot now be exercised. It would be useless therefore, now to insert or to make further allusion to them here.

By section 8, the Commissioners were, by the name of " The Tyne Improvement Commissioners," made a body corporate, with perpetual succession and a common seal.

And by section 36, the Commissioners were authorized to make by-laws with respect to the discharge of ashes, refuse, and rubbish.

The next Act which followed on the 21st July, 1859, was "An Act to amend the provisions of the Tyne Improvement Acts, to authorize an alteration of the piers at the mouth of the river and for other purposes."

At that time the piers were in course of construction, the Northumberland Docks had been made, and all hopes of a Coble Dene Dock had vanished.

The time for completing the piers limited by the act of 1852, was extended for a period of ten years, to be computed from the passing of the act on the 21st July, 1859; and powers of deviation from the lines of the piers, as delineated upon the plans of 1852, were granted.

The Commissioners were empowered to charge the pier rates upon outward, instead of inward vessels.

The 25th section relates to the consumption of smoke arising from the combustibles in fire-places or furnaces used *afloat*, in all such parts of the River Tyne, its creeks and inlets, and the docks and other lands covered with water adjoining thereto, as may be within the 'limits of the jurisdiction of the Commissioners, or within the several Boroughs of Tynemouth, South Shields, and Gateshead, as well as of the Borough of Newcastle-upon-Tyne; the penalty being 40s., for every days' use and consumption after one month's notice, in writing, by an Inspector of Nuisances, to remedy or discontinue the use of the same.

Next came the Act of 28th June, 1861, entitled "An Act to amend the Acts relating to the River Tyne; and to enable the Tyne Improvement Commissioners to construct docks and other works, and to remove and rebuild the Bridge of Newcastle-upon-Tyne; to make certain alterations in the rates charged by the Commissioners, and for other purposes."

The works which the Commissioners were by this act authorized to execute, comprised the following, viz :—

1.—The improving the navigation of the river, from the seaward extremity of the Tyne Piers, to a place at or near Hedwin Streams.

2.—The making and maintaining of docks, to be called the *Tynemouth* Dock, with one or more entrances into or from the River Tyne; and to be situate at or near the Low Lights, and upon part of the shore or bed of the river, and upon the lands adjoining, or near the river, and extending from or near to the Northern Pier, at the mouth of the river on the East, to Peggy's Hole on the West.

3.—The taking of water from the river at or near the Low Lights.

4.—The taking down and removing the bridge of Newcastle-upon-Tyne, and making a new bridge, of a different construction from that of the present bridge, and the constructing proper approaches on each side thereof, which said new bridge will be situate at or near to the site of the present bridge.

5.—The erecting of a temporary bridge near to the said bridge of Newcastle-upon-Tyne, and the maintaining it till such time as the new bridge shall be completed and open for traffic.

For the accomplishment of all which objects, financially and otherwise, comprehensive and special provisions were made by the act.

48

The Commissioners were also empowered to purchase by agreement, the ferries, and to maintain and charge for them, which they have done.

From and after the 1st of September, 1861, the charge for or in respect of the conveying or receiving ballast within the port was restricted to one shilling per ton; and the limits in which ballast might cost or unloaded were extended and defined.

Other clauses are therein which need no special notice here.

It is of importance however to make known, that except by the act of 1861, now under notice, expressly provided nothing therein shall amend, interpret, or alter, the acts of 1850, 1852, 1857, and 1859, or any of the powers or authorities thereof. Schedules of tonnage rates &c., are appended.

Lastly comes the act of 5th July, 1865, the title of which is "An Act to enlarge the powers of the Tyne Improvement Commissioners, and to facilitate the construction of the Tynemouth Docks, and for other purposes."

The works which the Commissioners were authorized by this act to execute, comprise the following, that is to say,

1.—The making and maintaining of a *graving* dock or docks, on the North side of the Northumberland Docks, at or near Howdon.

2.—The making and maintaining of a graving dock or docks, on the North side of the Tynemouth Docks.

3.—The making and maintaining of a *tunnel* under the River Tyne, commencing in Newcastle, at a point twenty yards or thereabouts Westward of the old Tyne Bridge, and terminating in Gateshead, at a point twenty yards or thereabouts Westward of Tyne Bridge aforesaid, for the purpose of receiving gas or water pipes, which may be displaced by the removal of Tyne Bridge.

The construction of Tynemouth Docks (which were stated to have been commenced before the expiration of three years, and which must have been so, for although I cannot make out the wall, I perceive an item of charge in the accounts under the head of "Tynemouth Dock Southern Wall" construction of £702 17s.) was carefully kept in view by this act, and certain Corporations and persons were empowered to contribute or guarantee portions of the £600,000 by the act of 1861, to be raised for the purposes of those Docks, in manner therein mentioned, viz.:—By

	£
Blyth and Tyne Railway Company	50,000
Owners of Lands, in the proportions named in the schedule, amounting in the whole to	50,000
Owners, Lessees, or Occupiers of Collieries, in the proportions named in the schedule, amounting in the whole to	50,000
Corporation of Newcastle	25,000
Corporation of Tynemouth	50,000
Tyne Improvment Commissioners	50,000

Further provisions are also made under the heads of water supply, protection of navigation, by-laws, towage, passage of swing bridges, ferry rights, borrowing powers, collection of rates, new works and lands, graving dock rates, and saving clauses.

The report of the finance committee of the Tyne Improvement Commissioners for the year ended 31st December, 1865, .was favourable and gratifying, the particulars of which may be ascertained by reference to the clear and admirable document itself, and the statements of accounts which accompanied it.

The borrowing powers of the Commissioners, under " *The Tyne Improvement Fund,*" stand as follows, viz.—

			£
Authorized by the Act of 1850			97,349
,,	,,	1861	600,000
,,	,,	1865	150,000
			747,349
Already borrowed			490,581
Unexercised powers			256,768

Sums amounting to £43,085 being also held by the Commissioners on call.

The mortgage debt of the Tyne Piers Fund is £245,920, and £25,300 is held on call.

The total quantity of material raised by the dredgers since the commencement in 1838, to and including 1865, is 16,610,678 tons. The quantity raised last year was 4,545,814 tons, at an average cost of 3½d., per ton. With such results even poetry herself comes rushing to my aid,

> "'Tis now, with all our comforts spread around,
> We hear the powerful dredger's welcome sound.''

The total quantity of coal shipped in the Northumberland Dock for export and river sale, from 1858 to 1865, both inclusive, was 13,784,890 tons, the total revenue for the same period having been £188,769 13s. 7d.

The total number of vessels cleared at Custom Houses on the Tyne during the year 1865, classified in an interesting table from below 100 tons to above 1000 tons register, was 19,663.

19,663 vessels, shewing a tonnage of 4,037,422 tons, paid Tyne Piers Dues during the year 1865, or claimed exemption therefrom for the remainder of the year as having paid 7 times, being sailing vessels, or 15 times being steamers.

The *Tyne Piers* account stands thus as regards income and outlay, from the 17th January 1852, (the date of the act) up to the 31st December, 1865, viz :—

INCOME.

	£	s.	d.
Total Piers dues	184,113	13	2
Mortgages contracted	245,920	0	0
	£430,033	13	2

OUTLAY.

		£	s.	d.
Expenses of collecting dues		1975	15	10
Salaries and engineering		16790	16	5
Parliamentary and law charges		9495	9	2
Trow Rocks purchase		6000	0	0
North Pier Works	212570 16 2			
Add apportionment of plant and stores account	10367 9 5			
		222938	5	7
South Pier Works	149925 8 2			
Add apportionment of plant and stores account	9260 18 5			
Repairs to craft during 1865	589 10 6			
	9850 8 11			
		159775	17	1
Miscellaneous		4741	2	10
Interest		39460	15	11
Commissions and stamps		333	12	9
		£461511	15	7

The total quantity of ships' ballast discharged on the Tyne, for the year 1865, was

	TONS.
Assessed ballast	372322
For private use	249833
Total	622155

There has been a considerable increase in both the number and tonnage of vessels using the port, and the average size of vessels has risen from 190 in the year 1864, to 205 in the year 1865.

The number of vessels above 500 tons register, which cleared from the port in 1865 was 1511, as against 975 in the previous year 1864, shewing an increase of 536 vessels of that description.

With which dry details I close this portion of my work, trusting that I shall be pardoned for setting them forth so minutely, for I deemed them of importance enough to justify insertion, knowing that they were of a nature to prove valuable to many who take a deep and anxious interest in all that concerns the river, and the works and operations which are connected with its improvement. By those who may desire still more extended particulars, they must be sought for in the Improvement Acts of Parliament themselves, the report of the finance committee, and the audited accounts of the Commissioners, as the same are annually published with every minute and necessary information, in a manner most creditable to Mr. Guthrie, the very able and deservedly popular Secretary to the Commissioners.

SOUTH SHIELDS LOCAL MARINE BOARD.

In my Custom House pamphlet, to which I must again refer, the particulars of our unsuccessful endeavours in 1862, for the establishment of a separate Local Marine Board for South Shields, will be found at page 61. This desideratum was however sure to follow, and it has speedily followed, as I foretold it would, the creation of South Shields a separate port, as is shown by the following official letter from the Board of Trade to our present Mayor.

Board of Trade, Whitehall,
9th December, 1865.

SIR,

        I am directed by the Board of Trade to inform you, that South Shields will be a place at which there will in future be a Local Marine Board, for carrying into effect the provisions of " The Merchant Shipping Act, 1854."

        I am therefore to call your attention to the provisions of "The Merchant Shipping Act, 1854," (17 and 18 Vic., c. 104, s. 110 to 120,) relating to Local Marine Boards, and to the fact that the election of members to the Local Marine Board of South Shields, must take place in January next.

        The attention of the Collector of Customs at South Shields. has been called to the provisions of the act, requiring that the list of voters shall be made out, signed, printed, and posted up.

I have the honor to be, Sir,
Your obedient servant,

T. H. FARRER.

The Worshipful the Mayor,
    South Shields.

By this, the only remaining link of the chain binding South Shields to North Shields, was broken; and both Boroughs are now in that really desirable state of independence and separation with regard to each other, which is best for those amicable relations which ought to exist between them. "South Shields and North Shields are now indeed placed; (I cannot help quoting, even if I quote from myself!) in no other position towards each other than that of friendly and laudable rivalry, having for its praiseworthy object the production of effects and benefits advantageous to the best interests of the entirety of that noble river, in the welfare and prosperity of which they are both so equally and so largely interested."

This being the proper triennial period, all the requisite measures have been gone through under the Merchant Shipping Act, and the South Shields Local Marine Board as it now exists in full blown independence, consists of the following members, viz.—

1. THE MAYOR OF SOUTH SHIELDS,
    (for the time being) Ex-officio,
2. JOHN ROBINSON, (East King-street)
3. JOSEPH WILSON,
4. JOHN LAWRENCE HALL,   ELECTED BY SHIPOWNERS.
5. JOHN BRODRICK DALE,
6. JAMES YOUNG,
7 JOHN ROBINSON, (Adelaide-st.,)
8. ROBERT INGHAM, M.P.
9. MATTHEW CAY,
10. JAMES MATHER,   APPOINTED by BOARD of TRADE.
11. HENRY FELL,

The first meeting of the board was held on the 28th of February, 1866, in the New Custom House Building, so wisely provided by the South Shields Corporation for Custom House and other purposes; and Mr. John Walker Lamb then became Secretary to the Board.

The business of the Shipping Offices, also now an independent South Shields establishment, is transacted in the same building, under the chief superintendence of Mr. John Rigby, whose nautical experience, knowledge of seamen, and other qualifications, are such as to fit him for the discharge of the duties of the responsible situation which he thus advantageously holds.

> "He had indeed thro' many a storm and tempest steered,
> And many a rock and coast of danger cleared."

THE SOUTH SHIELDS GAS WORKS.

" EX FUMO DARE LUCEM."

By a concluding paragraph to this subject of my Lecture in 1856, I ventured to assert that the Gas Company were alive to the requirements of a rapidly increasing population, and were prepared to meet them with promptitude and liberality. The Act of Parliament of the 26th June, 1857, "for lighting with Gas the Borough of South Shields and neighbourhood thereof, in the County of Durham," speedily proved the correctness of this assertion, and I proceed to disclose at once its chief provisions and results, as being a measure with which every inhabitant of South Shields is deeply interested, and should become intimately acquainted.

Its Recitals are,

That in or about the year 1824, certain persons formed themselves into a company for the purpose of supplying with Gas the Townships of South Shields and Westoe, in the county of Durham.

That by deed of settlement bearing date the 20th December, 1855, and made between the several persons named in the third part of the schedule thereunder written of the first part, and Robert Anderson and George Yeoman Heath, trustees for the purposes thereinmentioned of the second part. After reciting that the parties thereto of the first part, were the owners of certain freehold and leasehold hereditaments, and of machinery, pipes, and other chattels and effects which they had used in co-partnership, for the purpose of supplying the Borough of South Shields with Gas; and that being desirous of extending their works they had agreed to obtain a certificate of registration under the act passed in the 7th and 8th years of Her present Majesty, and chap. 110, generally to carry on their said co-partnership, under and subject to the provisions of the said act, and of the same deed; such persons formed themselves into a joint stock company, by the name of "The South Shields Gas Company," for the purpose of manufacturing Gas, and therewith lighting the streets, houses, and other places of the Borough of South Shields, and any of the parishes or places adjoining or near thereto; and of selling and disposing of Coke, Gas, Tar, and of all and every product and products, refuse or residue, arising or to be obtained from the substances or materials used in or necessary for the manufacture of Gas, with a share capital of £20,000, divided into 2000 shares of £10 each; with power to raise on bond, the sum of £5000, and to receive their share capital to the further extent of £15,000, or in lieu thereof, to borrow the whole or any part of such sum upon mortgage;

That the said company was completely registered under the act then in force, for the registration, incorporation, and regulation of joint stock companies;

That the company had obtained registration, under "The Joint Stock Companies Act, 1856.";

That no such increase of the capital of the company as was by the same deed authorised had taken place;

That the property of the parties interested in the company established in the year 1824, was valued and taken by the company established under the said deed of settlement at the sum of £11,200, and shares representing that amount were allotted to the parties so interested, and the same formed part of the said capital of £20,000, the whole whereof had been subscribed for and paid up and expended for the purposes of the undertaking of the said company;

That the company had not borrowed any money;

That the committee had extended and improved the Gas Works, but they required for the purposes of such works the additional lands thereinafter more particularly described, and it was expedient that they be enabled to purchase, take, and hold such lands for the purposes of their works;

That the company had laid down pipes and other apparatus for the supply of the said borough;

And that the population of South Shields and of its neighbourhood, had of late years greatly increased, and there was an increasing demand for gas, both for public and private purposes, and it was expedient that powers should be given to the company to enable them to afford such supply of gas; that their capital should be increased; that they should be enabled to supply gas within the district thereinafter mentioned; and that more effectual powers should be conferred upon them for the purpose of effectuating such supply; but the purposes aforesaid could not be effected without the authority of Parliament.

Whereupon it was enacted,

That, "The Company's Clauses Consolidation Act, 1845," "The Lands Clauses Consolidation Act, 1845," and "The Gaswork's Clauses Act, 1847," should be incorporated with, and form part of this act; and that in construing those acts respectively in connection with this act, the expression "The Special Act," shall mean this act; the expression "The Company" and "The Undertakers" respectively, shall mean the

Company by this act incorporated; and the expressions "The Undertaking" and "The Gasworks," shall include all the works of the Company executed, and to be executed.

That the expression "The Original Company," should mean the Company or Partnership existing under the said deed of settlement, and "The Joint Stock Company's Act, 1856," immediately before the passing of this act; and the expression "The Company," should mean the Company hereby incorporated, unless there was something in the subject or context repugnant to such construction.

That in citing this act for any purpose whatsoever, it should be sufficient to use the expression, "The South Shields Gas Act, 1857.

That the limits of the act, for the supply of gas, should comprise and include the Borough of South Shields, and the Parish of Jarrow, both without as well as within the Borough; and that the limits within which the Gasworks might be contained, maintained, created, or made, where the lands belonging to or used by the Original Company, for the purpose of the Gasworks, previous to the passing of the act, and also the lands which might be purchased by the Company under the powers of the act, all which lands were more particularly described in the schedule to the act annexed as follows, viz. :

"Certain lands and premises situate in the respective Townships of South Shields and Westoe, in the Borough of South Shields, and Parish of Jarrow, or the Parish of St. Hilda, being and commonly called the "The Gas Works," and certain tenements and ground adjoining or near thereto, called or known by the name of "Woodroffe Court," and contain tenements and ground, called or known by the name of "Wilson's Buildings," and certain cottages or ground, called or known by the name of "Grieve's Cottages," which said lands and premises are bounded on the North by Coronation Street, on the East by land claimed to belong to the Dean and Chapter of Durham, and under lease respectively to Mary Kirkley, George Potts, Edward Thompson, Andrew Stoddart, Robert Walter Swinburne, and others; on the South partly by Oyston Street, partly by land claimed to belong to the said Dean and Chapter of Durham, and under lease to the said Robert Walter Swinburne and others, and partly by land claimed to belong to the said Dean and Chapter, and in the occupation of the Manor Wallsend Colliery; and on the West by land claimed to belong to the said Dean and Chapter of Durham, and leased to the said Robert Walter Swinburne and others."

It then proceeds further to enact,

By Section 6. That the members of, or shareholders in the original company, and all other persons and corporations who had already subscribed, or should thereafter subscribe to the undertaking by this act authorised, and their executors, administrators, successors, and assigns respectively, should be, and they were thereby united and incorporated into a Company, for the purpose of making and supplying gas within the limits of this act, and for doing all acts necessary for that purpose, and for other the purposes of this act, and the said incorporated acts authorized, by and under the name of "The South Shields Gas Company," and by that name should be a body corporate, with perpetual succession, and should have a common seal, and should, and might sue, and be sued, and should have power to purchase, and hold lands for the purposes of the undertaking, subject to the restrictions and provisions therein, and in the said incorporated acts contained; but should not after the passing of this act be subject to any of the clauses or provisions of "The Joint Stock Company's Act, 1856," or of any other act for the registration, incorporation, and regulations of Joint Stock Companies.

Then follow clauses for the following objects, viz.

Clause 7.—Present property vested in the Company incorporated by this act.
8.—Deed of settlement to be void without prejudice to remedies for antecedent breaches thereof.
9.—Saving previous rights and liabilities.
10.—Contracts prior to act, to be binding.
11.—Actions &c. not to abate.
12.—As to recovery of debts of Original Company.
13.—Judgments in respect of existing liabilities may be enforced against individual shareholders.
14.—Shareholders against whom exection issued in respect of existing liabilities, to be reimbursed.

15.—Trustees of the Company to be indemnified.

By Clause 16.—That the Capital of the Company for the purposes of this act shall be £40,000, whereof £20,000 shall be called "The Original Capital," and £20,000 "The Additional Capital."

Clause 17.—The number of shares into which the said capital shall be divided, shall be £4000, and the amount of each share shall be £10.

Then follow clauses for the following objects, viz.

Clause 18.—Distribution of existing shares.

19.—Distribution of new shares.

20.—Rights and liabilities of subscribers to further capital.

21.—Calls.

22.—The prescribed rate of profits to be divided among the shareholders in any year, shall be £9 in the hundred by the year, on the capital in the undertaking for the time being paid up.

23.—Power for the Company to borrow on mortgage or bond, not exceeding £9800, viz. : at any time after the passing of this act, £5000, and when the additional capital of 20,000 shall have been subscribed for, and one half thereof paid up, the further sum of £4800.

24.—Application of money.

25.—Number and qualification of Directors.

26.—First Directors.

27.—Quorum of Directors.

28.—Officers to continue.

29.—Company to remove or appoint Secretary.

30.—Suspension of Secretary.

31.—First and other meetings.

32.—Manner of voting at meetings.

33.—Proxies.

34.—Number of shareholders to convene extraordinary meeting.

35.—First Directors, how long to remain in office.

36.—Supply of vacancies.

37.—Power to purchase the lands and hereditaments delineated on the plan, and described in book of reference.

38.—Compulsory purchase of lands, not to be exercised after two years from the passing of this act.

39.—Purchase of other lands by agreement; provided, that the quantity of land to be held by the Company does not exceed 5 acres.

40.—Gasworks to be erected only on the lands specified in the schedule.

Then come the following provisions which are important enough to be given in full, viz.

41.—Subject to the provisions of this act, and the said incorporated acts contained, it shall be lawful for the Company, from time to time, to make, construct, lay down, and maintain, alter, or discontinue such retorts, gasometers, receivers, drains, sewers machinery, and other works and apparatus, and also such houses and buildings, and approaches thereto, and to do all such other acts as they shall think necessary, consistently with the provisions of this act, for supplying gas within the limits of this act, and to sell, manufacture, and dispose of coke and other residuum arising, or to be obtained from the materials, used in the manufacture of gas, in such manner as the Company may think proper.

42.—The Company from time to time may enter into any contract with the Mayor, Aldermen, and Burgesses of the Borough of South Shields, the Local Board of Health, or any other persons having the control or management of any street, bridge, market, quay, pier, or other place within the limits of this act, for lighting or supplying the same or any part thereof with gas, and providing the same with lamp-pillars and posts, lamp-brackets, lamps and glass, and for the repair thereof respectively, and also from time to time may enter into any contract with any person for lighting or supplying with gas any church, chapel, shop, inn, tavern, dwelling house, mill, manufactory, warehouse, or other public or private building, or place, on such terms and conditions as the Company and such persons respectively agree on.

43.—The Company may, *with the consent of the owner and occupier* of any building lay any pipe, branch, or other necessary apparatus, from any main or branch pipe, into, through, or against such building, for the purpose of lighting it ; and may, *with the like consent*, provide and set up any apparatus necessary for securing to any building a proper and complete supply of gas, and for measuring and ascertaining the extent of such supply.

44.—The maximum charge for gas supplied by the Company shall be after the rate of 4s. 6d. per 1000 cubic feet of gas.

45.—If the Company shall be unable to agree with the Local Board of Health for the Borough of South Shields, as to the price to be paid for any gas which such Board may require, then such price shall be settled by arbitration, in manner prescribed by "The Lands' Clauses Consolidation Act, 1845," with respect to the settlement of disputes by arbitration.

46.—All the gas supplied by the Company, shall be of such quality as to produce from an argand burner, having 15 holes and a seven inch chimney, and consuming five cubic feet of gas per hour, a light equal in intensity to the light produced by 12 sperm candles of 6 in the pound, burning 120 grains per hour.

47.—The Company shall within 6 months after the passing of this act, cause to be erected in some convenient part of their works an experimental meter, furnished with an argand fifteen hole burner, and a seven inch chimney, or other approved burner or chimney, capable of consuming 5 cubic feet of gas per hour, with other necessary apparatus for testing the illuminating power of the gas.

Then follow clauses for the following purposes, viz.

Clause 48.—Power to Local Board to test the purity of the gas.
49.—Cost of experiment to be paid according to the event.
50.—Consumers may be required to use meters.
51.—Penalty for damaging, &c., the meter.
52.—Recovery of rent for gas and fittings under £20.
53.—Undisputed rates, &c., may be recovered by distress, under the warrant of a Justice.
54.—Costs of proceedings may be included in warrant of distress.
55.—Several names and sums may be included in one warrant. &c.

After which comes the following clause, which though last is certainly not least in importance,

56.—The Company, if they think fit, may sell, and the Mayor, Aldermen, and Burgesses of the Borough of South Shields, may purchase the undertaking of the Company ; and the 60th section of "The South Shields Improvement Act, 1853," shall be construed as if the Company incorporated by this act had been named in such section, instead of the Company of proprietors of the "South Shields Gasworks therein referred to."

That the objects contemplated by the act of 1857, have been judiciously and admirably accomplished during the interval which has since elapsed, must be apparent even to the most casual observer who knew the Gas Works as they *were* and now beholds them as they *are*. A large Gasholder has been erected and a set of larger purifiers constructed. A reduction in the price of Gas to the general body of consumers, and also to the large manufacturers has been satisfactorily made. The extension of the Company's mains to East Jarrow, and the replacing of them by considerably larger ones, for the supply of Jarrow itself, and its still rapidly increasing population have been effected. The purchase of the local Gas Works at the latter place, the discontinuance of them, and the superior supply of that neighbourhood as far as the Lead Works at Hebburn, wholly from the South Shields Works have been ably accomplished. And lastly the skilful construction of the works at South Shields under difficulties and without stoppage of the

57

supply of Gas to the consumers, which is so fresh in the memory of all, as
to have required only a passing remark, if it had not been thought necessary to record here as matters of local interest and importance,
a description of the works, the material changes and vast improvements
which have been systematically effected in their reconstruction, the
public spirit, and good management of the Directors, and the unquestionable ability, experience, and sound professional knowledge of
Mr. Warner, their Engineer, who has accomplished a revolution in the
works of no ordinary kind,

"Diruit, ædificat, mutat quadata rotundis,"

such in fact as to entitle him not only to the well merited confidence
of the Company, but the thanks of the public, and of all parties interested in a pure, a plentiful, and a cheap supply of an article which,
publicly and privately, has unquestionably become one of the most
absolute necessaries of every day life.

In the slight sketch which I gave at my Lecture, of the early history
of gas lighting, I noticed the simple Gas Work that was experimented
with " at the fireside all over the Kingdom," in the shape of a tobacco
pipe, in which coal was distilled, and this " Smoke Pipe" was perhaps
like many a simple lowly thing in the history of invention, the germ
of that which has revolutionized an important manufacture. For in
connection with it I may say, that the first idea of adopting fire clay as
a substitute for metal occurred to Mr. Grafton, of the Cambridge Gas
Works, in the year 1820, when he patented the invention. But Mr.
Grafton's labours in the improvement of the manufacture, did not end
with the substitution of fire clay for iron in the retorts, or vessels for
distilling the coal, for it was found necessary, with such a porous
material, to pump the gas from the retort as fast as it was expelled from
the coal by the heat, and in order to prevent any undue action of the
pump or exhauster, as it is technically termed, other apparatus had to
be devised for governing or controlling the action of the exhauster and
steam engine. Thus what was a rough and simple operation, now became a complete and delicate manufacture known as the "carbonizing,"
which is the gas making proper, or coal distilling part of the business.
But equally in other parts have improvements been made, for the
"condensers" for cooling the gas from the retorts, are now so arranged
as to obtain a greater control over the temperature of the gas, which
affects its quality. The operation of "washing, scrubbing and purifying are now more effectually performed than they were, through a better
arrangement of the apparatus for the purpose. In the "distribution"
of the gas a more judicious arrangement is also made than formerly,
for the town is " districted," and by self-acting valves or "governors"
any given pressure is maintained, and the supply regulated to the demand. "Tell-tales" and " Pressure Registers," are likewise now
employed, by which a constant check is maintained and records kept of

the make and supply. The *"testing"* apparatus too has been so much improved and admirably arranged, as to have become ratable, perfectly reliable. In not one of these essentials of a well arranged modern gas work is that of South Shields deficient, it being indeed in many points in advance of the most modern, for improvements have been made in the furnace arrangements of the retorts, in the condensers, in the purifiers, in the pressure registers, and even in the chimney, at the foot of which a furnace is arranged, by which an occasional annoyance has been got rid of, which arose from the burning out of the joints of old pipes, &c. All clearly indicating that much careful thought has been bestowed upon the arrangement and construction of the works, not only for a pure and plentiful supply of gas, but so as to avoid any nuisance or annoyance from the procuring of it and the carrying on of the business.

And what a change in two short years ! The fine well paved new street to the East of the works, in place of the dirty narrow lane of St. Hilda, that run through and inconveniently divided them, not forgetting the old ruinous soapery and filthy tenements. The well arranged, commodious offices and board room at the works, in lieu of the ordinary front parlour and humble first floor in Barrington Street and the old separated works for the present compact arrangement of them.

For the information of the absent I sketch the works in particular detail. They are nearly rectangular in plan, the boundaries being Oyston Street on the South, the Ballast Hill on the West, Coronation Street on the North, and the New Street on the East, the latter being parallel with the old lane of St. Hilda, and a little to the East of the South end of Cornwallis Street. About the middle of the new street on its West side, is the entrance, on one side of which are the offices, and on the other the gate and time-keeper's house and office, and weighing machine, forming the boundary point as it were of a large open yard for coke, between it and the Oyston Street boundary, along which is a range of brick buildings, comprising smith's shop, fire brick stores, sulphate of ammonia works, men's room, and a water cistern at an elevation sufficient to command the whole of the works. Continuous with those and facing the entrance to the works, is the retort house, which is about 100 feet square, the chimney being in the centre of the front, the retorts in three parallel rows, and the " through retorts" or those which are worked from both ends, in the middle, and immediately behind the chimney, and the " singles" on the other side of each entrance to the house. There will be when in full operation, considerably more than 200 retorts in action. The front of the house has a fire brick facing. Parallel with this there is another range of buildings comprising the engine room, stores, experimental rooms, meter shop, &c. The boilers are in the retort house, the guages being in the engine room, and also the pumps or exhausters for drawing the gas from the retorts as made. These exhausters, engines, boilers, &c. are all in *duplicate*, so that in case of accident, or any one of them becoming disabled or out of order, the others can be at once set to work, and thus prevent any interference with, or stoppage of the supply. The shafting for driving the exhausters, tar water, and gas liquor pumps, is all under ground, and so keeps the engine room free from the unsightly belts, &c. of the usual arrangements. Parallel again with these buildings is a double set of condensers, and by a judicious arrangement of Mr. Warner, viz.: a rotatory valve in the engine room, the gas can either be pumped direct from the retorts and forced through the condensers, or drawn through the condensers from the retorts. The two sets may be worked together or separately, and the current of hot gas may be changed from end to end of the set, by which, and the ventilating arrangement of condensing, great control is obtained over the temperature. At each end of the two sets is a " scrubber," a large cast iron cylinder with layers of pebbles, over which two pumps are constantly throwing large volumes of gas water, for washing the gas and depriving it of its ammonia. Here then the gas is deprived of two of its impurities, tar and ammonia, and it is passed on to the purifiers to be deprived of its sulphur, the purifying house being at right angles with the engine house, &c., and forming nearly a square space, in which is the large gasholder. The purifying vessels are four in number, and 14 feet square, and are placed on a raised floor of the house, leaving a clear space underneath for the purifying material. After passing through these vessels, the *manufacture* of the gas is *finished*, leaving it only necessary for me to state, that at the corner of the new street in a rectangular space formed by the purifying house and offices, is the meter and governor house, into which the gas next passes for *measurement*, and that from the meter it travels on to the gasholder, where it is stored, and from thence returns to the meter house, from which it flows by several distinct mains to the town, the supply or pressure being regulated by valves and self acting governors.

The gas rental for the past year amounted to £9,093 9s. 0d.

The present price of the gas is 3s. 8d. per 1000 cubic feet, with a liberal discount to large consumers, the maximum authorised to be charged by the act of 1857, being 4s. 6d.

On the death of Mr. John Dixon Lister, Mr. Jonathan Nelson became Secretary, and he died suddenly on the 22nd day of October last. Mr. John William Lawson is the present newly appointed Secretary.

Mr. Warner is the Engineer, whose works are the best and clearest evidences of his proved ability and capability.

The present directors are Robert Wallis, (Chairman,) William Anderson, James Anderson, William Harrison Fairbairn, Henry Hewison, William Shout, and Leonard Armstrong.

The accounts of the Company are periodically audited.

Such of the public street lamps as are not in the East Jarrow extended district, are supplied with gas, lighted, extinguished, cleaned, and attended by the Company under contract with the Corporation, acting as the Local Board of Health, at the rate of 1s. 2½d. per lamp per week; and such of them as are within that extended district, at the rate of 1s. 6d. per lamp per week.

The lamps with their appurtenant lamp posts and fittings, are likewise supplied to the Corporation by the Company, at the contract price of £2 5s. 0d. each, and the Company also keep them in repair by contract with the Corporation, at the price of 3s. 6d. each.

THE SUNDERLAND AND SOUTH SHIELDS
WATER WORKS.

On the 19th April, 1859, an amended Act of Parliament was obtained entitled "an act to enable the Sunderland and South Shields Water Company, to extend their works, and obtain a further supply of water, and to raise additional capital, and for other purposes."

Its explanatory recitals, are as follows :—

That by "The Sunderland and South Shields Waterworks Act, 1852," the Sunderland and South Shields Water Company were incorporated, and were authorized to supply water within the Boroughs of Sunderland and South Shields, and certain parishes, townships, and places in the Neighbourhood of such Boroughs respectively, in the County of Durham.

That the Company were authorized and required to purchase the undertaking of the South Shields Water Company, and such undertaking had been purchased accordingly.

That the share capital of the Company as authorized by the Act of 1852, amounted to £109,000, whereof £35,000 was distinguised as "Original Capital," divided into 7000 shares of £5 each, £19,500 was distinguished as "Additional Capital," entitled to preference. Dividends after the rates in such Act specified and £54,500 was distinguished as "Extension Capital," and was directed to be exclusively applied to the extension works authorized by such Act.

That in the Act of 1852, provision was made for the amalgamation of the original capital and extension capital, when the profits arising from the extension works should amount to £5 per cent. per annum, upon the capital expended thereon.

That that event had taken place, and such capital had become amalgamated accordingly, and such amalgamated capital was in the now reciting act called "The Ordinary Capital."

That the Company were by the Act of 1852, authorized to borrow on mortgage or bond the sum of £17,500, and also to borrow, for a period not exceeding 7 years, the sum of £10,000 for the purchase of the South Shields Water Works.

That the whole of the share capital, except the sum of £6870, represented by 1374 shares of £5 each had been raised, and the said sums of £17,500, and £10,000 had been borrowed.

That the population of Sunderland and South Shields and their respective neighbourhoods had greatly increased, and numerous houses and buildings had been erected, and in order to meet the increased and increasing demand for water, the Company required a further supply, and it was expedient that they be authorized to obtain that supply, and to construct additional reservoirs, aqueducts, and other works, and to borrow a further sum of money.

That the Company afforded to the inhabitants a constant supply of water, and it was expedient that more efficient provision should be made for preventing fraud and waste.

That it was expedient to establish a scale of rates in respect of the supply of water to dwelling houses, exceeding the annual value of £50.

And that for the purposes aforesaid it was expedient that the Act of 1852 should be amended.

It then enacts,

That " The Lands' Clauses Consolidation Act, 1845," and " The Water Works' Clauses Act, 1847," (except the 70th section of such last mentioned Act,) be incorporated with the Act.

And that the Act may be cited for all purposes as, " The Sunderland and South Shields Water Works Amendment Act, 1859."

After which come the following clauses, viz.—

3.—The interpretation clause.

4.—Giving powers to make new water works, according to deposited plans, with this proviso, "*provided always*, that the quantity of land to be purchased and taken compulsorily from the Rev. George Townshend Fox, his heirs or assigns, under the powers of this Act, shall not exceed in the whole 4 acres, exclusively of the land re-quired for the road of communication to the works of the Company and the pipe tracks, [...] ed reservoir and adjoining works, as shewn [...] ately adjoining the same, within the limits

[...] years, with this important proviso, " that [...] or be construed to extend, to restrain the [...] s, and pipes, from time to time whenever [...] ining a supply of water, for the use of the [...] ame, within the limits of this Act, and for

[...] tion of new shares.

[...] es.

[...] s original shares.

[...] sidered as part of the capital entitled to

[...] proportionable to the value of new shares. [...] bond not exceeding £50,000, including [...] mortgage or bond, under the act of 1852. [...] ave priority.

[...] s of " The Company's Clauses Consolid-

[...] e applied only to the purposes of act of

[...] uses which follow, and to some of be made known to all consumers, [...] sion that they will hereby have a [...] blicity, than through the chance [...] seen by very few of those who are

[...] by the Company, who shall use a cistern

A GLANCE AT OLD SHIELDS.

Mr Robert McKeith writes:—Previous to the Sunderland and South Shields water works, there was a small water works close to St. Hilda pit, which could only supply a few Pants where the people gathered for water, but seldom got it. When they did, it was as green as grass, having to be put through flannel bags as strainers, and then the bags were long green grass. It was a treat to see the girls carrying water in skeels. There was quite an art in carrying water. You would see some wet from head to foot, while others would be quite dry. When they could not get water at the Pants they had to resort to the natural springs, but where were they? One in the Long Bank, one in Shad-well Street, opposite Rennoldson's works, one at the Beacon where the pilots Look Out now, is a well in Bath Street near the farm, and they were sometimes glad to go as far as Trow Rocks for that beautiful spring water. But we had many watercarts which got their supply from the following pumps, one in what is now East Saville St., Westoe Village Pump, a spring at the Bents Farm, the Toll Gate Pump, and last, but not least, Cauldwell water, which was beautiful water. Just fancy those poor girls having to change clothes after carrying such a distance. Sir, we don't value water now an then, as it takes no seek-ing. In all my history I don't remember a spring in High Shields. Holborn itself is all forced land to a great depth. The springs all abound in and around the Roman Station. The good old times were hard old times all the country over.

Such of the public street lamps as are not in the East Jarrow extended district, are supplied with gas, lighted, extinguished, cleaned, and attended by the Company under contract with the Corporation, acting as the Local Board of Health, at the rate of 1s. 2½d. per lamp per week; and such of them as are within that extended district, at the rate of 1s. 6d. per lamp per week.

The lamps with their appurtenant lamp posts and fittings, are likewise supplied to the Corporation by the Company, at the contract price of £2 5s. 0d. each, and the Company also keep them in repair by contract with the Corporation, at the price of 3s. 6d. each.

THE SUNDERLAND AND SOUTH SHIELDS WATER WORKS.

On the 19th April, 1859, an amended Act of Parliament was obtained entitled "an act to enable the Sund.... Company, to extend their works, and .... and to raise additional capital, and for ....

Its explanatory recitals, are as follo....

That by "The Sunderland and South .... Sunderland and South Shields Water Compa.... rized to supply water within the Boroughs .... certain parishes, townships, and places in th.... spectively, in the County of Durham.

That the Company were authorized and i.... the South Shields Water Company, and s.... accordingly.

That the share capital of the Company as .... to £109,000, whereof £35,000 was distinguis.... 7000 shares of £5 each, £19,500 was distinguis.... preference. Dividends after the rates in suc.... guished as "Extension Capital," and was d.... extension works authorized by such Act.

That in the Act of 1852, provision was ma.... capital and extension capital, when the profits.... amount to £5 per cent. per annum, upon the .....

That that event had taken place, and suc.... cordingly, and such amalgamated capital wa.... Ordinary Capital."

That the Company were by the Act of 1.... or bond the sum of £17,500, and also to borro.... the sum of £10,000 for the purchase of the Sou....

That the whole of the share capital, exce.... 1374 shares of £5 each had been raised, and th.... been borrowed.

That the population of Sunderland and So.... bourhoods had greatly increased, and numerou.... and in order to meet the increased and incre....

required a further supply, and it was expedient that they be authorized to obtain that supply, and to construct additional reservoirs, aqueducts, and other works, and to borrow a further sum of money.

That the Company afforded to the inhabitants a constant supply of water, and it was expedient that more efficient provision should be made for preventing fraud and waste.

That it was expedient to establish a scale of rates in respect of the supply of water to dwelling houses, exceeding the annual value of £50.

And that for the purposes aforesaid it was expedient that the Act of 1852 should be amended.

It then enacts,

That "The Lands' Clauses Consolidation Act, 1845," and "The Water Works' Clauses Act, 1847," (except the 70th section of such last mentioned Act,) be incorporated with the Act.

And that the Act may be cited for all purposes as, "The Sunderland and South Shields Water Works Amendment Act, 1859."

After which come the following clauses, viz.—

3.—The interpretation clause.

4.—Giving powers to make new water works, according to deposited plans, with this proviso, "*provided always*, that the quantity of land to be purchased and taken compulsorily from the Rev. George Townshend Fox, his heirs or assigns, under the powers of this Act, shall not exceed in the whole 4 acres, exclusively of the land required for the road of communication to the works of the Company and the pipe tracks, *and such 4 acres shall be the site* of the intended reservoir and adjoining works, as shewn on the deposited plans, and the lands immediately adjoining the same, within the limits of deviation shewn on the plans.

5.—Power to deviate.

6.—Period for completion of works, 5 years, with this important proviso, " that nothing in this Act contained shall extend or be construed to extend, to restrain the Company from extending their works, mains, and pipes, from time to time whenever it shall be necessary, for the purpose of obtaining a supply of water, for the use of the inhabitants and other persons requiring the same, within the limits of this Act, and for distributing the same."

7 —Power to raise £141,000 by the creation of new shares.

8.—New capital to be divided into shares.

9.—New shares to be considered same as original shares.

10.—New shares to be sold by auction.

11.—Premiums on sales not to be considered as part of the capital entitled to dividend.

12.—Unissued shares may be cancelled.

13.—Rights of new shareholders to be proportionable to the value of new shares.

14.—Power to borrow on mortgage or bond not exceeding £50,000, including the £17,500, authorized to be borrowed on mortgage or bond, under the act of 1852.

15.—Former mortgages and bonds to have priority.

16.—Incorporation of certain provisions of " The Company's Clauses Consolidation Act, 1845."

17.—Monies raised under this act to be applied only to the purposes of act of 1852, and this act.

Considering that the stringent clauses which follow, and to some of which penalties are attached, should be made known to all consumers, I give them in full, under an impression that they will hereby have a better chance of obtaining local publicity, than through the chance medium of the Act itself, which is seen by very few of those who are brought within its operation.

18.—Every person supplied with water by the Company, who shall use a cistern or other receptacle for the water with which he shall be supplied, shall furnish the same with an efficient ball cock, or other like apparatus ; and the Surveyor or any other person acting under the authority of the Company, may, between the hours of 10 of the clock in the forenoon, and 4 of the clock in the afternoon, *enter into any house in order to examine if there be any waste, misuse, or undue consumption of water*, by means of any over-flow spout, waste pipe, or other means of contrivance; and in case any such waste, misuse, or undue consumption of water, shall be found to exist from the use of any such over-flow spout, waste pipe, or other means, or contrivance ; it shall be lawful for such Surveyor or other person to give not less than 3 days' notice in writing to the person so supplied with water, to alter, repair, and amend, or in default thereof, to remove such over-flow spout, waste pipe, or other means, or contrivance, and if the same shall not be forthwith altered, repaired, and amended, or removed, in accordance with such notice, it shall be lawful for the Company after 3 days' notice in writing, *to turn off the water from the house, and to cease to supply the same with water* until such over-flow spout, waste pipe, or other means, or contrivance, shall be sufficiently repaired, altered, or amended.

19.—Subject to the provisions of this Act and the incorporated Acts, it shall be lawful for the Company or the Directors thereof from time to time, to make such reasonable regulations as shall be necessary or expedient for the purpose of preventing the waste or misuse of water, and amongst other things to prescribe the nature, strength, size, and position of the pipes, cocks, and other apparatus to be used, and to interdict the use of any pipes, cocks, and other apparatus which may tend to such waste or misuse as aforesaid, and in the event of such regulations, or any of them not being observed by any person about to become a customer of the Company, or being a customer of the Company, the Company may refuse to supply water, or cut off the water supplied by them to such person or customer, as the case may be, until such regulations shall have been complied with, and in the event of any dispute as to whether such regulations are reasonable, or whether such regulations have been complied with by any person whose water shall have been so cut off as aforesaid, such dispute shall be settled by two Justices in manner provided by "The Railway Clauses Consolidation Act, 1815," with respect to the recovery of damages not specially provided for, and of penalties, and to the determination of any other matter referred to Justices; *provided*, that except in cases of accident, emergency, or necessary repairs, the Company shall not under this provision, cut off the water supplied to a now existing customer of the Company, unless he shall have had 5 days' notice in writing of their intention so to do, from the Secretary or other officer of the Company : *provided also*, that nothing hereinbefore contained shall alter or affect the obligations imposed upon the Company by the Water Works Clauses Act, 1847, to supply water to and within any house, nor shall any such regulations as aforesaid made by the Company, extend to prevent persons entitled to a supply of water, from placing water taps over sinks in the interior of their houses.

20.—Every person supplied with water by the Company, who shall wilfully suffer any pipe, cock, cistern, or other apparatus to be out of repair. so that the water supplied to him by the Company shall be wasted, shall forfeit to the Company for every such offence a sum not exceeding £5.

21.—The Company may in any such case require such person, by 3 days' notice in writing under the hand of a duly authorized officer of the Company, to repair any such pipe, cock, cistern, or other apparatus, so as to prevent any such waste of water, and in case of default so to do, within the said 3 days, the Company may repair the same ; and in such case the expenses of such repair shall be repaid to them by the person so allowing the same to be out of repair, and may be recovered as damages.

22.—Every person who, being supplied with water, or having agreed for a supply of water by the Company for domestic purposes, shall take or use any water for any purpose not included in the term "domestic purposes," as defined by the Act of 1852, and every person who, being supplied with water, or having agreed for a supply of water for trade or other purposes, other than domestic purposes, shall take or use the water for domestic purposes ; and every person who shall in any other manner, fraudulently take or use water so as to deprive the Company of the rates or payments to which they are entitled, shall forfeit to the Company, for every such offence, a sum not exceeding £10.

23.—When the rack-rent or annual value of a private dwelling house, supplied with water by the Company, for the domestic uses of the occupier shall exceed £50, the Company may demand, receive, and recover in respect of such supply, a rate per annum not exceeding £3 per centum on the rack-rent or annual value of the premises, any thing in the Act of 1852 to the contrary notwithstanding: *provided always*, that this provision shall not extend to any occupier of any such premises, who, on or before the 1st day of December, 1860, has agreed to be, or is supplied with water by the Company ; but such occupier during his occupancy, shall continue to be supplied with water by the Company for domestic purposes, at the rate prescribed by the Act of 1852.

The Sunderland and South Shields Water Company is one of the most successful of provincial companies, as must be admitted by all who trace it from its origin, have observed its progress, and notice its present advanced and prosperous condition. It originated in "The Sunderland Water Company," which was formed by "The Sunderland Water Works Act, 1846," as the same was afterwards amended by "The Sunderland Water Works Amendment Act, 1849." In 1852, it being considered for the public benefit, that the powers of the Company should be extended for the supplying the inhabitants of the town of South Shields and its Neighbourhood with water, and that the Company should be empowered to extend and enlarge their existing works, and to construct new reservoirs and aqueducts, and to obtain a further supply of water, and to increase the capital of the Company, "The Sunderland and South Shields Water Works Act, 1852," under the title of "an Act for better supplying with water the Boroughs of Sunderland and South Shields, and other places in the County of Durham," was obtained; and this was followed in 1859 by "The Sunderland and South Shields Water Works Amendment Act, 1859," being the Act from which full and copious extracts have already been given by me.

The three pumping stations of the Company are at Humbleton Hill, on the Durham Road, and Fulwell, and Cleadon, on the Sunderland and South Shields Road, and from them during the past year the enormous quantity of eleven hundred million gallons have been supplied.

New works are also in progress at Ryhope, on the road from Sunderland to Seaham, and a shaft for a further supply of water, in obedience to the still growing wants of the district, is now being sunk through the limestone at that place.

During the past year, 16271 yards of mains, and 1070 new services have been laid, and the income of the Company has now reached £22,919 17s. 10d., being an astonishing advance upon the humble £1600 revenue of the old Company, which can only have been accomplished through the discreet judgment, and enlightened management of the Directors, who may justly take credit for the sound state of still advancing prosperity, into which, assisted by the zealous aid of their efficient officials, they have succeeded in bringing these wonderful works of which all may feel proud.

Simultaneously with the increase of the *revenue*, was that of the *dividends* derived by the Shareholders, for creeping at first from something very small to 6 per cent., they steadly advanced from time to time to 6½, 7, 7½, 8, 8½, 8¾, 9, and 9½ per cent., the latter being the dividend paid to Shareholders for the year ended the 31st December, 1865.

After this it will not excite surprise when it becomes known, that the 850 tenants of the old Company, have now risen to the 40,000 customers of the new one, which are to be found in the wide spread stirring and thriving districts of Sunderland, Bishopwearmouth, Monkwearmouth, South Shields, Westoe, East Jarrow, Jarrow, and Hebburn, with the intermediate and adjacent villages and manufactories.

The *premiums* received from the sale last year of 1300 new shares, created under the authority of the act, amounted to £5670 7s. 2d., the whole of which in terms of the act was applied in reduction of the cost of works, which amounted for the year to £9465 1s. 2d., thus leaving £3794 14s. 0d. only, to be provided for by other means.

The old works at Sunderland and South Shields, have also been virtually paid for to the extent of £29,500, with the premiums derived from the sale of shares.

On the 22nd of February, 1866, 1000 five pound shares in the Company, were sold by auction under the authority of the Act, at prices averaging £9 6s. 7½d. per share, than which there could be no greater proof of the high estimation in which the undertaking is held by the public, as a safe and profitable investment.

Well may the Shareholders and their customers exclaim with Coleridge's "Ancient Mariner," though under circumstances widely different from those in which he was unhappily placed,

"Water, water, everywhere;"

but they cannot follow him when he thus despondingly concludes,

"Nor any drop to drink;"

for I have unanswerably shewn that in all the districts of this first rate Company, there is not only "water, water, everywhere," but many "a drop to drink," and that of the purest and most wholesome quality.

I acted on the part of South Shields as a joint Solicitor with Messrs. A. J. and W. Moore, in obtaining the Act of 1852, and it is one of the important public proceedings of my life, upon which I reflect with pride and satisfaction, as being connected with consequences most conducive to the comforts, the conveniences, and the health of my native town and its neighbourhood. South Shields might perhaps in part have monopolized the undertaking between the Tyne and the Wear, without a joint action with Sunderland, and by means of a shaft at Cleadon Hills, have obtained a sufficient supply of water on its own account for South Shields, Westoe, East Jarrow, Jarrow, and Hebburn, but the

joinder of South Shields and Sunderland, united the fresh water interests of both, and the peaceful, prosperous condition of the undertaking, " past and present," may be looked upon with confidence, as
a satisfactory proof of the wisdom and prudence of the course, which
was deliberately and successfully pursued by the far sighted promoters
of the measure of 1852, following as they did the wise advice of Solomon
in one of his well known proverbs,

"Let thy fountains be dispersed *abroad*, and rivers of waters in the streets,"

but rejecting it when at variance, as thus, with their own extended and
more liberal views,

"Drink waters out of thine *own* cistern, and running waters out of thine *own*
well."

THE TYNE FERRIES.

On the 30th June, 1862, the population of Newcastle-upon-Tyne,
Gateshead, South and North Shields, and other places adjacent or near
to the River Tyne, and the trade and commerce of the ports of
Newcastle-upon-Tyne and Shields, within that river having greatly
increased, and there being large manufactories and works established
on both banks thereof, and docks made on the North and South
sides of it, and the means of conveying traffic on, along, and across
the river then provided being insufficient, additional means were much
needed as a local and public advantage, and consequently an Act under
the title of " an Act for incorporating the Tyne General Ferry Company,
and for authorizing them to establish, make, and maintain ferries on,
along, and across the River Tyne, and landing places and other works ;
and for other purposes" was passed.

The following recitals were contained therein, viz. :

The Ferry Acts of the 1st June, 1829, and 30th June, 1848, for
which see my Lecture of 1856.

The purchase by the North and South Shields Ferry Company, of
the undertaking of the Tyne Direct Ferry Company, and the amalgamation of that Company with the North and South Shields Ferry
Company.

That the provisions of the first of those Acts restricting the establishment of ferries or passages across the River Tyne, promoted the
establishment of those means of communication across the river,
which the increasing population of the districts on its banks, and the
trade of the ports required, and it was expedient that those provisions
should be modified.

That by " The Tyne Improvement Act, 1861," the Tyne Improvement Commissioners were authorized (section 62) to provide or licence the making of public landing places on the River Tyne, and (section 63) to purchase and maintain any ferries established in and over the river.

That certain persons were willing at their own expense, to carry the undertaking into effect, on being incorporated as a Company for the purpose, it being expedient that they should be incorporated accordingly, and authorized to carry passengers, animals, and things, from any one landing place on the River Tyne, to any other landing place thereon.

That for the better attainment of those objects, it was expedient that arrangements should be made by the Company, so to be incorporated on the one hand, and the Tyne Improvement Commissioners, and other persons interested in ferries across the River Tyne, or having landing places on the river, should be authorized.

And that those objects could not be attained without the authority of Parliament.

It was therefore enacted (amongst other things) as follows :

This Act may for all purposes be cited as " The Tyne General Ferry Act," 1862.

The limits of this Act comprises the River Tyne, and all other places which under the Tyne Improvement Acts of 1850, 1852, 1857, 1859, and 1861 respectively, are from time to time within the jurisdiction of the Tyne Improvement Commissioners.

George Crawshay, Edmond Crawshay, John Rogerson, John Sharp, and William Scott, and all other persons who have already subscribed, or shall hereafter subscribe to the undertaking, or take shares of the capital of the Company, and their executors, and administrators, successors, and assigns respectively, are by this Act united into a Company, for the purpose of providing and using steam vessels for the conveyance of passengers, animals, and things on, along, and across the River Tyne, and between any landing places on the river, and of acquiring and maintaining ferries across the river, and landing places on the river, and other works, and of carrying this Act in other respects into execution, and for those purposes are by this Act incorporated by the name of " The Tyne General Ferry Company," and by that name shall be one body corporate with perpetual succession and a common seal, and with power to purchase, take, hold, sell, and dispose of lands, and other property, for the purposes, but subject to the restrictions of this Act.

The capital of the Company shall be £70,000, in 7000 shares of £10 each.

Section 85 of the first recited Act, (1st June, 1829,) restricting the user of ferries across the River Tyne, and imposing a penalty for ferrying across the river, shall not apply to any case in which the ferrying across the river, within the limits of the Parish of Tynemouth, and the Townships of South Shields and Westoe, takes place *in the course of a voyage or trip, commencing or ending at any place beyond those limits.*

The following clause (20) then occurs.

And whereas the Tyne Improvement Commissioners, are desirous that such provisions in this Act contained, should be made for the benefit of the public, with regard to the modification of the restrictions imposed by the 85th section of the first recited Act, (1st June, 1829,) and are willing to purchase the rights, powers, and undertaking of the North and South Shields Ferry Company, under the powers conferred upon them by the Tyne Improvement Act, 1861, and it is expedient that such provisions should be made with reference thereto, as in this Act expressed ; therefore it shall be lawful for the Tyne Improvement Commissioners, and they are hereby required, to purchase, and for the North and South Shields Ferry Company, with the consent of three-fifths of the votes of Shareholders, of that Company present, at a meeting specially convened for the purpose, to sell the undertaking, rights, and powers of the North and South Shields Ferry Company.

Provisions being then made in case of dispute, as to the amount of purchase, the clause ending as follows,

And all rights, powers, and liabilities of the North and South Shields Ferry Company shall, upon such purchase, be transferred to and exercised by the Tyne Improvement Commissioners, except so far as the same are altered by this Act; and the provisions hereinbefore contained, respecting the restrictions imposed by the first recited Act, shall not come into operation until the expiration of three months after the passing of this Act.

In addition to which it is provided by the Act,

That upon the completion of the sale and transfer by the said North and South Shields Ferry Company, of the whole of their undertaking in manner aforesaid, *such Company shall cease and determine.*

That the Tyne General Ferry Company, from time to time, if they think fit, with the consent of the Tyne Improvement Commissioners, but only by agreement, may take on loan, purchase, or otherwise acquire, any rights of ferry, on or across the River Tyne, subject to such conditions as may be from time to time prescribed by those Commissioners.

That the said Company may hire, purchase, or otherwise provide, maintain, repair, work, manage, regulate, and use steam and other vessels, and may work, and use the same for the conveyance of, and may, subject to the provisions of this Act, convey passengers, animals, and things on, along, and across the River Tyne, between any landing place *on one side* of the river, and any landing place *on the other side* of the river, and also between any landing place *on any part* of the river, and any landing place *on any other part* of the river.

That the said Company may, with the consent of the Tyne Improvement Commissioners, and subject to such conditions as they shall from time to time prescribe, and during the pleasure of the Commissioners, *but only by agreement,* take on loan, purchase, or otherwise acquire, and may maintain, repair, and use all or any of the now existing landing places on the River Tyne, at Quay Side, Newcastle-upon-Tyne, Mushroom, Felling, Saint Anthony's, Walker, Howdon, Hebburn, Jarrow, South Shields, North Shields, New Quay, and Prior's Haven, Tynemouth, now used by the Red Star Line of Packets Company, or any of them, and the works and conveniences connected therewith.

That the said Company may with the consent of the Tyne Improvement Commissioners, and subject as aforesaid, *but only by agreement,* take on lease, purchase, and otherwise require, and may provide, maintain, repair, and use, *any other* landing places, jetties, stairs, quays, approaches, and other works, lands, and buildings on the River Tyne, or the banks or shores thereof, or adjoining or near thereto, in the counties of Northumberland and Durham, and the town and county of the town of Newcastle-upon-Tyne respectively.

That for the purposes of the steam vessels provided, worked, and used by the Company, they, with the previous consent of the Tyne Improvement Commissioners, may provide, lay down, manage, and use in the River Tyne, and on the banks or shores thereof, and on, and at the Company's landing places, proper and sufficient mooring posts, moorings, rings, and other apparatus and conveniences, for the safe and convenient mooring of the steam vessels.

That the said Company shall (at their own costs and charges and without compensation,) on being requested by the said Commissioners, set back or extend, or elongate, all or any of the gears, stages, platforms, or other erections which may hereafter be fixed or set up, in or upon the shores or bed of the said River Tyne, under the authority of this Act, to such point or line in the said river, as shall be fixed by the said Commissioners, or the Company shall, if so required, altogether remove any such gears, stages, platforms, or other erections, and in case the Company fail to comply with such request, the Commissioners may execute the works required by such request, and the expense thereof shall be repaid by the Company to the Commissioners.

That the Tyne Improvement Commissioners, may contribute on such terms, and subject to such conditions as may be mutually agreed upon, to the undertaking of the Company, by making, improving, maintaining, or repairing any landing places on the River Tyne, or any works or conveniences thereat, to be respectively used by the Company, or providing or improving, by means of dredging, access to any landing places on the river to be used by them, or providing, or laying down any moorings to be used by them, or by making, providing, or executing any other works or conveniences in or upon, or in connection with the river, or the bed, or shores, or banks thereof, within the limits of the jurisdiction of the Commissioners, and the Tyne Improvement Commissioners may apply the Tyne Improvement Fund, and any monies authorized to be raised or borrowed on security thereof, for or towards any of the purposes or things by this Act authorized to be undertaken or done by the Commissioners.

Then follow clauses providing for the deposit of working drawings with the Admiralty; the exemption of certain vessels, &c.; local survey by order of the Admiralty; the removal by the Admiralty of works abandoned or fallen into disuse or decay.

After which come clauses, by which

The Company may demand and take for the conveyance in their steam vessels of passengers, animals, and things on, along, and across the River Tyne, such ferry tolls as the Company from time to time appoint, not exceeding the ferry tolls specified *in the schedule to the Act annexed.*

The Company may demand and take for the user of their landing places, and of any sheds or buildings, lifts, drops, cranes, weighing machines, and other conveniences provided by them thereat, such reasonable landing place tolls, as the Company, from time to time appoint.

The ferry tolls and the landing place tolls respectively, shall, at all times, be charged equally to all persons using, under like circumstances, the Company's steam vessels, and their landing places, and the works and conveniences thereat, but where a ferry toll shall be charged, no landing place toll shall be charged.

Whenever the Company work any steam vessel on, along, or across the River Tyne, all persons shall, on payment of the tolls, be entitled to use for the passage on, along, or across the river, such steam vessel, and the landing places provided by the Company for the purpose of the passage, and the Company's works and conveniences connected therewith.

Every passenger conveyed by the Company, may take with him his ordinary luggage, not exceeding 28 lbs. in weight, without any charge being made for the carriage thereof.

Provision is then made for the recovery of tolls, exemptions of certain persons from payment thereof; the setting up of lists of tolls on landing places and steam vessels; penalties for non payment of tolls; power to stop any person refusing to pay tolls; and penalties on toll collectors.

The Company are then authorized to let from time to time, by lease to take effect in possession, the ferry tolls and the landing place tolls, or any of them, to any person for any term not exceeding 3 years, such lessee to be entitled to demand and take the tolls, and have the like powers for recovering and enforcing payment thereof, as are by the Act granted to or vested in the Company.

And to compound and agree with any person using the steam vessels or landing places, for the payment of any sum, either monthly, quarterly, or yearly, instead of the ferry tolls or landing place tolls, or both.

A saving clause then follows for South Shields, in the following words.

"Except as by this Act expressly provided, nothing in this Act shall take away, lessen, alter, or prejudice any of the estates, lands, property, and effects of the Mayor, Aldermen, and Burgesses of the Borough of South Shields, or any of the tolls, rates, dues, duties, payments, issues, profits, or other income whatsoever, of or payable to them or any of their powers, authorities, rights, privileges, emoluments, or advantages, or shall amend, interpret, or alter, "The South Shields Improvement Act, 1853," and "The South Shields Improvement Amendment Act, 1861," or either of them, or any of the powers or authorities thereof."

And saving clauses are also introduced for the Tyne Improvement Commissioners; the Mayor, Aldermen, and Burgesses of Newcastle-upon-Tyne; the Crown; and the Duke of Northumberland.

Ending with the *schedule of tolls* referred to by the Act.

Having thus completed these useful, but tedious extracts from the "Tyne General Ferry Act, 1862," I may say that I have made them more copious than I would otherwise have done, if I had not been induced by the importance of the subject, to give the Act and its provisions a chance of being more generally known through the medium of this publication, to passengers going and coming by the steam vessels of the Tyne General Ferry Company, and the South and North Shields Ferry Boats, than they might have been if left to an uncertain sight of the Act of Parliament itself.

The Tyne Improvement Commissioners purchased and had conveyed to them, under the powers conferred upon them by the Tyne Improvement Act, 1861, the rights, powers, and undertaking of the North and South Shields Ferry Company, and such Company *then ceased and determined.*

The ferries across the Tyne at Shields, with embarking and landing places respectively, at the Market Place and Comical Corner, South Shields, West End of the New Quay, North Shields; and at Whitehill Point, in the Borough of Tynemouth; and Penny Pie Stairs, South Shields; remain in the possession, under the entire management, and control, and for the profit and advantage of the Tyne Improvement Commissioners.

All the other rights of ferry on the Tyne, are now by mutual arrangement and agreement with the Tyne Improvement Commissioners, exercised by the General Ferry Company, under the provisions of the Tyne General Ferry Act, 1862, in a manner which affords every accommodation, and gives satisfaction to the public. They have an efficient fleet of 20 swift and commodious steam vessels well adapted for the traffic, and their stations on the Tyne for embarkation and landing are at Newcastle Quay, Mushroom, High and Low Felling, St. Anthony's, High and Low Walker, Hebburn Quay, Hebburn, Howdon, Jarrow, Tyne Dock, Mill Dam, (South Shields,) East End of New Quay, and Low Lights, (North Shields,) and Tynemouth; and they work the direct ferries also between Jarrow and Howdon, and between Hebburn and Low Walker.

THE MASTER MARINERS' ASYLUM AND ANNUITY SOCIETY

Is an enrolled society with an unlimited number of members, and its object is to provide a fund for paying annuities to aged, infirm, and poor *master mariners,* their widows, and orphans, and to build asylums for their occupation, subject to certain conditions and restrictions contained in its rules, and agreeably to the several Acts of

Parliament for the benefit of Friendly Societies, and I brought it under notice in 1856, in connection with the name of Dr. Winterbottom.

By those rules, from which it is necessary to give some extracts, for general purposes, a donor of 10 guineas becomes an honorary member for 10 years; of £21 and upwards, for life; and an annual subscriber of one guinea, becomes an honorary member so long as the subscription is continued, is admissable at any age, but does not receive any benefit from the funds of the society.

The society is open to receive as its members all *master mariners* under the age of 40 years, but no member can receive any benefit until he has been a member for 7 years, unless from peculiar circumstances to be determined at a general meeting. Having been a member for 7 years, he becomes a *free member*, and as such entitled to all benefits. Whenever a member dies before becoming a free member, the amount of his contributions, without interest, is to be returned to his widow or children, if demanded.

The duties of the society are conducted by a Patron, two Vice-Patrons, five Trustees, a Treasurer and Secretary, and a Committee of twenty-one members.

The meetings are specially fixed by the rules.

The members are divided into three classes, and pay into the funds the following yearly subscriptions, viz. :—

1st. Class.—Consisting of persons under thirty years of age at the time of entering, to pay 30s. a year.

2nd Class.—Consisting of persons from thirty to thirty-five years of age, 35s. a year.

3rd Class.—Consisting of persons from thirty-five to forty years of age, 50s. a year.

Any member in arrear for one year, is to be placed on the subscription list for six months, and if within that period his arrears and fines are not paid up, he is to be expelled.

Any member through old age, sickness, or other cause, becoming unable to follow his employment, is eligible to be placed on the books as an *annuitant* or an *inmate of the asylum*, and receive such annual sum as the society shall, at the general meeting preceding such member becoming eligible, have fixed for the current year; but no free member or annuitant possessing an annual sum of £60 from any source, is eligible to receive any benefit from the society; and any member who is an inmate of the asylum, becoming possessed of that income, is immediately to yield up the possession of such cottage or tenement as he may then occupy.

On the death of a free member, his widow is eligible to be placed on the books as an annuitant, or as an inmate of the asylum, and to receive such annual sum during her widowhood as the society shall then be paying.

No widow of any member who shall have married such member

while an annuitant of the society, is to be entitled to any benefit therefrom, unless she happened, previous to her so contracting marriage with such annuitant, to be an annuitant herself, in which case during the life of her husband, her annuity is to be reduced to one half; but in case she survives her husband, she immediately becomes entitled to the full annuity; with this proviso always, that no widow is to receive any benefit from the society who possesses an income of £40 per annum.

On the death of a free member, his sons and daughters, being orphans, are eligible, or such of them as have not obtained the age of 12 and 14 years respectively, to be placed on the books as annuitants, until the boys obtain the age of 12 years, and the girls the age of 14 years respectively; and they are to be paid such annual sums as the society shall see fit, to be applied for their benefit, according to the discretion of the Committee, who also have power, if they think expedient,.altogether to withdraw the same for reasons to be stated at the general meeting of the society.

Any member having been a contributor to the funds of the society for 10 years, may withdraw therefrom on giving notice to the Secretary, and thereafter such member becomes exonerated from all payments, and ceases to be entitled to any benefit.

All the unappropriated monies forming the stock of the society, are to be invested from time to time, either with the Commissioners for the reduction of the national debt, or in real or other approved securities in England, (pursuant to 10 Geo. 4, c. 56, s. 13.)

The society had its origin at a meeting of ship masters, held at South Shields, on the 28th of January, 1839, and without entering upon the history of its growth, and present position, it is sufficient now to state, that commencing then with the very liberal donations of private individuals, it can now boast of a funded and realized capital of £8973 0s. 9d., consisting of twenty-one cottages of freehold tenure, on the North side of the road leading from South Shields to Bent House, the estimated value of which is £3011 3s. 6d., and seventeen cottages of the same tenure, on the South side of that road, the estimated value of which is £4661 9s. 9d., money invested with the National Debt Commissioners, and other monies, as particularly set forth in the published annual statement of the Committee for the past year. To the characteristic generosity of the late Dr. Winterbottom, the society is altogether indebted for the twenty-one North cottages first erected,

"His ninetieth year was passed, and then was seen
A building rising on the Northern green,
A doctor's gift, who without children died,
When he to generous gifts his wealth applied."

The 17 South cottages having since been built out of the accumulations arising from the rents of the others, interest, annual subscriptions of contributing members, and donations.

There are now forty-four annuitants on the books, viz. : eleven males, and thirty-three females, and the payments to them for the year 1865 amounted to £354. Only £115 7s. 6d. were received from contributing or benefit members, the absence of others being evidence of a want of that thoughtful appreciation of the benefits of the society, on the part of those for whom it was so considerately formed, and by whom it ought to be freely supported. The annuitants increase and the members decrease, shewing that there is something "rotten in the state of Denmark."

The rents received from the North and South cottages, amounted last year to £483 17s. 6d., and they are all let and likely to continue so.

According to the abstract of the Treasurer's account for 1865, the total amount of receipts from all sources was £688 9s. 9d., and of expenditure £562 15s. 2d., leaving a balance in favor of the society of £125 14s. 7d.

In addition to the twenty-one cottages so built for the society at the entire cost of Dr. Winterbottom, the library and washhouse buildings were likewise his liberal and voluntary gifts. The keeping in order of the grounds in front of the North cottages, was also considerately provided for by the good old man, through an investment of £100 in Trustees for the purpose ; and the periodical painting of the North cottages is secured by means of his investment for that special purpose of £303 17s. 4d., in the three per cent. consols. A telescope, night glass, thermometer, map of the world, and books, were also judiciously placed by him in the library, for the use of its frequenters, commanding as it does a wide spread view of the German Ocean.

For all which generous acts and also others, of such extent as never before were bestowed upon the town by any citizen of it, had South Shields to thank its largeh-earted benefactor, Thomas Masterman Winterbottom, of whom it may with truth be sung,

> "A two fold taste he had ; to *give* and *spare*,
> Both were his duties, and had equal care."

With this concluding expression of our fervent praise,

> "May after ages long repeat his praise,
> And fame's fair meed be his, for many days."

Mr. George Daglish Robson has been for many years the Secretary of the society, and the well drawn annual reports, with their accompanying statements of clearly explained receipts, expenditure, and realized capital, are of a nature to entitle him to well merited praise. Oft has he thereby urged upon master mariners in encouraging language and with forcible arguments, the claims of the society for their support and the benefits which they and theirs would derive by the prudent bestowal of it, but all alas ! in vain, the outlay for the hopeful "present" when in youth, strength, and full employment, appearing from the paucity of contributing members to have more deterring weight and influence than a forethought of "future" advantages, to be derived from membership, in the distant time of failing strength, increasing age, and diminished means. This should be "reformed altogether" in future, as Hamlet said to the players, not only for selfish motives connected with themselves, but disinterestedly for the sake of him who having poured down his benefits upon them, is entitled to such grateful appreciation as can only be expressed by that support of the institution, which they, and they only as master mariners, can legally give. Active, and perhaps extraordinary means would likewise seem needful, to awaken the society from that torpid state of dreamy inactivity, into which it is considered to have fallen, and those seafaring men who can become members in terms of the rules, should pointedly be reminded of the special advantages afforded by a society of this peculiar description, with a productive capital of such realized amount as that which I have named.

SALMON FISHERIES.

In an able, but too flattering review of my work of 1856, by a popular townsman of mine, he noticed amongst some few omissions the great abundance formerly, and trade of Shields in salmon. Since then

> "Another term is past; ten other years,
> In various trials, troubles, views, and fears."

And I now prove by my recollection of his suggestion, even at this distance of time, and by my present attention to it, how greatly I still value his favorable notice of my work.

The Tyne was indeed once famous for this the king of British river fish, and Shields partook of the benefits which were derived from its abundance, cheapness, and capture, for on the 20th March, 1765, 149 large salmon were taken at one draught near the bar at South Shields; and on the 9th of June, 1775, 265 salmon were caught by one draught, at the Low Lights, North Shields; I myself having frequently witnessed when young the abundant success of the fishermen at the fishery for salmon, on the edge next the river of the Herd Sand, at South Shields.

The take of salmon in other parts of the Tyne, away from South Shields, was sometimes also amazing, as proved by the following extracts from Sykes' Local Records.

1755, June 12th, upwards of 2400 salmon were taken above bridge in the River Tyne, and sold in Newcastle at one penny and a penny farthing per pound.

1758, July 20th, upwards of 2000 salmon were taken in the Tyne, and being brought to Newcastle Market, were sold at one penny three farthings per pound.

1760, May 29th, a remarkably large salmon was taken in the River Tyne, and sold in Newcastle Market for eleven shillings; it weighed 54 lbs.; was 4 ft. 4 in. long; and 33 in. round.

1761, Aug. 6th, 260 salmon were taken in the Tyne at Newburn, near Newcastle, at a draught.

1764, May 14th, many large salmon were taken in the Tyne at Newburn; one in particular which measured 5½ feet in length, was 28 inches round, and weighed 54 lbs.

1764, July 20th, such a great quantity of salmon was taken in the Tyne, that it was sold for one penny farthing per lb.

1771, July 15th, upwards of 4000 salmon were exposed for sale in Newcastle fish market, which sold for about one penny farthing per lb. 107 salmon were caught that morning at one fishery above Tyne Bridge.

1825, October 12th, a pair of spectacles in steel case was taken out of the maw of a salmon, in the fish market Newcastle.

1833, June 13th, a prodigious and almost unprecedented take of salmon occurred in the Tyne. Nearly 500 were exhibited for sale in Newcastle fish market, and sold readily at about sixpence per lb.

A comparison of this the plentiful "past," with the meager "present" of the salmon fisheries on the Tyne, at South Shields and elsewhere, is melancholy and disheartening, for owing to the deepening of the channel of the river, by the necessary dredging operations of the Tyne Improvement Commissioners, the fishery at South Shields has been injured, while the decrease in the number of salmon caught at New-burn and the other fisheries of the Tyne, can safely be attributed in a great degree, to such defilement of the river by human agency, "that the fastidious salmon will not suffer itself to be poisoned by the hateful mixture of evil odours and polluted waters," and therefore does not venture now to ascend the stream in such multitudes as in former years, when the river was sufficiently pure to encourage their entrance into and ascent up it, for breeding purposes, for "the salmon" says Izaak Walton, "is the king of fresh water fish," and he adds quaintly, "he has like some persons of honor and riches, which have both their winter and summer residences, the fresh rivers for summer, and the salt water for winter to spend his life in."

The murderous array of nets, weirs, and all kinds of salmon traps, was also another operating cause of the decrease in the numbers of that noble fish, but it is to be hoped that the legislative interference of recent years, and the consequent prevention of the justly termed "infernal machines," to which I have alluded, will prevent that extirpation of the salmon, which would otherwise have taken place, and give the fish a fair chance of re-establishing itself in part, if not wholly, in something approaching to its former plenty.

The increasing scarcity and consequent high price of salmon, has not only caused the legislative measures and proceedings thereon to which I have referred, but has directed public attention during the last few years to artificial means for the increase of the fish, which has been practised with considerable success on the Continent, as well as in some parts of our own country. Whether the Tyne as a salmon river, has participated in this I have not the means of stating, but it is satisfactory to know that the importance of the subject has been recognized, and that the production of cheap food, by the artificial propagation not only of the salmon, but of other kinds of fish, has been entertained and found practicable.

At the same time it cannot be lost sight of by calculating people, as a sure cause of diminished production in fish, as well as in other animals, and therefore of that decreased supply for the wants of man, which is now complained of, the enormous reduction in the sources from which that supply is obtained, arising from the capture and consumption as human food for our continually increasing population, of so many of the parent fish. As it always has been with the goose and the egg, so it as certainty is with the fish and its roe, the loss of the future egg and gosling in the one case, and of the future roe and fish in the other, being the inevitable consequence of the destruction of the producing power, and that to an extent in the cases of fish and their offspring, which cannot be disputed, when we consider the multitudes of young which are involved in the life and safety even of a single parent fish. As 100 fish will of course produce more roe than 50, so with equal certainty, will our supply of fish be proportionately lessened by the annihilation of 50 for human food, an arithmetical fact so self-evident, that Cocker himself could not have denied it, even when applied to so common, and so prolific an animal as a fish.

The facility of communication between our coasts and the populous interior of the country, by means of railways and their wide spread ramifications in every direction, must however not be lost sight of as an important auxiliary in that increased destruction and consumption of fish as food, to which I have ventured to attribute its growing scarcity; and thus even have the occupants of the deep been affected by that revolution which has happily banished from our roads, the slow stage coaches and carriers' carts of our younger days, and replaced them by that brilliant railway system under which cheap, rapid, and unlimited accomodation has been provided for the trade and traffic of the country, and an interchange of commodities, fishy, fleshy, and otherwise, secured, which has proved so beneficial to the inhabitants, and is now so essentially necessary for their supply and accommodation.

"WEEL MAY THE KEEL ROW"

Is still the popular tune which accompanies that "success to the coal

trade," which is usually toasted and sung on our public festive
occasions, but it is now alas! a mere "lucus a non lucendo," for
though by the coal trade the district of the Tyne is still enlivened and
enriched, there is now no keel to row, and no blue bonneted keelmen
with dimples in their chins, to win the hearts of those Sandgate beauties,
who watched with eager eyes in bye gone days, the black and accustomed
craft in which their lads were known to be.

> " Weel may the keel row, the keel row, the keel row,
> Weel may the keel row, that my lad is in,
> He wears a blue bonnet, a blue bonnet, a blue bonnet,
> He wears a blue bonnet, and a dimple in his chin."

In explanation of which local revolution in the coal carrying trade
of the Tyne as a river, it is unnecessary for me to travel out of the
record, by entering into any extraneous particulars of the coal itself,
its formation, extent, or probable duration, it being sufficient for my
present purpose to state, that before the introduction of steam ships,
and public railways, the trade in coal from the Tyne, was through the
medium of sailing vessels alone, into which the coals were conveyed
either by staiths at the terminus next the river, of the private railway
attached to each colliery ; or by keels which conveyed them from the
staiths to the ships in Shields Harbour. These keels were sharp at
both ends, carried eight chaldrons of coal, sailed fast, and were
efficiently manned by three men and a boy, by whom, whether under
sail, or propelled laboriously by oars or puys, they were dexterously
navigated and managed. Vast numbers of keelmen were well employed
in this industrious manner, both on the Tyne and Wear, and riots were
not unfrequent, arising chiefly from a jealous dislike of the staiths, and
a well founded dread of future evil to arise therefrom, to them and
their employment as keelmen ; they having had the same " auld warld"
feelings and notions, I suspect which found such humorous and sar-
castic expression in that immortal "Clishmaclaver" between the "Brigs
of Ayr," which was the happy production of Scotland's Ayrshire
Ploughman, Robert Burns,

> " A' ye douce folk I've borne aboon the broo,
> Were ye but here, what would ye say or do ?
> How would your spirits groan in deep vexation,
> To see each melancholy *alteration !*

The " auld brig" itself being answerable for the contemptuous opinion
given of the *authors* of those *alterations*, in its colloquy with the " new"
one,

> "Men three parts made by tailors and by barbers,
> Wha waste your woel kaind gear on brigs and harbours."

By the creation of public docks on both sides of the Tyne at South
Shields and Howdon, with railways connected therewith, for the loading
and unloading of ships, without the intervention of keels ; and by the
use of powerful steam colliers of large tonnage, for the rapid and

regular conveyance by sea of coal, in preference to the slow sailing colliers, (which by the bye are gradually dying out,) the keels and their crews were no longer wanted, and have therefore succumbed and been ousted from the trade, the appearance of a solitary coal keel on the Tyne, being now a " rare avis" indeed, black but not " similima cygno," painfully reminding us when it does occur, of those fleets of keels and their stalwart crews, with which in former days the coaly Tyne was plentifully dotted from Blaydon to Shields, their absence being proof of another of those progressive revolutions in which steam, all powerful steam, has been the conquering agent.

THE RAILWAYS.

South Shields would be an exceptional instance if it were not, as a large sea port town, connected by means of direct railways, and their various ramifications with most parts of England and Scotland. It has three stations within the Borough, one intended for the centre and Eastern parts, another for the Western portion, and a third specially for and near Tyne Docks and the neighbouring District, and the traffic in passengers, goods, and minerals is amazingly extensive. The Brandling Junction Railway was the commencement of the system here, and the North Eastern Railway Company are now the local colossus, if not of *Rhodes,* most certainly of rail-*ways* at South Shields. Their truly magnificent Tyne Docks, happily within our Borough and for which we have such cause for thankfulness, have already been described by me, and I have nothing further to add respecting them. Wonderful, most wonderful indeed is the revolution which steam and rails have effected, not only here but throughout the world, and sound was the advice to the nations, since in some respects most wisely followed, which the poet thus by verse conveyed.

"Lay down your *rails,* ye nations near and far,
Yoke your full *trains* to *steams* triumphal *car* ;
Link town to town, unite in *iron bands,*
The long estranged and oft embattled lands.
Peace, mild eyed seraph, knowledge, light divine,
Shall send their Messengers by every *line,*
Men, joined in amity, shall wonder long
 That hate had power to lead their fathers wrong,
Or that false glory lured their hearts astray,
And made it virtuous and sublime to slay."

The *direct* passenger line of railway now preparing to be *reopened* between South Shields and Sunderland, by which the long and circuitous route by, and weary detention at Brockley Whins, will be avoided, is a forced concession which we owe I fancy, to the threatened

Tyne, Wear, and Tees Railway. I say *re-opened* becau.· it was once a line in direct operation between the two towns, the rails having been taken up, doubtless for economical reasons.

THE CEMETERY AND THE CHURCH YARDS OF ST. HILDA AND HOLY TRINITY.

The unsatisfactory state of the church yards in England, had for many years previous to 1850, occupied the anxious attention of sanitary reformers, whose enlightened efforts resulted that year in the passing of an Act, under the auspices of the then General Board of Health, entitled " The Metropolitan Interments Act, 1850." Proving to be inoperative owing to certain defects, it was repealed in 1852 by the 15 and 16 Vic., c. 85, entitled " an Act to amend the laws concerning the burial of the dead in the Metropolis," thereby laying the foundation of the law for the establishment and regulation of burial grounds throughout the country. Its provisions were extended in 1853, to England and Wales by the 16 and 17 Vic., cap. 134, entitled " An Act to amend the laws concerning the burial of the dead in England, beyond the limits of the Metropolis, and to amend the :Act concerning the burial of the dead in the Metropolis," afterwards amended in 1854, by the 17 and 18 Vic., cap. 87, entitled " An Act to make further provisions for the burial of the dead in England, beyond the limits of the Metropolis." And lastly the whole were amended and consolidated in 1855, by the 18 and 19 Vic., cap. 128, entitled " An Act further to amend the laws concerning the burial of the dead in England."

These Acts have happily accomplished their objects not only in the Metropolis, but universally throughout the provinces, the establishment of " The South Shields and Westoe Burial Board," in 1854, and the formation by it of the now existing cemetery, being practical results of the success of the legislative endeavours, so far as they have come under our own observation within this Borough.

The cemetery contains 17 acres of ground or thereabouts, and is of freehold tenure. There are two chapels upon it, one for churchmen, and the other for dissenters, the burial ground itself being divided into two distinct portions, of consecrated and unconsecrated, to which may be noticed in addition, a separate allotment for Roman Catholics. There are also a house and offices for the residence and use of the Superintendent, who is likewise the Registrar; and an entrance lodge or house, in which the Sexton lives. The whole is interspersed with wide gravel walks, surrounded by a brick wall of sufficient elevation, and planted with trees, shrubs, and flowers tastefully arranged.

> " With awe, around these silent walks I tread ;
> These are the lasting mansions of the dead."

The interments therein since its consecration by the Bishop of Durham, on the 24th April, 1857, amount to 5967, being at the average rate of 663 per annum.

Judging from the sum borrowed, the cost of the whole may be fairly taken at £11,000, which is now reduced by repayments of £2450, to an existing mortgage debt of £8550.

The fees payable, and the apportionment of them are in strict accordance with the published table, to which all may have access.

The Burial Board consists of two separate boards, of South Shields and Westoe united, each of them having nine members.

William Anderson, Esq. J. P. is the chairman of the board, and the following are its officers, with their respective yearly salaries, and other advantages, viz :—

	£	s.	d.
Thomas Salmon, clerk	40	0	0
David Reed, superintendent and registrar, being an increase this year of £10, and a house and ground rent free	80	0	0
James Ramsey, sexton or grave digger, a house and ground rent free, and his fees as sexton			
Thomas Scott, treasurer	10	0	0

The accounts are annually audited by auditors, and printed and circulated for public information.

Saint Stephen's Church Yard still remains open for interments under certain restrictions. To Westoe Chapel and Saint Mary's Church, no grave yards are attached.

With respect to the church yards of Saint Hilda and Holy Trinity, thereby hangs a tale which I *gravely* proceed to narrate.

And first as to Saint Hilda, which thus appears prominently in the order of Council of the 18th October, 1854, according to the following extract.

"South Shields—No burial to take place in *St. Hilda's Church Yard* within twenty feet of the church, or of any dwelling house. One body only to be buried in each grave; no burial to take place in any grave without a covering of earth four and a half feet in depth at the least, measuring from the upper surface of the coffin to the level of the ground, and burials to be wholly discontinued therein from and after the *1st July*, 1855."

The following being the extract from the order in council of the 28th, February, 1855, having reference to burials in *Holy Trinity Church Yard*.

"South Shields—To be wholly discontinued in *Holy Trinity Church Yard*, from and after the *1st July*, 1855."

Entertaining a strong opinion of the great injustice that would be done to, and the serious loss in property that would be sustained by, the owners of family vaults and brick graves in the church yards of St. Hilda and Holy Trinity, by the carrying out of those prohibitory orders in council on the 1st of July, 1855, I voluntarily and without aid, assistance, promise, or expectation of reward from any body, prepared and forwarded to Sir George Grey, the Home Secretary, the following petition, with the thirty-two signatures attached, first remarking that the number of petitioners does not by any means represent the number of vaults and brick graves actually interfered with, my reasons for their limitation having been sufficient and politic under the circumstances of the application.

TO THE RIGHT HONORABLE SIR GEORGE GREY, BART., HER MAJESTY'S PRINCIPAL SECRETARY OF STATE FOR THE HOME DEPARTMENT.

The humble petition of the undersigned inhabitants of the Parish of Saint Hilda, in the County of Durham,

Sheweth—That your petitioners are entitled to right of interment in vaults and brick graves for the burial of the dead, in the church yards severally attached to the churches of Saint Hilda and Holy Trinity in the said Parish, as the same has been legally acquired before the passing of the existing burial acts or any of them.

That both the said church yards are now closed by an order in council, in pursuance of the provisions of the said burial acts.

That to the closing of those church yards on sanitary grounds, so far as regards the burial of the dead in common graves, your petitioners do not object, but inasmuch as the sanitary reasons which may be applied to that description of graves, do not extend to such vaults and brick graves as are owned by your petitioners, your petitioners respectfully but earnestly ask for an exception in favor of the latter; and this they do with the greater confidence, in consequence of the legislature having itself admitted the principle of the exception, by the fourth section of the 16 and 17 Vic., c. 134, intituled "An Act to amend the laws concerning the burial of the dead in England, beyond the limits of the Metropolis," whereby it is rendered lawful for one of Her Majesty's principal Secretaries of State, on being satisfied that the exercise of such rights will not be injurious to health, to grant licence for the exercise of the same, during such time and subject to such restrictions as such Secretary of State may think fit; your petitioners in this being further encouraged by the fact, that by an order in council of the 22nd of October last, relating (inter alia) to the burial ground Christ Church, in the neighbouring Borough of Tynemouth, burials are allowed therein in vaults and brick graves, of a nature similar to those in which your petitioners have such right of interment in the church yards of Saint Hilda and Holy Trinity, as aforesaid.

Your petitioners therefore humbly pray that for the reasons before stated, all persons having right of interment in vaults and brick graves in the church yards of Saint Hilda and Holy Trinity aforesaid, may be permitted to exercise the same, as in the case of Christ Church, Tynemouth, your petitioners being willing to be subjected to the same regulations and restrictions, as with a due regard to the public health, have been prescribed by the exceptional order in favor of the latter, to which your petitioners have made allusion.

And your petitioners will ever pray, &c.

Thomas Salmon,	Mary A. Davison,	J. S. Denham,	Ann Roxby,
Andrew Stoddart,	Mark Foreman,	Ann Sharpe,	Henry Lawson,
C. A. Wawn,	George Hudson,	Alex. Strachan,	George Denham,
Ann Mackay,	R. H. Bell,	Ann Blagburn,	Jonathan Nelson,
Henry Anderson,	Thomas Forsyth,	James Blumer,	John Rudd,
Thomas Young,	Mary White,	Elizabeth Edwards,	Henry Mayors,
W. W. Fairles,	J. W. Kirkley,	Robert Wallis,	Ann Thompson,
Thomas Forrest,	Robert Dobby,	W. Anderson,	Thomas Railton.

South Shields, 10th February, 1857.

The answer which I received from the Home Secretary was satisfactory, and from an order in council of the 20th March, 1857, I make the following extract for the information of all whom it may concern, feeling myself to have been well rewarded by the success of my unassisted endeavours, and the qualified salvation of the property.

And whereas by two orders in council of the 11th December, 1854, and the 1st May, 1855, burials were directed to be discontinued in *St. Hilda's* Church Yard, South Shields, from and after the 1st of July, 1855, (afterwards extended to the 1st of January, 1856,) and in Holy Trinity Church Yard, also in South Shields from and after the said 1st of July, (afterwards extended to the 1st of January last,) and it seems fit that the *said orders be varied*; now, therefore, Her Majesty, by and with the advice of her privy council, is pleased to order, and it is hereby ordered, that such now existing vaults and brick graves in the said two church yards, as can be opened without disturbing soil that has already been buried in, may be used for the interment of widowers, widows, parents, and unmarried children, and brothers and sisters of those already buried therein, provided that each coffin be imbedded in charcoal and separately entombed in an air tight manner.

WM. L. BATHURST.

Reverting back after this digression, to the cemetery itself, by some it may be said, " *et ubi solitudinem faciunt, pacem appellant,*" but there can be no doubt that not only solitude but peace *has* prevailed within its walls, with the living as well as the silent dead, for its affairs have been prudently and ably conducted by the general board and its managing committee, who have never lost sight of the real objects of its establishment, the opposite principles and opinions of all those " sorts and conditions of men," for whose use and convenience, and at whose expence it was created and carried on, and the duty which became vested in them as the appointees of the ratepayers, for the gradual reduction and eventual extinguishment of the debt.

Many sepulchral monuments have been erected in remembrance of the departed dead, and Harvey himself might not unprofitably renew once more his solemn " meditations amongst the tombs," in the secluded cemetery of South Shields and Westoe.

" Blessed is the turf, serenely blessed,
Where throbbing hearts may sink to rest,
Where life's long journey turns to sleep,
Nor ever pilgrim wakes to weep,
There shall no vain ambition come
To lure them from their quiet home."

MARINE INSURANCE CLUBS.

The following tabular statement for the year 1866, when compared with former years, and with that for 1856, shews an absence much to be regretted of many well known clubs, the names of which were familiar to me even as household words, from boyhood. As I am not aware of any similar decrease in the mutual insurance capital of the shipowners of North Shields, Newcastle, or Sunderland, and as the administrative talents of the shipowners who formed the Committees here, and of their Secretaries, were equal I imagine to those of the towns which I have named, the change in our case becomes exceptional and remarkable, and can only be attributed to some special operating cause or causes, which I should be glad to have explained, and which ought to be met and removed, for the system was one of mutual convenience, the loss of which is not only a discredit to our shipowners, many of whose ships are actually insured on a mutual principle at North Shields, Newcastle, Whitby, Scarborough, Topsham, and London ; but an unsatisfactory withdrawal of that which added materially to the mercantile character and importance of the Borough. The whole amount secured on ship by mutual insurance amongst ourselves is at present only £224,000, and that is a very small proportion indeed of the tonnage of shipping owned by the registered shipowners of South Shields, the value of which is little short of £900,000. Let this I pray be looked into and corrected, for the honor and interest of the Borough.

NAME OF CLUB.	WHEN ESTAB-LISHED	NATURE OF INSURANCE.	NAMES OF SECRETARIES.	AMOUNT OF CAPITAL.	
				IN MONEY.	KEELS
				£	
Coal Trade -	1811	On ship -	John Davison -	23000	
Shields A1 - -	1857	On ship - -	Do. - - -	55000	
Eligible Cargo -		On freight -	Do. - -		450
Sun - - -	1836	On ship - -	Chris. A. Wawn	41000	
Sun - -		On cargo, freight, and outfit -	Do. - -		500
Standard - -	1850	On ship - -	John Walker Lamb	25000	
So. Shields Protecting Society -	1819	Casualties not covered by ordinary insurance	Do. - -	1076800 being on 134,600 tons at £8 per ton.	
Port of Tyne A1 -	1855	On ship -	Stout & Bainbridge	25000	
North Eastern -	1866	On ship - -	Do. - -	30000	
Alliance - -	1865	On ship -	Do. - -	25000	
Alliance - -	1865	On freight -	Do. - -		450

THE TYNE PILOTAGE.

The long and severe local and parliamentary struggle in both houses, having happily ended by the passing of an Act on the 19th of June, 1865, entitled " An Act for confirming a provisional order made by the Board of Trade, under The Merchant Shipping Act Amendment Act, 1862, relating to the pilotage of the River Tyne," it is unnecessary to enter here into the circumstances and details of the memorable and well fought contest, which would really supply material for a volume in itself.   Suffice it to say, that the pilots and their friends of whom I glory to be considered one, came off victorious, but not to that full extent as regards the constitution of the Board of Commissioners, which I and others, had at one time anticipated.   We are however thankful for that which we have moderately received from the legislature, and the time may perhaps be not far distant, when by experience, that best and safest of teachers, defects may be discovered leading to such further reformation, as will bring the provisions of the order and its confirmatory Act, still more into accordance with "the spirit of the age." In the meantime the Pilotage Board, of which I have the honor myself to be a member, by appointment of the Board of Trade, works peaceably, and hitherto upon the whole, satisfactorily.

The object of the provisional order and its confirmatory Act was, it is well known, to transfer the jurisdiction and powers in pilotage matters, from the Trinity House of Newcastle-upon-Tyne to a body of incorporated Commissioners, by the name of " The Tyne Pilotage Commissioners," and having a common seal.   That body, as now constituted for the first time, is as follows, viz :—

	NO.	NAMES.
By the Board of Trade	2	Thomas Salmon Matthew Hall Atkinson
By the Tyne Improvement Commissioners	2	James Cochran Stevenson John Ormston
By the sea pilots of the Tyne, and the pilots licensed for any part of the River Tyne, or the entrance thereof	2	John Hutchinson Robert Blair
By the registered shipowners of Newcastle-upon-Tyne	2	Henry Milvain Thomas Kemp Betts
By the registered shipowners of North Shields	2	George Cleugh John Morrison
By the registered shipowners of South Shields	2	Matthew Cay John Lawrence Hall
And by the master pilots and seamen of the Trinity House of Newcastle-upon-Tyne	5	John Johnson Robertson Thomas Brown Bell Richard Swan Joseph Swan George Arnott

The chairman of the board is James Cochran Stevenson; the law clerk, Thomas Carr Lietch; the secretary, George Lyall; the pilot superintendent, John Osborne; the treasurer, John Brodrick Dale; the auditor, John Walker Lamb; and I am myself the chairman of the Finance Committee.

The offices and board room of the Commissioners, are in the South Shields Custom House, where the meetings are held, and the committees sit, and thus has another institution of real importance, not only been added to those which already exist in South Shields, but is located in a building provided by the Corporation with prudent forethought, for the supply of that anticipated accommodation, the want of which would of necessity have been detrimental to the best interests of our town, and serviceable to those of our active rivals.

Reverting back to "The Tyne Pilotage Order Confirmation Act, 1865," I may state that by it,

The costs and expenses of the elections of Commissioners, are to be paid by the Commissioners, out of money coming to their hands as such.

Certain parts of "The Commissioners Clauses Act, 1847," (10 and 11 Vic., c. 16,) are incorporated therewith, by which (inter alia) the prescribed number constituting a quorum of Commissioners at a meeting, is fixed at seven; and the annual meeting of the Commissioners is to be held on, or within one week after the 1st of October in each year.

The Pilotage District of the Tyne, includes the whole of the River Tyne, and seaward over a radius of seven miles.

The jurisdiction in pilotage matters within that district, is transferred from the Trinity House of Newcastle-upon-Tyne, to and vested in the Commissioners.

All pilots licensed for the Tyne or its entrance, by the Trinity House of Newcastle, at the commencement of the order, are entitled to act as such pilots under the Commissioners for one year after the commencement of the order, without further license or payment in respect of that year, but in all other respects are to be subject to the authority of the Commissioners and the provisions of the order, as if they had been severally licensed originally under the order.

The Commissioners are to examine every person who applies to them for a pilot license, for the purpose of ascertaining his skill, knowledge, and experience in relation to the navigating, piloting, and conducting of vessels into, out of, and within the district; and may if they think fit, license by writing any person examined and found qualified to act in the capacity of pilot as aforesaid, provided he has served five years in the pilot service.

Every pilot to be licensed under the order, is on receiving his license trom the Commissiouers, to pay to them the sum of forty shillings for such his license ; and every pilot licensed for the district aforesaid, or any part thereof, by the Trinity House of Newcastle-upon-Tyne at the commencement of the order, or to be licensed under the order, are annually to pay to the Commissioners, the sum of ten shillings for the renewal ot his license ; *provided* that the Commissioners may from time to time, increase or diminish the license and renewal fees, or either of them, subject to the approval of the Board of Trade.

The following *pilotage rates* are to be paid, namely,

From and including the 1st of April to the 1st of October in each year, 1s. 3d. for every foot of water which any ship or vessel shall draw ; and from and including the 1st of October to the 1st of April in each year, 1s. 6d. for every such foot of water.

And such pilotage dues are to be paid to the Commissioners, or to the pilot performing such pilotage duty, within five days after the performance thereof ; provided that the Commissioners may from time to time increase or diminish the said pilotage dues, subject to the approval of the Board of Trade.

Nothing in the order to extend to oblige the owner or master of any vessel, to employ or make use of any pilot, in piloting or conducting such vessel, if he is not desirous so to do, or to pay pilotage dues when not employing or making use of a pilot.

The following clauses are of such importance as to warrant their introduction here *in full.*

1.—All money standing in the books of the Trinity House of Newcastle-upon-Tyne, to the credit of, or lawfully applicable to the Tyne Pilotage District hereby transferred to the Commissioners, and also all money held by the said Trinity House for, or on behalf of the Sea Pilots or the River Pilots of the said District, at the commencement of this order, shall be paid to the Commissioners incorporated by this order.

2.—The costs, charges, and expenses of the promoters of this order, and of the Master Pilots and Seamen of the Trinity House of Newcastle-upon-Tyne, in relation to this order, and of the proceedings consequent thereon in Parliament, including the costs, charges, and expenses incident to the application for, and obtaining the order of the Board of Trade, and the proceedings relating thereto in the last session of Parliament, shall be paid by the Commissioners out of the first monies coming to their hands under the provisions of this order.

3.—All compensation money payable by the Commissioners of Her Majesty's Treasury, under the provisions of section 12, of the 24 and 25 Vic., cap. 47, to the said Trinity House of Newcastle-upon-Tyne, for differential dues for Pilotage, payable in respect of the said district, shall, after the commencement of this order, be paid to, and received by the Commissioners.

4.—If the services of any persons at the commencement of this order, permanently employed by the Trinity House of Newcastle-upon-Tyne, on duties connected with the Pilotage within the Tyne Pilotage District, are not continued by the Commissioners, the Commissioners shall grant compensation to such persons, out of the monies to come into their hands by virtue of this order, such compensation not to be granted except under such circumstances, and to such an amount as might be granted under the Act or Acts for the time being in force, with respect to compensation for abolition of office in the public civil service.

In terms of the Act and its incorporated order, the first meeting of the Pilotage Commissioners was fixed by the Board of Trade to be held, and was held, in the rooms of the Tyne Improvement Commissioners at Newcastle-upon-Tyne, on the 21st of July, 1865. By appointment since of the Pilotage Commissioners themselves, also in terms of the act and order as to subsequent meetings, they are now fixed to be held, and are from time to time held in the Custom House Building at South Shields, on the the first Friday in every month.

By a saving clause nothing in the order is to exempt the Pilotage Commissioners, or the Pilotage District from the provisions of any General Act of Parliament in force or to be passed, relating to pilotage or pilotage dues, or to merchant shipping, or to ports, harbours, or docks, or to dues on shipping, or on goods carried therein, or from any future revision and alteration, under the authority of Parliament, of the pilotage dues authorized by the order, or of the limits of the district defined by the order.

The intended common seal of the Pilotage Commissioners is consistently local, the bold promontory of Tynemouth, its ruined castle,

> " Where from the lighthouse brighter beams arise,
> To show the shipman where the shallow lies,"

the entrance to Shields Harbour, the Southern Pier, and a coble with her crew, forming its component parts. " In Portu Salus," is the appropriate and well chosen motto, for many a ship and crew have found " safely" in the hour of need, and been conducted into " port" securely, by the aid, skill, and experience of a gallant South Shields Pilot, who, with the permission always of Him,

> "That commandeth the waters and ruleth the sea,
> Bringeth them into the haven were they would be,"

I did hope to have ended by announcing the transfer by the Trinity House to the Pilotage Commissioners, of the funds to which the latter are entitled, but "dark and more dark the dreary prospect grows," and it looks at present as if *that* would be an event to be recorded in the next decennial supplement.

THE SOUTH SHIELDS LITERARY, MECHANICAL, AND SCIENTIFIC INSTITUTION

Still pursues the even tenor of its way after a steady constitutional reign of forty-one years, the particulars of the first thirty-one years having been made known by me in 1856, leaving its important doings for the last ten years, to be now set forth, first remarking with regret, that during the latter period the Institution has been deprived by death of three of its original and valued office holders, viz. :—Thomas Masterman Winterbottom, Matthew Hutchinson, and John Nevison. It also having lost by death, a friend in the person of John Twizell Wawn, a Vice-President.

It was in 1855 that the committee felt the necessity of seeking greater accommodation for members, and of supplying the requirements of a rapidly increasing population. Serious attention was given to this, and in 1856 plans were procured for the alteration of the old building in Fowler Street, by raising and extending it by the contemplated purchase of adjoining property in Denmark Street, the estimated cost of all which was £650.

To accomplish this a vigorous canvass for subscriptions was set on foot, and a large committee of twenty-six members appointed, who after long and careful deliberation, wisely decided upon an entire abandonment of the Fowler Street building, and the acquisition of a new one on a totally different site, sufficient to embrace a hall for one thousand people, rooms for classes, library, news room, dwelling rooms, kitchen, and all such other appliances and facilities, as would make it available for any of the purposes for which it might be required by the inhabitants. The Fowler Street property was therefore sold, and the present site of the new building secured and enfranchised, and in 1858 all having been matured, plans were advertised for, and the one sent in by Mr. Wardle, Architect, of Newcastle-upon-Tyne, was selected out of the very small number offered for competition, the Architects generally having objected to the terms offered, and conspired together to withhold tenders, an act of selfish illiberality towards a public Institution, which deserves to be held in lasting remembrance. The work itself was likewise offered to the open competition of builders resident in the Borough, and the contract was fairly obtained by Mr. Joseph Wright, Senr., and executed in a manner which gave the most complete satisfaction, as was indeed to be expected from one who had been himself an active and useful member of the Institution, from nearly its commencement.

At this stage of the proceedings, it being felt that the Committee was too large, an executive one was appointed consisting of Robert Walter Swinburne, Evan Hunter, Robinson Elliott, Edward Corder, Richard Howse, William Henderson, Isaac Tweddell, George Daglish Robson, Luke Mackay, and Thomas Salmon, and the two Secretaries John Pearson Elliott, and Christopher Tate,

"An honest and an upright dozen,"

To whose correct judgment, indefatigable attention, and resolute perseverence, under difficult and sometimes disheartening circumstances, the successful accomplishment of the undertaking is so undoubtedly to be attributed, as to have originated a suggestion from an old friend of

Mechanics Institution, South Shields.
Erected 1859.

the Institution, for the names of the Committee and Builder to be recorded on a marble tablet in the Hall of the Institute, as a lasting remembrance of those who were immediately connected with the erection of a local work of real importance to the public, and had performed their duties so judiciously and so well. If I had not been myself a member of the Committee, I would personally have used exertions for the carrying out of this just suggestion, but this I doubt not, will now be done without further delay, by some who concur in its propriety, and are in a disinterested position for securing its early and effectual accomplishment.

The Committee while prosecuting their active canvass for subscriptions, in aid of the great object which they had before them, did not lose sight of an additional mode by which the building fund could be materially assisted, through the medium of a *Ladies' Bazaar*, and to the ladies therefore they applied, whose noble response to the important appeal, is in the grateful recollection not only of the members of the Institution, but of the inhabitants at large, for nothing could exceed the willing kindness, the energy, and the generosity with which that Bazaar was got up. It is not indeed too much to say, that it was pre-eminent for the variety and beauty of the articles contributed, the tastefulness of its arrangements, and the success which proudly attended it, as proved by the realization as net proceeds for the Institution, of no less a sum than £810; and well do the names of the generous warm-hearted ladies of management deserve to be placed upon record here, those who held stalls were Mrs. John Williamson, (Mayoress), Mrs. Captain Blackett, Mrs. James Carr, Mrs. Thomas Salmon, Mrs. William Marshall, Miss Wallis, Mrs. Cooke, Mrs. T. J. Swinburne, the Misses Wawn, (of West Boldon,) Mrs. James Anderson, Mrs. Aisbitt, and Mrs. Whinney; and they together with Mrs. Dale, Mrs. Miller, Mrs. Buckland, Mrs. G. B. Stoddart, Mrs. Maxwell, and Mrs. Greenwell constituted the Committee of management; with Mr. R. B. Dawson as their Honorary Secretary.

The Bazaar was open on the 10th, 11th, and 12th days of April, 1860.

The foundation stone of the building was laid with all due formality on the 18th of August, 1859, by the President, Robert Ingham, and he was supported on the occasion by the Mayor, Corporation, and Town Clerk, the Rev. James Carr, R. W. Swinburne, Robert Wallis, and many other influential individuals. The building was completed and opened with the Bazaar on the 10th of April, 1860.

It would be unfair to enumerate some inhabitants, and pass by others who assisted with donations, but it will not be deemed invidious to particularize the liberality as *non-residents*, of Hugh Taylor, of Chipchase Castle, the Earl of Durham, Dean of Durham, and Joseph Simpson, of Manchester, who were contributors to the building fund.

I had myself the privilege which I highly prized, of being permitted to shew my devotion, as Vice-President and Honorary Member, to the cause of the Institution, by the preparation, without charge, of the numerous deeds, contracts, and documents connected with the old and new buildings, and by a gift of the requisite stamps; and most gladly did I avail myself of it, as a means by which in money's worth, I contributed my cheerful help to an Institution which I love so well, with which I have been so long and so intimately connected, and which is deserving of much better support than that which it receives.

The building is under the Trusteeship of the South Shields Corporation, which is a convenient arrangement, by which the trouble and expense of a change of Trustees in the event of death or resignation is avoided.

In 1865, the hall was ornamented, wood panelled round to a considerable height from the floor, and otherwise improved by a heavy outlay then made. The two large pictures by Robinson Elliott, which constitute so great an ornament to its walls, were the valuable gift of that talented artist and steady friend of the Institution, the subjects of them being "The finding of the cup in Benjamin's sack," and "Emancipation," as symbolized in Cowper's "Morning Dream."

On the 1st of June, 1860, *a newsroom* was established in connexion with the Institution. A very low charge was encouragingly made, so that it might be open to all classes, the prices fixed being 2s. 6d. per annum to members of the Institution, 6s. per annum to non-members, and 1d. per visit to transient visitors, who had thus an opportunity of reading the newspapers and periodicals lying daily on the table. Notwithstanding the great advantage thus offered, comparatively few avail themselves of it, which is much to be regretted.

Since March, 1861, the business of "The Marine School of South Shields," and the Lectures connected therewith, have been carried on and delivered in part of the building, a pecuniary advantage of some consequence, which is likely to be lost to the Institution, by the erection of a building expressly for the school itself, as contemplated by its founder.

Encouraged by the success of the Ladies' bazaar, and urged on by pecuniary necessities, it was determined in 1863, to hold a polytechnic exhibition in the Institute, for the two-fold purpose of giving to the public the pleasure and benefit of inspecting superior works of art not commonly available in South Shields, and at the same time of realizing means for the discharge of existing liabilities. The first object was fully secured, for an admirable exhibition was gathered together at much cost, and with great discrimination and labor, but the support given to it by the public fell very far short of that which the Committee had a right to expect for such a purpose, and the consequence to the society was, a pecuniary loss instead of that gain which would have ensued, if those for whose pleasure and instruction the exhibition was held had proved their taste by giving their attendance.

So it was with the concerts of the higher class which from time to time were given, under the management of the Committee, for their results also have been such as not to justify a repetition of them.

The history of the proceedings of a local Institution from year to year, is marked with incidents presenting such a similarity, that little more respecting the South Shields one need to be stated. It is one of the oldest, and though its numbers have never been such as to satisfy the wishes of its friends, or of those who are sensitively anxious for the literary character of the Borough, yet it has worked steadily in its vocation, and not been subject to fluctuations so great as to necessitate at any time a re-organization. During the whole of its existence it has preserved its character as a purely literary and scientific Institution, and been a source of incalculable advantage to many young men who have wisely availed themselves of it.

Lectures have been delivered yearly by some of the most distinguished men of the day, but with scarcely an exception, the attendance has been most unsatisfactory, with the usual return of " nulla bona ! "

Classes form another and most important part in the operations of a scientific and literary Institution, the drawing ones being under the able teaching and superintendence of Mr. Robinson Elliott, while the French and German ones are under Mr. Thompson, now of North Shields. Both those gentlemen are most assiduous and indefatigable in the attention they give, and I should not omit to make known, that some of the students of the drawing classes having settled in London, have taken prizes in the Kensington School of art. The excellent President of the Institution, has for many years given three guineas annually to be appropriated in prizes for the drawing classes. An amalgamated engineer's class has also been established for the purpose of preparing the young engineer for examination. It is very desirable that more classes should be formed.

A microscopical exhibition has also been held, which as usual was no source of profit. A microscopic society in connection with the Institution has likewise been organized, but at present its meetings are suspended.

There has been during the whole existence of the Institution, a steady and rapid circulation of *books*, there being evidently some who concur in the declaration made by the Leicestershire Squire, in a moment of unusual intellectual enthusiasm, " that upon his honor there were some books which it was a positive pleasure to read !" The number of volumes now in the library is about 6000. The best leading periodicals are taken in, and allowed to lie during the day on the news room table. What books can do has thus been well described by him who was truly a poet in every respect of peculiarly English character, whose delineations were ever vigorous, stern, uncompromising, and true.

> "Thus *books* can give
> New views to life, and teach us how to live;
> They sooth the grieved, the stubborn they chastise,
> Fools they admonish, and confirm the wise,
> Their aid they yield to all: they never shun
> The man of sorrow, nor the wretch undone;
> Unlike the hard, the selfish, and the proud,
> They fly not sullen from the suppliant crowd;
> Nor tell to various people various things,
> But shew to subjects, what they shew to kings."

An enumeration of bibliothical advantages so tempting and so correct, as to excite feelings of wonder and regret, that so few comparatively of the inhabitants of this large and populous town, should avail themselves of them; for alas! alas! out of a rapidly increasing population amounting in 1861 to 35,239, only 300 friends of literature and science are to be found, who prove their intellectual intelligence by giving their countenance and support as members, to " The South Shields Literary, Mechanical, and Scientific Institution," the managers of which are left to struggle against the financial difficulties of a harassing position, arising out of a mortgage debt of £1900, and a floating one of £252, all of which, be it remembered, has been patriotically incurred in the creation of an admirably contrived building of admitted internal convenience, which having sprung out of a craving necessity of public utility, ought to be emancipated from debt, either wholly or in part, by the assistance of those for whose benefit it was erected, and is now maintained. The twin Institution at Tynemouth, is now altogether free from the debt which at one time paralized its efforts and obstructed its progress, and surely that which is now an accomplished fact at Tynemouth, should not only be an encouragement to us at South Shields to go and do likewise, by following our neighbours' spirited example, but be viewed by us in the meantime as an existing humiliation, of which we ought speedily and effectually to get rid. How this is to be done is matter for serious consideration and contrivance. All ordinary schemes have already failed for want of public support, with the exception always of the gratefully remembered Ladies' bazaar. The polytechnic, from which much was fairly expected, was, to the discredit of the town, an undeserved failure; lectures and concerts have been tried and found wanting; an available surplus of receipts over expenditure, is hardly to be looked for in the present state of the concern; and the register of members proclaims too sadly that from it assistance is not to be hoped. Unless therefore some modern dives with the riches and public spirit of a Northumberland Hugh Taylor comes to our aid, as he and Mr. Lindsay did to that of our North Shields neighbours; or some wealthy testator remembers us, as some could have done long since, by a seasonable bequest; for

> " Much do we need, and therefore will we ask,
> Kind friends to aid us in our present task;
> From them with special cause we beg for aid,
> When of our subject we are most afraid;"

I fear that we of the Institute will continue to be left to our own insufficient resources, with a prospect for the future of dispiriting aspect, involving of necessity an abandonment of those hopes of a free library in which some of us have fondly indulged, and of those other advantages which might have arisen to all, from that total or even partial relief from debt, which is so immensely important, and to which allusion has already been anxiously made by one, who painfully alive to the wants of the Institution, regrets his own inability to do that in aid of it, which others who rejoice in the multitude of their riches, could afford to bestow at any time, with ease and convenience.

The President of the Institution, is Robert Ingham, M.P.; and its Vice-Presidents are Richard Shortridge, Robert Walter Swinburne, Robert Wallis, Evan Hunter, Christopher McDonald, and Thomas Salmon; Thomas Scott is the Treasurer; the Secretaries being John Pearson Elliott and Christopher Tate. Where all have served the Institute so faithfully and so long, a selection of any for special acknowledgment, could not perhaps be justified under ordinary circumstances, but the valuable services for 28 years of Mr. J. P. Elliott as a Secretary, (always admitting most thankfully those for 11 years of his shorter lifed colleague Mr. Tate,) have been so extraordinarily constant and unwearied, as eminently to deserve this special encomium, which is thus freely offered under a sense of the weighty obligation which the society has incurred.

THE WORKING MEN'S INSTITUTE.

The committee of this Institute and Club, in presenting their 16th report to the annual meeting of the 27th November last, offered their congratulations on the success which had attended every operation of the society during the past year. It appears from the report that sixteen years ago, the society was commenced by a few earnest working men, who desirous of improving their minds, met together and laid the foundation of it, they being doubtless aware, without perhaps being able to quote, or refer to the high authorities of Sallust, Plautus, or Bacon, that

" Every man is the architect of his own fortune—
That the prudent man really frames his own fortunes for himself—
AND,
That the mould of a man's fortune is in his own hand."

The beginning was small, but the willing few having strong faith, struggled on, and every succeeding year was one of success and progress. Books were added to the library,

> "Books which to one of these four ends conduce,
> For wisdom, piety, delight, or use."

Classes were held, lectures given, generous friends contributed, and hundreds of working men have passed through the society, cultivating habits of reading and thinking, sowing the seeds of future usefulness, and carrying to the homes, manufactories, and workshops of the Borough, a taste for the good and the true. The politic removal of the society from King Street to East King Street, provided increased accommodation in the shape of news-room, library, class rooms, conversation and smoking room, rooms for bagatelle, chess, and draughts, and a large yard for quoits; and the wisdom of it has been encouragingly proved by the entry of 268 new members during the year, making the number on the register 643.

The funds are in a healthy condition, and the society last year was self supporting, the subscriptions of the members having amounted to £92 15s. 11d., while the expenditure was £88 6s. 7d.

The news room is well attended, and supplied with eight daily, seventeen weekly, and twelve monthly papers and periodicals.

> "The news! there scarcely is a word, I'll venture here to say,
> That o'er men's thoughts and fancies holds more universal sway;
> The old, the young, the grave, the gay, the wealthy, and the poor,
> All wish on each succeeding day, to hear it o'er and o'er,
> Though on each day 'tis always chang'd from what it was before."

The library has been steadily increasing, and numbers 1293 volumes, 93 of them having been added during the year. The lectures have been so crowded that the room was not large enough for the accommodation of all who applied for admission.

The objects of the society as declared by the committee, are partly recreative and partly educational. The one being to furnish comfortable apartments, suitably supplied with books, newspapers, periodicals, and games of various kinds. The other the establishment of classes for instruction in the various departments of literature and science, so as to "unite the thinking head with the working hand, to teach the young members the hatefulness of evil, to imbue their minds with such a portion of that wisdom, manliness, and strength of character, as will, with God's grace, preserve them untainted from the many corruptions which beset them in their walk through life;" and in short to make them useful, moral, well conducted members of society in their several stations; reminding them as I do with the privileged freedom of old age, that they

> "Who fame or bliss would share,
> Must *learn* by labour, and must *live* by care."

And further bringing under their notice by way of encouragement in their own honest, humble position, that

"A prince can mak a belted knight,
A marquis, duke, and a' that,
But an *honest man's* aboon his might,
Gude faith he manna fa' that!

"For a' that, and a' that,
Their dignities and a' that,
The pith o' sense, and pride o' worth,
Are higher ranks than a' that."

The office bearers are Solomon Sutherland, President; John Bell, Vice-President; W. Swinburne, Treasurer; Thomas Pyke and Charles Weatherburn, Secretaries; the Committee consisting of twenty members. The success of the Institute and its present prosperous condition, are proofs of their administrative capabilities, and experienced knowledge of the wonted requirements, and wishes of those who usually become members of societies of this useful description. Freedom from debt of any kind, being happily a main ingredient in this peaceful and encouraging state of affairs.

THE SOUTH SHIELDS GEOLOGICAL CLUB,

The motto of which should be,

"Sermons in stones, and good in every thing,"

was established on the 9th October, 1862. Its affairs are managed by a President, Vice-President, Treasurer, Secretary, Curator, and a Committee of six members, who are elected annually by ballot. Mr. George Lyall, F.G.S. has been the President; Mr. William Brockie, the Vice-President; Mr. Luke Mackey, the Treasurer; and Mr. Thomas John Bell, the Secretary, from its commencement; and Mr. Joseph Wright, Jun., is the Curator. The laudable object of the club, is the cultivation and diffusion of a theoretical and practical knowledge of Geology and its cognate sciences, with more especial reference to the study and development of geology and palæontology of the surrounding district. The club consists of about fifty members, who meet weekly during the winter months, in the lecture room of the Working Men's Institute, and who take excursions during the summer months, to various places of geological or scientific interest, in this and the neighbouring counties. A considerable number of excellent specimens of fossils has been collected by or presented to the club, with which it is intended ultimately to form a museum, and it has a small library for the use of its members. The club I am glad to state has progressed satisfactorily, and has made several important discoveries, which have extended our knowledge of the fossil bearing strata of the district, the value of which has been duly recognized by Sir Roderick Impey Murchison, F.R.S., F.G.S., and Director General of the geological survey of the United Kingdom, and have been submitted by him to the British Association for the advancement of science.

Without entering upon the many speculative and difficult questions connected with the wide field of geology generally, it may truly be said without exaggeration, that it has well repaid in a mining and mineral sense, the large debt which it owes to the practised experience of the miner and the engineer, for there is hardly now a district where the discoveries and reasoning of geology have not checked extravagant expenditure, in the vain search after coal or metallic ore, where they were not to be found, and conquered the credulity of selfish ignorance ever ready to listen to the delusive advice, or erroneous notions of some designing Dousterswivel or merely working colliers or miners. The false and deceitful promise of finding coal by going deeper, will not again lure the landed gentry, or speculative companies, to such adventures as the sinking for coal in the oolites of Oxford, the sandstones of Sussex, or the silurians of Radnorshire. While to its credit can the assertion be made, that geology has not confined itself to merely aiding the mining interest by preventing foolish and wasteful expenditure in search of imaginary treasures, for it is within my memory that the eminent practical viewers of these our great Northern coal fields, doubted, nay even denied the existence of coal under the magnesian limestone, yet now, thanks to geology and the knowledge derived from it, and particularly from Mr. W. Smith's geological report in 1822, enormous quantities of first rate coal so situate, have been dug out and sent to the London market, securing by its ready sale the realization of magnificent profits, which would otherwise have been lost, by the continuance of the valuable coal itself an unsuspected treasure in the bowels of the earth. Facts most important to which I allude for the express purpose of making known the peculiar adaption of this immediate district of the coal field, as a suitable locality for a society such as that, which, with its praiseworthy objects, has been established here amongst ourselves, by Mr. Lyall, and his scientific coadjutors, such objects being as widely different as the poles asunder from those of Captain Grose and his "Antiquarian Trade," when he peregrinated through Scotland in search of antiquities, the acquisition of which was so humorously described and ridiculed by Burns,

> "He has a fouth o' auld nick-nackets,
> Rusty airn caps and jingling jackets,
> Wad haud the Lothians three in tackets,
>   A towmont gude;
> And parritch pats, and auld saut backets,
>   Before the flood."

To which he added in that spirit of genuine wit and Scotch humour, which gave delight even to the *Gross* and ponderous antiquary himself, the following well known articles, the antiquity of which will not be doubted even by the most sceptical.

> " Of Eve's first fire a cinder,
> Auld Tubal Cain's fire shool and fender,
> And a broom stick o' the witch of Endor,
> Weel shod wi' brass."

The readers and admirers of Burns (and who are not ?) need not be reminded by me, that to him and the well known verses from which I have thus briefly quoted, the *great* Captain acquired a world wide celebrity, more lasting than he could have obtained from his own antiquarian researches, and published " Antiquities of Scotland," for the names ot Burns and Grose are indissolubly united by immortal verse and will be held and recollected in humorous fellowship together, so long as the English language and the broad Scotticisms of our Northern neighbours, in which their poet delighted to indulge, shall endure.

THE MARINE SCHOOL OF SOUTH SHIELDS.

Dr. Winterbottom, the generous founder of this school died on the 8th of July, 1859, at the advanced age of 93 years, and was buried with well merited public honors, in the South Shields Cemetery. At his death the machinery of the deed of settlement, by which the school was organized, with a magnificent endowment of £27,000, came into operation ; but upon it and its provisions, I purposely avoid any particular observations, leaving them to be handled by the Rev. Robert Eli Hooppell, the head, and at present only master, who is engaged in the careful preparation as a labour of love, of the life of the venerable Doctor, and is doubtless from his superior knowledge and experience as to the real working of the school since its opening, best qualified to give all such information as the public look for from his book, and will be thankful to receive. I am however free myself independently to admit, for I am in no way connected with the school or its management, that with all proper respect for the Rev. Master, his talents, his qualifications, and his zeal in the discharge of his duties, the interests of the town and of humanity itself, would have been better advanced if the Doctor's well meant but mistaken generosity, had exhibited itself in the more natural direction, (he having been himself a member of the medical profession,) of a much wanted eleemosynary hospital or infirmary for sick and needy sufferers, rather than of a school for the nautical education or improvement of those, who, judging from their apparent indifference, do not seem to be sensible of its intended advantages, or to appreciate the founder's affectionate liberality towards them. In support of which preferential impression of mine in favor of an endowed hospital or infirmary, the following descriptive lines which all must admire, may aptly be quoted and brought forward thus,

> " On either side,
> The wards appear, all airy, warm, and wide,
> And every ward has beds by comfort spread,
> And smooth'd for him who suffers on his bed ;
> There all have kindness, most relief,—for some
> Is cure complete ; it is the sufferer's home :
> Fevers and chronic ills, corroding pains,
> Each accidental mischief man sustains ;
> Fractures and wounds, and wither'd limbs and lame,
> With all that, slow or sudden, vex our frame,
> Have here attendance ; here the sufferers lie,
> (Where love and science every aid supply,)
> And healed with rapture live, or soothed by comfort die."

A description so faithfully explanatory of the comforts and advantages of a local hospital, under varied circumstances of sickness and disease, relief and cure, as to cause it now to be matter of unavailing regret, that the school and not the hospital, was the favored object, through which the Doctor's good intentions towards his native town, were generously manifested.

With respect to the very costly building which the Sanhedrim of the school are intending to erect for its future use, it would perhaps be wise if they were to act upon the cautious principle so prudently propounded by Mrs. Glass, when she recommended the hare to be caught before it was skinned ; for the result of the school as an experiment is understood to have not hitherto been such as to justify so rash a speculation ; and if the object be to fish for scholars through an architectural bait, to be skilfully placed on the hook by Mr. Clemence, it is my opinion that the fishing will be unsuccessful on their part as "fishers of men." But *that* it may be answered is a question of responsible trust and administration which concerns the seventeen Governors alone, and their application of the fund with which they are entrusted, and *that* I am not disposed to dispute at present, feeling contented as an inhabitant of South Shields, with the knowledge that the town under any circumstances of success or failure in the matter of the school, will be beautified without public cost, by a building of the handsome description alluded to, the erection of which will be another addition to those ornamental ones which already exist, and have sprung up in our streets of late years, not only for ecclesiastical, but for civil purposes.

THE SWIMMING CLUB.

"RARI NANTES IN GURGITE VASTO."

It has been remarked that probably not one in ten of our sailors, in the navy or merchant service, can swim, and that when a ship is wrecked, even within a short distance of the shore, and no boats or other assistance are at hand, few on board can save themselves by swimming, and those few usually passengers. This was the case even so far back as the memorable shipwreck at Melita, so minutely described by Saint Paul, a portion only of those on board having been saved by swimming, the rest escaping to land on boards and broken pieces of the ship, leaving us fairly to conclude, that the swimmers only would have been saved, if it had not been for the fragmentary portions of the vessel, which proved the other happy means of safety and escape. Familiarity with the element doubtless breeds contempt of its dangers, in the minds of seafaring people, and hence this melancholy indifference, and its too often fatal consequences.

But it is not to sailors alone that this carelessness is to be attributed, for many bathers on our coasts are annually drowned under distressing circumstances, for want of this useful, healthy, and easily acquired accomplishment, and great is the loss of valuable life, so frequently arising from boat accidents on our navigable rivers, in consequence of inexcusable ignorance in the art of swimming. I say inexcusable, for it is in the power of every body to swim who possesses a moderate degree of health and activity, although all will not swim equally well, even with the same amount of practice and opportunity.

Well aware of all this, the promoters of "The South Shields Swimming Club," established it formally in the month of May, 1862, and it has gone *swimmingly* on ever since, its praiseworthy object being, as declared by the preamble to the rules, "To associate bathers, to encourage the art of swimming, and to raise it to the position which it is entitled to occupy amongst other sports, and by prize competitions to stimulate the young in becoming proficient in this useful, pleasant, and healthful accomplishment." It embraces 280 members, being an increase of 175 since its commencement in 1862, and its officers are a Patron, Vice-Patrons, President, Vice Presidents, Honorary Swimming Master, Treasurer, Auditors, Committee, and Honorary Secretary; the Committee of Management consisting of the President, two Vice-Presidents, Secretary, Treasurer, two Auditors, and nine members of the club, who are chosen annually. The bathing season commences on the 1st of May, and closes on the 30th September in each year, the place of bathing being the South Shields Pier at half-past six each Tuesday Morning during the season. The annual subscription for Honorary Members is five shillings; for Ordinary Members, two shillings and sixpence; and tor Youths under the age of seventeen years, one shilling; The Committee meet on the first Tuesday in each month for the transaction of business, and the annual general meeting of the members takes place on the first Tuesday in October. The Committee have power to offer competitive prizes for excellence in "Natation," and this they do with great judgment and spirit, the day of such competition being always an annual gala day at South Shields, when the proceedings are witnessed from the crowded South Pier by assembled thousands of delighted spectators, and from steam and other boats likewise.

To the steady attention, personal co-operation as swimmers, and hardy, unflinching example of Mr. Henry Nelson, the President, and Mr. Alexander Allen, the Honorary Swimming Master, much of the popular success of the club is to be attributed, and it can now be looked upon with pride, as a successful and valuable Institution, having an undisputed right fairly to reckon amongst its members, some of the most graceful swimmers in the North of England.

> "I saw him beat the surges under him,
> And ride upon their backs; he trod the waves,
> Whose enmity he flung aside, and breasted
> The surge most swollen that met him."

THE ESTABLISHED CHURCHES.

I have already bestowed a separate article upon Saint Mary's Church, and I now proceed to explain the changes which followed the promotion of the Rev. James Carr from South Shields to Sherburn, which took place in 1862. The rev. gentleman during his sojourn of thirty-one years at South Shields, as the successor of the Rev. William Maughan, who died on the 8th of June, 1831, was the Incumbent of Saint Hilda, including Westoe Lane and Harton Chapels, in all of which services were performed on the sabbath day, namely, at Saint Hilda's Church in the morning and afternoon, at Westoe Lane Chapel in the morning and evening, and at Harton Chapel in the afternoon, Saint Hilda's Church during the whole of that long period having been kept closed on the sunday evenings. A complete separation of the three, was the consequence of Mr. Carr's removal to Sherburn; Saint Hilda's Church falling to the Rev. Thomas Henry Chester; Westoe Lane Chapel, with a district to the Rev. Samuel Stewart; and Harton, with a district, to the Rev. Arthur Archbold Phillpotts. On the death of Mr. Stewart, on the 13th of May, 1865, Westoe Lane Chapel and its district, were bestowed upon the Rev. Edmund Lyde Butcher. Mr.

Carr received a public testimonial on his departure, and his familiar form, and ever happy remarks on many a platform, and public and private occasion, will long be remembered here in pleasant connection with the past.

The division of the Chapelry into the six distinct perpetual curacies, or districts of Saint Hilda, Holy Trinity, Saint Stephen, Jarrow Docks, Westoe, (in South Shields), and Harton, with an Incumbent in charge of each, bears a favorable contrast with its early state and condition, when one Incumbent only, who was not always resident, a Curate, and an afternoon Lecturer chosen and willingly paid by the congregation of Saint Hilda, were the only ecclesiastics of which Saint Hilda's widely extended Chapelry could boast, and which were certainly not sufficient even for the spiritual wants of the limited population of that day. By all parties interested were those seasonable district divisions not only submitted to but encouraged, and all are deserving of praise and thanks, for their co-operation in all that was necessary for bringing about, according to their several means, that divisional revolution which has proved so beneficial and satisfactory to the various congregations.

The particulars of the separation, under orders in council, of Saint Hilda from Jarrow, and the subsequent creation of the ecclesiastical districts of Holy Trinity, Saint Stephen, Jarrow Docks, Westoe in South Shields, and Harton, will be interesting and useful. They all took place under the powers and authority of the following Acts, or some of them, viz : 59 Geo. 3, intituled "An Act to amend and render more effectual an Act passed in the last session of Parliament, for building, and promoting the building of churches in populous Parishes," the 1 and 2 Vic., c. 106, intituled "An Act to abridge the holding of benefices in plurality, and to make better provision for the residence of the clergy ;" and the 2 and 3 Vic., c. 49, intituled "An Act to make better provision for the assignment of ecclesiastical districts to churches or chapels augmented by the governors of the bounty of Queen Anne, and for other purposes ;" and in pursuance of representations or schemes, consented to by the Patrons and Incumbents, made according to law, by the Bishop of the Diocese to the Archbishop of York, sanctioned and reported by the latter to Her Majesty in council, and by Her Majesty in council, approved and ordered to be carried into effect.

And first with regard to the *separation of Saint Hilda from Jarrow*, which was effected under an order in council of the 30th June, 1845, embracing and carrying out the whole of the following *schemes*, as approved of by all parties interested, viz.,:

"The whole of the parochial chapelry of Saint Hilda to be separated from the Parish of Jarrow to which it belongs, and constituted a separate and independent Parish, and a perpetual curacy, of which the Church belonging thereto to be the Parish Church.

Such perpetual curacy to be subject to the same ecclesiastical jurisdiction as the Parish Church of Jarrow, and all the ecclesiastical rights and authority of the Incumbent of Jarrow within the said chapelry of Saint Hilda, henceforth to cease and be transferred to the Incumbent of Saint Hilda.

All Easter dues and other ecclesiastical dues, rates, and payments now belonging to the Incumbent of Jarrow, within the said parochial chapelry of Saint Hilda, to henceforth belong to the Incumbent of Saint Hilda.

Baptisms, churchings, marriages, and burials to be as heretofore performed in the Church of the Parish so to be constituted, and the fees for all such offices performed within the said Parish, as well as all ecclesiastical dues, offerings, and other emoluments arising from or in respect of the said Parish, and usually payable to the Incumbent of a benefice, to belong to the Incumbent thereof.

The Incumbent of the said intended perpetual curacy, to have exclusive care of souls within the limits of the Parish so to be constituted.

The right of nominating a minister to the Church of such Parish, to continue as heretofore to be vested in the Dean and Chapter of Durham.

The inhabitants of the said chapelry to contribute as heretofore to the repairs of the Parish Church of Jarrow.

Next with respect to *Holy Trinity and Saint Stephen*, to which ecclesiastical districts were respectively assigned by an order in council, of the 11th of August, 1848, the following being a copy of the representation upon which such order was made.

Your Majesty's Commissioners for building new churches, beg leave humbly to represent to your Majesty, that having taken into consideration all the circumstances of the Parish of *Saint Hilda*, South Shields, in the county and diocese of Durham, it appears to them to be expedient, that particular districts should be assigned to the consecrated churches of Saint Stephen and the Holy Trinity, severally situate in the said Parish, under and by virtue of the power, or authority for this purpose contained in the 16th section of an Act, passed in the 59th year of the reign of his late Majesty King George the 3rd, intituled " An Act to amend and render more effectual, an Act passed in the last session of Parliament for building and promoting the building of additional churches in populous Parishes," or under, or by virtue of any, and every other power or authority in this behalf, vested in your Majesty's said Commissioners by the church building Acts, and that such proposed chapelry districts should be respectively named, " *The chapelry district of Saint Stephen, South Shields*," and " *The chapelry district of the Holy Trinity, South Shields*," with boundaries as hereinafter mentioned.

The chapelry district of *Saint Stephen, South Shields*, is bounded on the East by the German Ocean, on the West by the Stanhope and Tyne Railway, on the North by the River Tyne, and on the South by German Street, as such proposed chapelry district is more particularly delineated on the map or plan hereunto annexed, and therein tinted green."

The chapelry district of the Holy Trinity, South Shields, is bounded on or towards the East by the Boldon Turnpike Road, and the Stanhope and Tyne Railway, on the West by the Parishes of Monkwearmouth and Jarrow, on the North by the River Don and the River Tyne, to an inlet called the Mill Dam, and from thence by Commercial Road, along a cart road called the Jingling Gate Lane, to the Stanhope and Tyne Railway, and on the South by certain lands adjoining Harton Green Lane, in the Parish of Whitburn ; as such proposed chapelry district, is now particularly delineated on the map or plan hereunto annexed, and thereon colored pink.

That it also appears to be expedient that banns of marriage should be published, and that marriages, baptisms, churchings, and burials should be solemnized or performed in the said churches of *Saint Stephen* and the *Holy Trinity ;* and that all the fees to arise therefrom should be paid and belong to the Incumbents for the time being of the said two churches.

Next as to the *chapelry of Harton*, (not in the Borough of South Shields,) which was separated from the Parish of Saint Hilda, by order in council of the 27th of August, 1864, the following being the scheme embraced and carried into effect by that order :—

The church of the Holy Trinity in South Shields celebrated the one hundredth anniversary of its foundation on the 22nd day of May. The revd. Canon R. E. Holmes, now of Bywell St. Peter's but for a quarter of a century vicar of Holy Trinity, has given our library a copy of his history of the parish—a very thorough piece of work worthy of study by any clergyman contemplating the composition of a parish history—from which the following notes are taken. They may be of historic interest some day ; what would we not give for just these facts about the first hundred years of, for example, St. Nicholas, Newcastle !

Holy Trinity church was the eighth to be erected in the diocese of Durham in the xixth century and was part of the Church of England's response to the post-war problems of the " industrial revolution." The site was given by the Dean and Chapter of Durham, who endowed the parish with £150 a year, and also paid for the building. It cost the moderate sum of £4 3s. 4d. for each of its 1200 sittings and was, it must be admitted, built of the very cheapest materials available. Anthony Slavin, a young Durham architect, afterwards to become a fashionable as a moderniser of mediaeval castles, designed the church and though it was neither as original as the earlier works of John Dobson nor as archaeologically correct in its details as A. W. N. Pugin would have made it, it might have been a great deal worse in 1833. It had a nave with side aisles and western tower but no constructional chancel. In 1836 a gallery was added, and in 1839 a clock for the tower, in 1863 an organ, and there were other minor improvements till 1878 when the ever increasing population and prosperity[1] of the district led to an important scheme of reconstruction, designed by R. J. Johnson. A chancel was added, and double aisle-transepts, the nave was raised and given a clerestry, new woodwork of more pleasing design and more substantial workmanship was installed. Apart from a rebuilding of the east end and the introduction of a German reredos designed by Kempe, and a font canopy by H. S. Hicks, both fine pieces of craftsmanship in wood, there have been few subsequent alterations to the structure nor are there likely to be many in these days. Which is a pity, for the composition of the building would be greatly improved by a spire. A spire gives pleasure to all the beholders of a town, while a reredos, however beautiful, only benefits those who come close to it !

---

1 During the Franco-Prussian war a South Shields biscuit works worked continuously night and day for over twelve months making rations for the French army ; but the main source of Shields prosperity was the development of the Tyne as a port and a centre of engineering and shipbuilding.

HOLY TRINITY'S CENTENARY

History of South Shields Church

PARISH TO CELEBRATE

(23 : 5 : 1933)

Yesterday was the hundredth anniversary of the laying of the foundation-stone of Holy Trinity Church, South Shields—the second oldest Anglican church in the town.

It was on May 22, 1833, that the foundation-stone of the church was laid by the Rev James Carr, of St. Hild's, and in the absence owing to illness of Bishop Van Mildert, Dr Sumner, of Chester, afterwards Archbishop of Canterbury, performed the consecration on September 18, 1834.

The Rev R. E. Holmes, now Canon Holmes, of Bywell St. Peter's, Stocksfield, a former Vicar of Holy Trinity, who wrote a history of the parish, gives some interesting particulars of the days of its foundation

1896, and in 1913 he was succeeded by the Rev A. R. Steggall, in whose memory the Bishop of Durham unveiled memorials on Sunday evening. Mr Steggall died in 1929, was succeeded by the Rev C. Booth, 1929-1931, and the present Vicar—Rev O. N. Gwilliam—was appointed in January, 1932.

There are 6,200 residents in the parish and over 1,000 children attend the church's day school, the largest of its kind in the diocese.

Mr Gwilliam told a *Newcastle Journal* representative that centenary celebrations were already being contemplated.

The *chapelry of Harton* to be separated from the Parish of Saint Hilda, South Shields, to which it belongs, and constituted a separate Parish for ecclesiastical purposes, and a perpetual curacy and benefice by the name or style of "The perpetual curacy of Harton," of which the church or chapel within the said chapelry of Harton, and the burial ground adjoining and belonging thereto, shall be the Parish Church and church yard or burial ground.

The said proposed separate Parish or benefice of Harton, to be subject to the same ecclesiastical jurisdiction as the said Parish of Saint Hilda, and the Incumbent of the said separate Parish and benefice to have sole and exclusive cure of souls within the limits of the same.

Two Churchwardens to be annually chosen in the customary manner, and at the time when Churchwardens are usually appointed in and for such separate Parish and benefice, and every person so chosen to be duly admitted and do all things pertaining to the office of Churchwarden, as to ecclesiastical matters within the said separate Parish and benefice.

Baptisms, churchings, marriages, and burials to be performed in the church of the said Parish or benefice, and all fees and payments for such offices performed within the said separate Parish and benefice, and all ecclesiastical dues, offerings, and other emoluments arising from or in respect of the said separate Parish and benefice, and usually paid and payable to the Incumbent of a benefice, to belong to, and be received by the Incumbent of the said separate Parish and benefice of *Harton*.

The patronage or right of nominating a Minister to the said separate Parish or benefice of *Harton*, to be vested in and be exercised by the said Dean and Chapter of Durham, and their successors for ever.

The parishioners of the said separate Parish and benefice of *Harton*, to be henceforth exonerated from all rates to be made for or in respect of the Parish of Saint Hilda, or of any other church or chapel not within the limits of the said separate Parish and benefice, but to be liable exclusively to rates, to be made for the maintenance and repair of the church of the said separate Parish and benefice of *Harton*, and the expenses incidental to the due performance of Divine Service therein.

The parishioners of the said separate Parish and benefice of *Harton*, not to be entitled to accommodation in the said church of Saint Hilda, nor shall the parishioners of the other portions of the said Parish of Saint Hilda, be entitled to accommodation in the said church of Harton.

Next as to the *chapelry of Westoe,* which was also separated in like manner, and by the same last mentioned order in council of the 27th of August, 1864, from the Parish of Saint Hilda, the following being the scheme embraced and carried out by that order, viz. :—

The *chapelry of Westoe* to be separated from the Parish of Saint Hilda, South Shields, to which it now belongs, and constituted a separate Parish for ecclesiastical purposes, and a perpetual curacy and benefice, by the name or style of "The perpetual curacy of Westoe, in South Shields," of which the church or chapel within the said chapelry, to be the Parish church.

The said separate Parish and benefice to be subject to the same ecclesiastical jurisdiction as the said Parish of Saint Hilda, and the Incumbent of the said separate Parish and benefice to have sole and exclusive cure of souls within the limits of the same.

The Churchwardens to be annually chosen in the customary manner, and at the time when Churchwardens are usually appointed in and for such separate Parish and benefice, and every person so chosen, to be duly admitted, and do all things pertaining to the office of Churchwardens as to ecclesiastical matters within the said separate Parish and benefice.

Baptisms, churchings, marriages, and burials to be performed in the church of the said separate Parish and benefice, and all the fees and payments for such offices performed within the said separate Parish and benefice, and all ecclesiastical dues, offerings, and other emoluments arising from or in respect of the said separate Parish and benefice, and usually paid, and payable to the Incumbent of a benefice, to belong to, and be received by the Incumbent of the said proposed Parish and benefice of *Westoe in South Shields.*

The patronage or right of nominating a minister to the said separate Parish or benefice of *Westoe in South Shields,* to be vested in, and be exercised by the Dean and Chapter of Durham, and their successors for ever.

The parishioners of the said separate Parish and benefice of Westoe, in South Shields, to be henceforth exonerated from all rates to be made, for, or in respect of the Parish Church of Saint Hilda, or of any other church or chapel not within the limits of the said separate Parish or benefice, but shall be liable exclusively to rates, to be made for the maintenance and repair of the church of the said separate Parish and benefice of " Westoe in South Shields," and the expenses incidental to the due performance of Divine Service therein.

The parishioners of the said separate Parish and benefice of " Westoe in South Shields," not to be entitled to accommodation in the said church of Saint Hilda, nor shall the parishioners of the other portions of the said Parish of Saint Hilda, be entitled to accommodation in the said church of " Westoe in South Shields."

And lastly, as to the chapelry of *Jarrow Docks,* which was likewise separated in a similar manner, by the said order in council of the 27th of August, 1864, from the Parish of Holy Trinity, the following being the scheme embraced and carried out by that order, viz. :

The said chapelry of Jarrow Docks to be separated from the Parish of Holy Trinity to which it belongs, and constituted a separate Parish for ecclesiastical purposes, and a perpetual curacy and benefice by the name of " *The perpetual curacy of Jarrow Docks,*" of which the church or chapel of "Saint Mary," within the said chapelry of Jarrow Docks shall be the Parish church.

The said separate Parish and benefice to be subject to the same ecclesiastical jurisdiction, as the said Parish of Holy Trinity, and the Incumbent of the said separate Parish and benefice to have sole and exclusive cure of souls within the limits of the same.

The Churchwardens to be annually chosen in the customary manner, and at the time when Churchwardens are usually appointed in and for such separate Parish and benefice, and every person so chosen to be duly admitted, and shall do all things pertaining to the office of Churchwarden, as to ecclesiastical matters within the said separate Parish and benefice.

Baptisms, churchings, marriages, and burials to be performed in the church of the said separate Parish and benefice, and all fees and payments for such offices performed within the said separate Parish and benefice, and all ecclesiastical dues, offerings, and other emoluments arising from or in respect of the said separate Parish and benefice, and usually paid and payable to the Incumbent of a benefice, shall belong to the Incumbent of the said Parish and benefice of *Jarrow Docks.*

The patronage or right of nominating a minister to the said separate Parish and benefice of *Jarrow Docks,* to be vested in and be exercised by the Dean and Chapter of Durham, and their successors for ever.

The parishioners of the said separate Parish and benefice of *Jarrow Docks,* to henceforth be exonerated from all rates to be made for or in respect of the Parish Church of Holy Trinity, or of Saint Hilda, or of any other church or chapel not within the limits of the said separate Parish and benefice, but shall be liable exclusively to rates to be made for the maintenance and repair of the church of the said separate Parish and benefice of Jarrow Docks, and the expenses incidental to the due performance of Divine Service therein.

And the parishioners of the said separate Parish and benefice of Jarrow Docks, not to be entitled to accommodation in the said church of Holy Trinity, nor shall the parishioners of the other portions of the said Parish of Holy Trinity, be entitled to accommodation in the said church of Saint Mary, at Jarrow Docks.

The limits and boundaries of the chapelry of Harton, of the chapelry of Westoe, in South Shields, and the chapelry of Jarrow Docks, are set out and defined by the plans severally marked A B and C referred to in the representation of the Lord Bishop of Durham, and which are lodged in the registry of the Diocese of Durham. The boundary plans of the districts of Holy Trinity and Saint Stephen are lodged there also.

SAINT MARY'S CHURCH.

There are many senses in which the term *church* is used, when it is applied with any propriety, but it is the English National Church, of which I am myself an unworthy member, to which allusion is intended, when I speak of a church, well knowing at the same time that there are multitudes of devout and well informed Christians, who thought-fully abstain for various reasons, from connecting themselves in any manner with a national church, and have their own system of order, ritual, and doctrine, as a branch, not of the national church, but as they term it, of the great catholic or universal church. I candidly own that according to my judgment, the union of church and state, which is in effect nothing more than a union of the people in one christian society, the affairs of which are regulated by the national will, as that will is collected on other subjects, as the safest, the soundest, and the best for any people, but I do not therefore quarrel with those Christ-ian friends whose opinions are opposed to mine, believing on my con-science that minor differences will in no wise affect our eternal salvation, if our life, conversation, belief, and practices be in strict accordance with the doctrines and commands of that wonderful and blessed book, which is open to all for the wisest and best of purposes, whether they be churchmen or non-conformists.

By him, whom Byron truly characterised as "Nature's sternest painter, yet the best," has those various differences of opinion amongst Christians been quaintly propounded after a fashion of his own, and it is well that they became known in so pleasing, poetical, and popular a form.

First, by Truth and Reason are the question supposed to be answered,

> " *What is a Church!* ' Let Truth and Reason speak,
> They would reply : The faithful, pure, and meek,
> From Christian folds, the one selected race
> Of all professions, and in every place;' "

Then by the " *Vicar*" in true " established" form,

> " *What is a Church !* ' A flock,' our *Vicar* cries,
> ' Whom Bishops govern, and whom Priests advise ;
> Wherein are various states and due degrees,
> The bench for honor. and the stall for ease ;
> That ease be mine, which, after all his cares,
> The pious, peaceful prebendary shares ;' "

And then by the Sexton, in a manner the *gravest* of all,

> " *What is a Church!* our honest *Sexton* tells,
> ' 'Tis a tall building, with a tower and bells,
> Where Priests and Clerk with joint exertion strive,
> To keep the ardour of their flock alive ;
> *That*, by his periods eloquent and grave ;
> *This*, by responses, and a well set stave ;
> These for the living ; but when life be fled,
> I toll myself the requiem for the dead." "

The foundation stone of Saint Mary's District Church, of which it is my purpose now to speak, was laid on the 22nd of October, 1861, by Robert Ingham, Esq., the member for this Borough, and it was consecrated by the Lord Bishop of Durham, on the 22nd of October, 1862, with all the usual forms and ceremonies. It is situated at the junction of two principal roads leading to the Tyne Docks, and the new town adjoining, the site on which it stands having been jointly presented by the Dean and Chapter of Durham, and the Jarrow Chemical Company. My old esteemed friend the late Mr. John Dobson, of Newcastle-upon-Tyne, was the able architect, and Mr. Joseph Elliott, of North Shields, was its builder by contract. It is in the Gothic style of architecture, and consists of a nave, terminating with a chancel or altar recess, having open timber roofs. There is also a vestry at the East end of the South aisle, and a gallery at the West end of the church. It contains sittings for 528 adults on the ground floor, and 136 children in the gallery, making a total of 604 free sittings, and is so constituted as to be capable, at a comparatively trifling outlay, of having side galleries added, should they be found indispensable to meet the demands of an increased population. The pews are all open, with broad seats, sloping backs, and kneeling boards. The pulpit is on the North side, and the reading desk on the South side of the chancel. The church is lighted with gas and fitted with polished brass standards, which are exceedingly ornamental ; and it is comfortably warmed with hot water apparatus. The interior altogether is fitted up in every respect according to the modern notions of ecclesiastical furnishing, and every attention has been paid to the comfort and accommodation of the numerous congregation by which, under the active and popular ministration of its well selected Incumbent, it is steadily filled.

The church is designed to have a tower at the West end of the North aisle, of the height of 100 feet from the ground, with a peal of bells and suitable clock, but it has only at present been carried to the height of 40 feet and is covered temporarily with an ornamental pitched slate roof. The lower part of the tower serves as the main entrance to the church.

The grand, new, costly organ built by Herr Schulze, the celebrated German Organ Builder, and munificently presented to the church by Mr. John Williamson, stands in the West gallery, and is possessed of all the modern improvements. It was opened with great ceremony and under most auspicious circumstances, on the 24th of June, 1864, everything possible having been done that was worthy of so very important an occasion. Saint Mary's thus became possessed of the best organ at that time, in the North of England, and can boast likewise of one of the most refined and able organists in the person of Mr. William Rea. No wonder therefore that the attractiveness of the services are such as always to command a numerous body of attentive worshippers.

"It is a good thing to give thanks unto the Lord, and to sing praises unto thy name, O most high."

"Upon an instrument of ten strings and upon the psaltery; upon the harp with a solemn sound."

This new church, of which the Rev. James Jeremy Taylor is the first Incumbent, has been erected for a district in the vicinity of the Tyne Docks. It is endowed to the extent of £300 per annum., by the Dean and Chapter of Durham, who on disposing of their land on Jarrow Slake to the North Eastern Railway Company for the purposes of the Tyne Docks, devoted a portion of the purchase money as an endowment fund. The Dean and Chapter also subscribed towards the erection of the building, the cost of which was £4182 15s. 3d., provided in the following manner, viz. :—

	£	s.	d.
Dean and Chapter of Durham	1510	0	0
Mr. John Williamson	862	1	11
Church Societies	575	0	0
Donations	917	18	6
Sundry Collections	240	2	5
Collecting Boxes	77	12	5
Total	£4182	15	3

The particulars of the separation from Holy Trinity, of the district of "Jarrow Docks," with Saint Mary as its church, by order in council will be found under the head of "The Established Churches."

THE NEWSPAPERS.

"Sing drooping muse the cause of thy decline,
Why reign no more the once triumphant nine?"

Was the question jealously asked by one of the most honest and popular of our modern poets, now deceased, and this was the querulous answer returned by himself,

"Alas new charms the wavering many gain,
And rival sheets the reader's eye detain;
A daily swarm, that banish every muse
Come flying forth, and mortals call them *news*,"

the following being an aspect of a very opposite nature, as cleverly taken by a still surviving friend of progress, who thus, also in verse, the "mighty" *press* approves,

> " But mightiest of the mighty means,
> On which the arm of progress leans,
> Man's noblest mission to advance,
> His woes assuage, his weal enhance,
> His rights enforce, his wrongs redress,
> Mightiest of mighty is the *press*,"

with which contradictory views of men equally capable of judging, eminent and distinguished alike in their respective circles, and moving sincerely in very different directions, I introduce my Newspaper subject, which it is not my intention to confine to the narrow bounds of South Shields and North Shields, but to extend to the local press of the immediate district, as to which however my remarks will be chiefly chronological.

It was so far back as the 1st of August, 1711, that the *Newcastle Courant* was published at Newcastle-upon-Tyne by John White, being at the time of its commencement the only newspaper North of the Trent. For several years it was published three times a week, price two-pence, including stamp one half-penny. Mr. White afterwards joined in partnership with Thomas Saint, who on Mr. White's death on the 26th January, 1769, became sole proprietor, By Mr. Saint the publication was continued until his death on the 31st of July, 1788, when it passed to Messrs. Hall and Elliott, and by the executors of Mr. Hall, was in the year 1796, sold to Edward Walker, by whose executor Charles Henry Cook, on the death of Mr. Walker on the 23rd June, 1831, it was continued until the 7th July, 1832, when he sold it to "John Blackwell and Company," by whom it is still published in Newcastle on Friday as a weekly paper. This is the oldest established Journal in the North, and was the first in the Kingdom which was printed on a Stanhope Press, that press on improved principles, having been made in Newcastle. It was afterwards and now is printed with a machine. The Courant, although the oldest existing Newcastle Paper, had a short lived predecessor established by Baker, the King's Printer, in the year 1639, when Charles the First was in the town with his army. This however was but a temporary news sheet; and many years elapsed from that time, before the provinces of England had a periodical journal, the "Lincoln and Stamford Mercury," founded at Stamford in 1695, on the Great North Road, having been, I believe, the first, and it was followed by the " Worcester Journal" in 1709, and the " Nottingham Journal" in 1710, the Newcastle Courant making its first appearance, as already stated, in 1711.

On the 8th November, 1735, " *The North Country Journal or the Impartial Intelligencer*," a newspaper in small folio, was printed and published in Newcastle by Leonard Umfrevile at the head of the Side. It had previously been printed and published by Leonard Umfrevile and Isaac Lane, and was afterwards by Leonard Umfrevile and Co. Leonard died on the 9th of March, 1837, after which the publishers were Thomas Umfrevile and Co., Thomas having been the brother of Leonard. The Umfreviles appear to have been decendents of one of the greatest names and most illustrious families in the North, tracing back their pedigree to the family of Robert Umfrevile, Lord of Toures and Vian, in the time of William the Conqueror. They disappeared in poverty from the Newcastle horizon.

In 1835, and perhaps in 1736 and 1737, there appears to have been a "*Durham Courant*" newspaper in existence, of which the publisher was probably Patrick Sanderson, bookseller.

On the 7th of April, 1739, the first number of a newspaper in folio entitled "*The Newcastle Journal*," was published in Newcastle by Isaac Thompson and William Cuthbert, at their office, on the head of the Side. The establishment was afterward removed to the Burnt House Entry, where the paper was regularly published until the death of Mr. Thompson, on the 6th of January, 1776.

Did not cease till 1788.

On the 16th of October, 1755, the publisher of a weekly newspaper under the title of "*The Newcastle Intelligencer*," was commenced by William Cuthbert and Co., at the printing house, in the Custom House Entry, Quayside, Newcastle. It was a small folio, with columns on each page. It appears to have been continued between two or three years, but to have met with only partial success.

On the 24th of March, 1764, was published the first number of "*The Newcastle Chronicle or General Weekly Advertiser.*" The publisher was Thomas Slack, and on the death of him its founder, on the 14th of January, 1784, he was succeeded by his son-in-law Solomon Hodgson, in whose hands it remained until April the 4th, 1800, when he died. His widow Sarah Hodgson, who continued to carry on the paper, survived him till the 10th of September, 1822, and his sons Thomas and James Hodgson, then became its proprietors, and so remained to the close of 1849, when they disposed of it, after it had been in the family upwards of 85 years. On the 4th of January, 1850, the Chronicle was published by M. W. Lambert for himself and other Proprietors, and on the 24th May following, the publication was removed to new premises in Grey Street, the printing machinery being put in motion by one of Armstrong's hydraulic engines. On the 1st of May, 1858, it appeared as a daily paper, (the weekly issue being still continued.) It is now printed and published at St. Nicholas's Buildings, Newcastle, but new and extensive premises are in preparation for it in Westgate Street, to which it will shortly be removed. There are also publishing offices in South Shields, North Shields, and Sunderland, (where the Sunderland Weekly News is published in connection with the Newcastle Daily Chronicle and the Weekly Chronicle.) The present proprietor is Joseph Cowen, Jun. As the Chancellor of the Exchequer bore more and more hardly upon the press, the price gradually rose till it reached seven-pence, and it afterwards fell in proportion as the Government lessened the burden of taxation. With the compulsory stamp wholly abolished, the daily edition is now sold at a penny, and the weekly edition at two-pence. The price of the Sunderland News is a penny.

On the 18th of October, 1788, the first number of a newspaper, entitled "*The Newcastle Advertiser,*" was published in Newcastle by Matthew Brown. After his death in 1803, it was purchased by John Thompson and Charles Hutchinson, and afterwards by John Thompson. On the 3rd October, 1811, it was sold to Edward Humble, bookseller, who tried different days of publication under the new title of "*The Freemen's Weekly Post,*" and for some time with a second title of "*The General Hue and Cry.*" At last it was discontinued in Newcastle, and "*The Durham County Advertiser*" arose from it, the first number of which was published in Durham, on the 10th September, 1814, under the firm of "Francis Humble and Co." It is now printed and published at Durham weekly, under the same title by Sarah Duncan, sole proprietress, the price being two-pence halfpenny.

On the 1st of June, 1802, was published in Newcastle by John Mitchell, the first number of "*The Tyne Mercury and Northumberland and Durham Gazette.*" It was afterwards published by his son and successor, William Andrew Mitchell, the editor; and on the 9th of May, 1843, it appeared for the last time under the editorship of the Mitchells. It was continued by Messrs. Fordyce, and in July, 1844, the day of publication was altered from Tuesday to Wednesday. On the 11th of February, 1846, the then proprietors Messrs Cathrall and Macliver, announced their intention of discontinuing it, and starting a new periodical; and on the 21st of that month, they published the first number of the "*Newcastle Guardian,*" at No. 37, Grainger Street, the Tyne Mercury having then been established for nearly 40 years. In the beginning of 1847, Mr. Cathrall retired from the Guardian, and in February, George Bradley the editor of the Sunderland Herald Newspaper, became joint proprietor with Mr. Macliver, the day of issue at that time being Saturday. In 1858, Mr. Macliver retired, and Mr. Bradley became sole proprietor. The offices were successively changed to Pilgrim Street and Clayton Street. Mr. Bradley died in 1863, and the paper is still published weekly in Clayton Street by his widow.

On the 1st of June, 1820, the first number of "*The Durham Chronicle or General Northern Advertiser,*" was published in the city of Durham by John Ambrose Williams. It was afterwards published by John Hardinge Vietch, who was succeeded as proprietor by John Wheeler. By him it was disposed of to a company of local gentlemen connected with the city of Durham, including Messrs Robertson and Calvert, who are now the only proprietors. It is published weekly at the price of two-pence.

On the 29th January, 1831, the first number of "*The Sunderland*

and Durham Shipping Gazette and Mercantile Advertiser," was published at Sunderland by William Gracie. It was discontinued after a few months.

On the 28th May, 1831, the first number of *" The Sunderland Herald and Stockton Observer, and General Advertiser,"* was published at Sunderland by Thomas Marwood and Co. From the 1st of January, 1841, it was, and still continues to be published by Vint and Carr. It is a weekly paper with the original price seven-pence, afterwards reduced to four-pence halfpenny, and now to three-pence.

On the 4th August, 1831, the first number of *" The Albion or Shields, Newcastle, and Durham Weekly Advertiser,"* was printed and published at South Shields by B. G. Sharp and Co., gratis. It contained nothing but advertisements, and this was the only number that appeared.

On the 31st of August, 1831, the first number of *" The Northumberland Advertiser, and North and SouthShields Gazette of Agriculture, Shipping, and Commerce,"* was printed and published at North Shields by William Fordyce. It was discontinued on the 10th of July, 1832, but a new series was begun August 21st, 1832, by W. H. Young, which terminated on the 25th March, 1834. The advertisements averaged from six to twelve a week.

On the 12th May, 1832, the first number of the present *"Newcastle Journal,"* was printed and published in Newcastle by Hernaman and Perring, the proprietors, at No. 69, Pilgrim Street, Newcastle, there having been a newspaper under the same title formerly published in Newcastle from 1739 to 1776. On the 2nd of January, 1861, it was changed from a weekly to a daily journal, and is now published as such by the proprietors A. and J. M. Carr, at No. 108, Grey Street, Newcastle-upon-Tyne.

On the 13th July, 1833, the first number of *" The Newcastle Press,"* was published at No. 85, Pilgrim Street, in that town. It existed until October 4th, 1834, on which day the last number was published.

On the 26th November, 1836, the first number of *" The Newcastle Standard"* was published. It was edited by Charles Larkin, but was discontinued on the 15th April, 1837.

On the 21st October, 1837, *" The Northern Liberator,"* a Chartist Newspaper, was published for the first time in Newcastle by John Turnbull. It was edited by A. H. Beaumont, the proprietor. The last number was published December 19th, 1840.

On the 18th November, 1837, the first number of *" The Gateshead Observer,"* was published in that town by John Lowthin and William Douglas. It is now published by its sole proprietor William Henry Brockett, being the only newspaper within the area of the Gateshead Poor Law Union, which contained in the year 1861, a population of 59,411 inhabitants, forming with Newcastle, (with which Gateshead is connected by two bridges, one being the famous "High Level," designed by Robert Stephenson,) an aggregate of 200,000 inhabitants. It is a weekly paper, price two-pence, and there are three editions published, one on Friday night in time for the mails, a second on Saturday morning, and a third on Saturday afternoon, with the latest political, market, and other intelligence of the day.

On the 19th April, 1839, the first number of " *The Port of Tyne Pilot, and Counties of Northumberland and Durham Courier,*" was published at No. 7, Dean Street, South Shields. It was discontinued on the 30th December, 1842, after 193 numbers had been published, but not until the locally patriotic object for which it had been established by Dr. Leitch, had been accomplished in the emancipation of " *Old Father Tyne,*" and his advancement to his naturally true and high position. For that we Eastenders are in no small degree indebted to the public spirited North Shieldsman of that day, to whom I have just thankfully alluded, who by his paper, his pen, and his talents, his encouragement of others, and his own dogged pertinacity, caused "Justice to reign on the Tyne," at Shields as well as Newcastle, the five-eights of the coal dues still continuing to be exacted by the latter, "always excepted."

On the 4th October, 1839, was published at Sunderland the " *Sunderland Beacon,*" the name of which was afterwards changed for a short time to the " *Northern Times.*" After undergoing some changes of proprietorship, it came into the hands of Alderman Williams in 1857, and so now continues. It is published twice a week, viz. : on Tuesday and Friday, the price on Tuesday, (four pages) being a penny, and on Friday, (eight pages) two-pence.

On the 24th December, 1840, the first number of an advertising sheet entitled " *The Great Northern Advertiser and Commercial Herald,*" was published at No. 89, Side, Newcastle. It was distributed gratuitously till March 25th, 1841, when it was enlarged and a charge of three-pence made for it, a price which was raised and lowered a number of times. On the 30th September, 1843, it was issued under the new title of " *The Newcastle Advertiser.*" In January, 1845, it was purchased by the proprietors of the Newcastle Courant, who discontinued its publication on the 1st August, 1848.

On the 4th February, 1842, the first number of a monthly newspaper entitled the " *Tyne Courier,*" was published at South Shields, but it existed only five weeks.

On the 24th February, 1849, the first number of a weekly newspaper called " *The North and South Shields Gazette,*" was published in South Shields by Henry Augustine Yorke. It is now a daily paper under the title of " *The North and South Shields Gazette and Daily Telegraph,*" and is published for the proprietor by Thomas Shields, at South Shields, North Shields, and Sunderland.

On the 1st January, 1854, the first number of " *The Northern Tribune*," a monthly publication edited by Joseph Cowen, Jun., was published in Newcastle, and discontinued the following year.

On the 12th May, 1854, the first number of " *The Northern Examiner*," was published in Lambton Street, Sunderland, by Mr. Welford. After publication of sixteen numbers, the office was removed to Newcastle, where No. 17 was issued on the 1st September. It was published for the last time on the 25th January, 1856.

On the 5th January, 1855, the first number of the " *Shields Advocate*," a new weekly newspaper, was published in South Shields. It was printed in Sunderland by William Hardie, and afterwards removed to North Shields, and there discontinued.

On the 30th June, 1855, the first number of the " *North of England Advertiser*," was published in Newcastle by Robert Ward, whose property it still is, and by whom it is issued weekly at the central offices, Newcastle, and the branch office, Sunderland, the price being two-pence, and the sworn average weekly sale 11,409 copies since its commencement.

On the 3rd July, 1855, the first number of " *The Newcastle Messenger and Advertiser*," was published by the proprietors of the Newcastle Courant thrice a week, but it was discontinued on the 28th March, 1857, after 273 numbers had been published.

In 1855, was first published in Newcastle " *The Northern Daily Express*," by John Watson, subsequently by William Christie Marshall, and now by " *The Northern Daily Express Company (Limited.)*" It is published daily, with a weekly edition every Saturday.

On the 1st August, 1857, the " *Northern Weekly Standard* was published in Newcastle for the first time.

The " *Shields Daily News*," was first issued on the 22nd August, 1864. It is printed and published by Richard Whitecross, of North Shields, and Henry Augustine Yorke, of South Shields, at the offices in North and South Shields.

And lastly, on the 6th November, 1865, the first number of " *The Sunderland Daily Shipping News*" was issued, price one half-penny, and continues to be published in Sunderland by Thomas Carr and John Samuel Burton.

By some these particulars, which I have gathered with trouble and care, will be considered tedious and unnecessary; by others they will be deemed interesting and valuable; but by all it will be admitted that coming like shadows, and so departing, the evanescent movements of many of the newspaper speculators as described by me, bring them within the well known similitudes immortalized by Tam o'Shanter's wondrous tale and " Alloway's auld haunted kirk."

> " Or like the snowfalls in the river,
> A moment white, then gone for ever,
> Or like the borealis race,
> That flit ere you can point their place,
> Or like the rainbows lovely form,
> Evanishing amid the storm ;

their disappearance amid "storm" being more strictly in accordance with truth, than any loveliness of "form" which can erroneously be attributed to them, even by their warmest admirers.

But in the steady and firmly established publications of which I have already made honorable mention, with sincere gratification, there has been nothing of this evanescent mutability. They still survive and prosper, and singling out from amongst them for my present comparative purpose, as arising out of its more remote antiquity the venerable Courant, reigning still in Newcastle where it first saw the light in 1711, how strange and altered a restrospect can its editor now take in comparison with its "past and present," and how true generally in a newspaper point of view ! *Then* with its scanty population of 18000, was the now great Newcastle, a pasture bare and meagre for a journalist, and *there* would no modern short-hand reporter, with all his admitted cleverness, have gained his daily bread. To scenes in Town Councils and Local Boards of Health, and quarrels among Poor Law Guardians, the quiet Courant was an utter stranger—Tea Gatherings were not in vogue—Total Abstinence was unknown—and "small beer," though drank, went certainly "unchronicled"—no mail to catch and none to lose—few pitiless letters, and no pelting telegrams—no assaults of rival contemporaries—no fret and fever—no worry and worret—no editorial imaginary correspondence—and no railway whistle. All was calm within the undisturbed sanctum of the placid editor of that day, leisurely preparing at his own convenience and pleasure for the patient press, and under no responsibility, real or fancied, to trouble society with his speculations or opinions. Very different now is the constant craving of the hungry public, and the ceaseless editorial whirl, and truly may the hard worked editor of modern days exclaim, in the words of the astonished parent, to his unsatisfied offspring,

> " Crowdie ! ance ; crowdie ! twice ;
> Crowdie ! three times in a day :
> An ye crowdie ony mair,
> Ye'll crowdie a' my meal away,"

following it up with the confession "*in extremis*" of the bothered Leicestershire Boor,

> " Wat wi' faath, and wat wi' the earth a tuning round the sun, and wat wi' the railroads a fuzzen and a whizzen, am' clean stonied, muddled, and bet ;"

which last dying speech and confession of his, are said to sum up with great emphasis, the intellectual results of scientific discovery in a great part of mankind.

The following are the newspapers now in existence within the area to which I have confined myself,

> "Diurnal most, some thrice each week affords,
> Some only once—O avarice of words."

SOUTH SHIELDS AND NORTH SHIELDS.

North and South Shields Gazette and Daily Telegraph—daily—price one half-penny.
Shields Daily News—daily—price one half-penny.

NEWCASTLE-UPON-TYNE.

Newcastle Chronicle—price one penny—daily—and a weekly edition every Saturday price two-pence.
Newcastle Journal—price one penny—daily.
Northern Daily Express—price one penny—daily—and a weekly edition every Saturday—price one penny.
Newcastle Courant—price three-pence
Newcastle Guardian—price two-pence   } Weekly.
North of England Advertiser—price two-pence

GATESHEAD.

Gateshead Observer—weekly—price two-pence.

CITY OF DURHAM.

Durham Advertiser—price two-pence half-penny } Weekly.
Durham Chronicle—price two-pence half-penny

SUNDERLAND.

Sunderland Herald—price three-pence—weekly.
The Daily Shipping News, in connection with the Sunderland Herald—daily—price one half-penny.
Sunderland Times—twice a week, viz. :—on Tuesday and Friday—price on Tuesday, (four pages) one penny, on Friday (eight pages) two-pence.
A Shipping List is daily published by Barnes—price one half-penny.
Sunderland Weekly News—published by the Newcastle Chronicle—Weekly—price one penny.

And now agreeing with Bowring, rather than with Crabbe, in the opinions poetically but oppositely expressed by them concerning the press, I rejoice that it was foreign to the limited object of my book, to enter, as I otherwise should have done, upon the subject *generally* of newspapers. Something notwithstanding may still be said in approval, and something in condemnation of them, for well as we have been told, and confidently as we believe, how noble and mighty are its means for assuaging our woes, enhancing our weal, enforcing our rights, and redressing our wrongs, the press we also know has its abuses as well as its uses ;

> " So here compressed within a single sheet,
> *Great* things and *small*, the *mean* and *mighty* meet;"

and the utmost care should therefore be exercised by all in whom a wholesome power of control is vested by proprietorship or otherwise, to prevent its ever being made the painful instrument of private annoyance, revengeful feeling, sectarian prejudices, false allegations, or distorted facts. In the local area of a provincial newspaper where gossip, slander, personalties, bigotry, and petty jealousies arising from divisional cliques in society are sure to prevail, there is the greater necessity for this precaution, for the *individuality* attached to a newspaper is lost sight of by multitudes of the credulous people by whom it is read, the oracular dicta and bold assertions of the editorial *We*, being accepted with all the confidence and credence which were attached of old to the mysterious delivery of the ancient oracles,

> " And so the sibylline leaves were blown about,
> Disjointed scraps of fate involved in doubt."

THE VALUE OF PROPERTY

Within the Borough, as taken in 1856 and 1866 for ratable purposes in connection with the relief of the poor, was, and is as follows :—

TOWNSHIPS.	GROSS ESTIMATED RENTAL.				RATABLE VALUE.			
	1856.		1866.		1856.		1866.	
	£	s.	£	s.	£	s.	£	s.
South Shields ..	30869	0	28314	11	23024	10	21013	0
Westoe	45923	10	82053	10	34386	0	62948	10
Totals	76792	10	110368	1	57410	10	83961	10

There being it will be perceived, a decrease during the ten years in the Township of South Shields, and a very considerable increase in that of Westoe, arising in both cases from causes so well known as not to require explanation.

THE NUMBER OF PARLIAMENTARY VOTERS

On the list for the Borough was in the year

1832 540
1856 1073
1865 1211

THE POPULATION OF THE BOROUGH.

Still acting upon the well known command of old,

"To increase, multiply, and replenish the earth."

our Borough population has increased, having been according to the census of

1841 22908
1851 28293
1861 35239

shewing an increase in the twenty years of 12331.

NUMBER OF BURGESSES ON THE MUNICIPAL ROLL

In 1850, being the first year of Incorporation....... 879
" 1856 1570
" 1865 2300

The increase on the roll in the fifteen years has been 1421.

THE MAYORS SINCE 1856.

"COME LIKE SHADOWS, SO DEPART."

7th year of incorporation, Matthew Stainton, elected 9th Nov., 1856
8th " " Terrot Glover, elected 9th Nov., 1857
9th " " John Williamson, elected 9th Nov., 1858
10th " " " re-elected 9th Nov., 1859
11th " " Robert Wallis, elected 9th Nov., 1860
12th " " " re-elected 9th Nov., 1861
13th " " John Brodrick Dale, elected 10th Nov. 1862
14th " " Richard Baty Ridley, elected 9th Nov. 1863
William James, elected 5th Aug., 1864, on the death of R. B. Ridley
15th " " William James, re-elected 9th Nov. 1864
16th " " Thomas Moffett, elected 9th Nov., 1865

THE BATHS AND WASHHOUSES

Are now under the management of the Town Improvement and Public Health Committee of the Corporation, and are carried on by Mrs. Robson, as the widow of the late Christopher Garbutt Robson deceased, who was, at the time of his death, the tenant of the Corporation, under a lease for three years, commencing the 26th of March, 1864, at a yearly rent of £50. The mortgage debt upon them is now reduced from £3000 to £1200, by the payment of twelve annual instalments of £150 each, to the Public Works Loan Commissioners, who are the mortgagees.

THE UNION WORKHOUSE

Is now free from debt, the mortgage of £2400 by which it was originally encumbered, having been paid off by annual instalments of £120 each.

THE DISPENSARY, INDIGENT SICK SOCIETY, OLD CHARITY SCHOOL, AND SAVINGS' BANK

Still exist and prosper under continued good management, the two first having been considerably benefitted during the decennial period to which I am confined, by the pecuniary bequests of charitable individuals. A Savings Bank in connection with the Post Office, is likewise now in operation.

GLAZONBY'S CHARITY.

The Trustees are now Robert Ingham, Richard Shortridge, Thomas Salmon, Robert Wallis, and William Anderson, they having been appointed on the 27th of December, 1858, in the places of Christopher Bainbridge, Thomas Wallis, James Wardle Roxby, Robert Dawson, and Thomas Forsyth, deceased.

THE SUBSCRIPTION LIBRARY

Did not become resuscitated according to the confidence in public support, which I mistakingly expressed in 1856, and it is therefore now,

I say it with regret, a thing of the " past," with its volumes dispersed, and without the slightest hope of restoration. It is well therefore that the library in connection with the Mechanics' Institute affords a substitute worthy of support, but which is *not* properly supported, and that a library is also praiseworthily attached to the flourishing Institute of the Working Men.

THE LOYAL STANDARD ASSOCIATION

Steadily pursues its way, by enabling its members to make provision to a certain extent, against the dangers and uncertainties of a sea-faring life. The present Trustees are Robert Wallis, John Robinson, and Robert Walter Swinburne. John Robson became the Secretary on the death of his predecessor, the late John Jobling, on the 28th of November, 1865. Full publicity is comprehensively given from time to time to the affairs of the society, through the annual statements of receipts and expenditure, and the encreased watchfulness of the Committee and Trustees are such as will secure the confidence of the members.

According to the published statement, the receipts for the year ended the 2nd December, 1865, arising from the contributions of members, were £2177 10s. 1d., and from miscellaneous sources £143 1s. 5d., making together £2320 11s. 6d. The disbursements for death benefits, sick and shipwrecked members, Secretary's salary, &c., were £2031 9s. 1d., shewing a gain I am happy to say of £289 2s. 5d.

The capital at that date was £2567 3s. 9d., including a balance then due from the late Secretary of £257 8s. 2d.; and the number of members 1800.

The total amount paid to members from 2nd December, 1824, to 2nd December, 1865, was £54764 12s. 6d.

THE LIFE BOAT

" Walks the waters like a thing of life,
And seems to dare the elements to strife."

Still retaining *her* character for safety, as the Pilots by whom she continues to be fearlessly manned on all occasions of danger, preserve *theirs* for courage and humanity. Connected with those noble fellows more closely now than ever, through the medium of my Tyne Pilotage

Commissionership, it is my pride to possess their entire confidence, for which the only return I can make, is by that watchful attention to their rights and interests which I am enabled as a Commissioner to give, and which I shall gladly and most steadily continue to do. No longer under the dominion of their ancient master the Trinity House of Newcastle-upon-Tyne, their allegiance as Pilots is now altogether withdrawn from those foreign potentates, and willingly yielded to the new authorities who mildly hold sway, at South Shields, in which and to which as a colony, mixing with and yet in some respect distinct from the inhabitants generally, the Pilots live and completely belong.

CHURCHES, CHAPELS, AND SCHOOLS.

Following exactly the same course which I pursued in 1865, I have with the assistance of the Rev. Gentlemen connected with the various Churches and Chapels in the Borough, obtained the interesting statistics which I have embodied in a separate tabular statement annexed.

Persons who are curious in such matters may by a comparison between the tables of 1856 and 1866, ascertain the changes (progressive or otherwise) which have taken place in the last ten years ; and by way of facility I may make known the following comparative totals, viz. :

1856—Total number of Day Scholars in Table	1633
Deduct 500 which were returned erroneously as if in connection with Laygate Presbyterian Church	500
Real number of Day Scholars then connected with Churches and Chapels	1133
1866—Total number now so connected	1636
Increase in ten years	503
1856—Total number of Sunday School Scholars	3143
1866— Do. do.	5070
Increase in ten years	1927
1865—Total number of gratuitous Sunday School Teachers	344
1866— Do. do.	625
Increase in ten years	281

The only places of religious worship with which *Day* Schools are connected, are it will be perceived, the established Churches of Saint

Hilda, Holy Trinity, Saint Stephen, and Saint Thomas, and the Roman Catholic Church in Cuthbert Street. As regards *Sunday* Schools they are, I rejoice to notice, in connection without a single exception with every Church and Chapel within the Borough.

> " To every sect, we have a school assigned,
> Rules for all ranks, and food for every mind."

ADDRESSES.

The loyal attachment of the inhabitants of South Shields to the reigning Sovereign, has at all times been a disinterested feeling of pure loyalty, uncontrolled or affected by the political principles for the time being of the Ministers of the Crown, and hence the manifestations so constitutionally displayed towards the Sovereign, even when those principles of Government happened to be disapproved of by the majority of the inhabitants. So it was in the time when " George the Third was King," and so it is and has been during the reign of Her present Gracious Majesty, to whom addresses from South Shields on every fitting occasion, of congratulation or condolence, have been affectionately presented.

Other addresses have also being presented during the period to which I am restricted, and I now proceed to particularize them all as follows,

FEBRUARY 18TH, 1858.—Address to the Queen on the Marriage of the Princess Royal, presented at a Levee, by a Deputation from the Corporation, consisting of the Mayor (Ald. Glover,) Ald. Wallis, and myself as Town Clerk, when we were most graciously received, and had the honor of kissing the Queen's hand.

APRIL 3RD, 1861.—Address of condolence to the Queen on the death of her mother, the Duchess of Kent.

DECEMBER 23RD, 1861.—Address of condolence to the Queen, on the death of the Prince Consort.

OCTOBER 8TH, 1862. Address of congratulation to Mr. Gladstone, the then Chancellor of the Exchequer, on the occasion of his visit to the Tyne, presented on the South Pier, South Shields, by the Mayor (R. Wallis, Esq.,) myself as Town Clerk, and Corporate Deputation.

MARCH 10TH, 1863.—Address of congratulation to the Queen on the Marriage of the Prince of Wales, which was forwarded through the usual channel of the Home Office. The rejoicings on the occasion were of the most generous, judicious, and spirited description. Bells were rung, flags displayed, salutes fired, fire works exhibited, the Town Hall illuminated, bonfires on the hills, the children entertained, and the inmates of the Workhouse plentifully regaled ; a public subscription breakfast, with the Mayor presiding, a public procession through the streets of no ordinary character, a public meeting in the Market Place at which addresses were voted, and a ball in the Evening. All being evidences of that continued Loyalty to the Throne, for which South Shields has ever ranked proudly conspicuous amongst her Northern Neighbours of Durham and Northumberland.

MARCH 10TH, 1863.—Similar address to the Prince of Wales, which was presented to him and the Princess at Marlborough House, on the 29th April, 1863, by the Mayor (Ald. Dale,) and myself as Town Clerk.

It was meant also to have congratulated Garibaldi by an address on his intended visit to the Tyne, as had been done by a few of his admirers in 1854. The visit however did not take place, and the address was simply forwarded to him.

CONCLUSION.

Having now reached the extent of my limits, I can only generalize the remainder of my subjects, first congratulating my fellow townsmen on the accomplishment of some of the prophecies which I foretold in 1856. For the then anticipated impetus to our trade, *has* taken place through the medium of the Jarrow Docks, and Bar and Harbour Improvements; our town *has* extended in almost every direction, and population *has* rapidly increased; streets and houses *have* sprung up to meet the requirements of that population; and cleanliness and health *have* been cared for by a perfect system of underground sewerage, private connecting drains, and surface scavengership; the adaptation of our beach to bathing purposes has *not* been over-looked, for bathing machines are now thereon; the public cemetery *has* been formed; and a public quay *has* been supplied, with such important results as are patent to all.

In addition to which, my readers may briefly be reminded of those other improvements and acquisitions to the Borough which have likewise come to pass, though not the subjects of prophecy; such as the new road to the South pier and the pier itself, affording as it does an invigorating promenade; the repavement of the Market Place, removal of the obstructive old parsonage, and the widening of Church Row; the illumination of Saint Hilda's Church Clock, and its useful chimes; the time gun, and electric telegraph wires; new streets and footpaths, and others of greatly amended character, reminding us of those Highland roads which were thus commemorated in somewhat of an Irish fashion,

> "Had you seen these roads before they were made,
> You'd lift up your hands, and bless General Wade ;"

the making of one extensive graving dock, and the enlargement of others; an effective Police Force and Fire Brigade, with dwelling houses for the latter, most convenient for prompt assistance in cases of fire ; a regular system for the inspection of weights and measures ; the new Mechanics' Institute, Theatre, Custom House, and Freemasons Hall ; Building Societies, Penny Banks, Flower Show, Agricultural Association, Swimming Club, Life Brigade, Volunteers, Pilotage and Local Marine Boards, Shipping Offices, Marine School, Ecclesiastical Districts, one new Church and some Dissenting Chapels, with others which Phœnix like have risen from the old ones, to the embellishment of our streets, and the increased accommodation of their respective Congregations ; reconstructed Gas Works and banished lanterns from our streets ;

> "No more with dog and lantern comes the maid,
> To guide her mistress when the rubber's play'd."

while in all directions shops have sprung up and old ones been re-suscitated, to meet the taste and fashion of an advancing generation.

For these and all other benefits, *we* as a community have reason to be thankful, and for that continued health and those many blessings which Almighty God has been graciously pleased to bestow upon me, I offer up *my* humble and hearty thanks, grateful that I have been spared to add in this my ripe old age, to those other particulars of my native town, which ten years ago were published by me ; reminding the inhabitants now, as I earnestly did then, of that increasing great-ness and advancing prosperity, which I believed to be looming in the distance, and exhorting them by union and a community of purpose, to work " shoulder to shoulder" in obtaining for South Shields those shipping, commercial, and manufacturing advantages which her well adapted situation as a Seaboard and Harbour Town can surely com-mand. "Evening and Morning, and at Noon," must we cry aloud and spare not in the pursuit, and as our cause is good, so will our success be certain,

> " Man through all ages of revolving time,
> Unchanging man, in every varying clime,
> Deems his own land of every land the pride,
> Belov'd by heaven o'er all the world beside :
> His *home* the spot of earth supremely blest,
> A dearer, sweeter spot than all the rest."

COMMERCIAL PRINTING OFFICES :

H. HEWISON, MARKET PLACE, SOUTH SHIELDS.

The Index to the supplementary part is at the beginning

INDEX

TO

SOUTH SHIELDS, ITS PAST, PRESENT, & FUTURE.

1856.

A NEW HISTORICAL BALLAD.

(*Air*, "The Troubadour.")

"HANDSOME CONDUCT OF SOUTH SHIELDS.—Whatever may be said of North Shields, whose municipal magnates have certainly dealt poor Newcastle some hard knocks, South Shields has behaved most generously to the Conservators, now that they are on their last legs, having sent them up, during the pending inquiry at the Guildhall, a Spring treat of Salmon and Lamb !"—*Gateshead Observer*, (Feb. 23, 1850).

SLILY the Tynemouth-Clerk came up to clutch

NEWCASTLE *versus* SHIELDS 180 YEARS AGO.
[FROM A SHIELDS SURVEYOR OF THE SLAKE.]

LOOKING over some old papers, the other day, I fell in with a copy of the speech of the Attorney-General (Sir Heneage Finch) on behalf of the Corporation of Newcastle, in a cause which was tried at Westminster, in 1669, between that body and the Dean and Chapter of Durham, as to the right of the Chapter to erect a ballast quay at JARROW SLAKE without the license of the Corporation. The sentiments expressed at that time, by the Attorney-General of King Charles, are so ... what the Attorney-General for the JARROW DOCK ... essed at the present time, had he been so ... re geese in the Council tha ... one so)— that I can ... for the am ...

Among ... said :— " ... ago, quences ... " eve think it ... bett and inter ... tow by erecti ... wo *miles off* ... be town ha ... v *tion had* ... new inv ...

TYNE TUNNEL PROJECT
60 M.P.H. TUBE PLAN FOR N. AND S. SHIELDS
CAN BE ...

THE erection of a synagogue by the Jewish community at South Shields marks the beginning of an important chapter in the history of the congregation, which has been established in the town for just over one hundred years. The congregation consisted originally of 12 families; to-day it numbers at least 70 financial members, and the new synagogue will provide for over 300 souls. In the early days the religious meetings were held in the homes of members. A house in Charlotte Street was ...

Milton Keynes UK
Ingram Content Group UK Ltd.
UKHW020635230124
436534UK00008B/377